NEW ENGLAND

Country Inns and Back Roads

Other books by Jerry Levitin

Country Inns and Back Roads, North America
Country Inns and Back Roads, California
Country Inns and Back Roads, Britain and Ireland

Country Inns and Back Roads

NEW ENGLAND

1993–1994

Jerry Levitin

HarperPerennial
A Division of *HarperCollins*Publishers

FIRST EDITION
Designed by Joan Greenfield

ISSN: 1060-3778
ISBN: 0-06-273193-9

93 94 95 96 ◆/RRD 5 4 3 2 1

CONTENTS

PREFACE

When I became responsible for revising the late Norman Simpson's Berkshire Traveller series in February 1989, I was surprised to learn that most books on inns and bed and breakfast establishments are written by authors who do not visit the inns they write about. In fact, many reviews are simply paid advertisements, written by the innkeepers, and the publisher receives a payment for the inclusion.

You can feel assured that the inns and B&B's in *Country Inns and Back Roads: New England* are visited on a regular basis and the reviews are updated each year. And since there is no cost for inclusion, you can be doubly sure that each inn listed is based on its own merits.

I have also noticed that few guidebooks take into account the personalities of the innkeepers. Guidebooks will list facts regarding the inns' settings, locations, and interior decoration, but as Norman Simpson believed, the key to a successful inn is the traveler's feeling of being welcomed. An efficiently run, beautifully decorated inn situated on a lovely site will not be listed between the covers of any of the *Country Inns and Back Roads* books if it is missing that intangible human warmth. Of course, to determine that extra ingredient, the inn and its innkeepers need to be visited.

In past years, I have distinguished between full-service inns that serve lunch and dinner and bed & breakfast inns, which serve only the morning meal. These were reviewed in two different books, *Country Inns and Back Roads: North America* and *Bed & Breakfast American Style*, respectively. However, In 1992 I decided to combine the two to list the best of both worlds, plus a few select small hotels that never quite fit into either of the old books. You'll find this new format to continue in the future for *Country Inns and Back Roads: North America* and in my two new regional guides, *Country Inns and Back Roads: New England* and *Country Inns and Back Roads: California*.

The change is based on our nation's traveling habits. Many states and areas within states do not offer many traditional inns, but may have plenty of B&Bs. For example, the West tends to have inns that spread out with cottages or single-story lodges. Classic inns, with the restaurant on the ground floor and the rooms above, are generally found in the East. Why not, then, let you select from one book only?

In addition, many readers told me that going from inn to inn made them crave a respite from the full-course dinners that they were being served each night. For a change, they welcome a B&B or a hotel where many meal options are available.

But all the books in the series still share that *Country Inns and Back Roads* feeling—a hospitality, a warmth that makes you want to return again and again.

Although there are exceptions to every rule, this book generally lists lodgings that have five or more rooms to rent, but no more than 40; a common area where guests can congregate away from the public; private baths; high standards of cleanliness; and innkeeper involvement. The meals are freshly prepared and served in a relaxing atmosphere.

I look for a place that caters to the overnight guest first, rather than the dining guest. This preference eliminates some very fine restaurants with guest rooms above. My ideal is the inn that only serves houseguests. However, financial considerations often require the innkeeper to open the dining room to the general public.

HOW THE BOOK IS ORGANIZED

This book is divided into geographical sections. Each of these sections has its own keyed map showing the approximate location of every accommodation. Of further assistance is the Index, which lists the establishments alphabetically and another index that lists the towns alphabetically and the Inn's rates. We have also compiled some new indexes that can help you locate inns offering special activities or amenities.

The paragraphs following the narrative accounts of my visits contain essential information about the amenities offered and nearby recreational and cultural attractions. Reasonably explicit driving directions are also included here.

If you are displeased with one of my selections, or if you feel that a wonderful inn has inadvertently been overlooked, please let me hear from you by using the form printed in the back of the book.

MEAL PLANS

You'll notice references to the following "plans" throughout the text and also in the index of rates. Here are some thumbnail definitions of the terms.

"European plan" means that rates for rooms and meals are separate. "American plan" means that all meals are included in the cost of the room. "Modified American plan" means that breakfast and dinner are included in the cost of the room. The rates at certain inns-commonly known as "bed and breakfasts" include a continental or full breakfast with the lodging.

RATES

I include a listing of rates in the Index. Space limitations preclude any more than a general range of rates for each inn, and these should not be considered firm quotations. Please check with the inns for their various rates and special packages. It should be noted that many small inns do not have night staffs, and innkeepers will appreciate it if calls are made before 8:00 P.M.

RESERVATIONS & CANCELLATIONS

At most of the inns listed in this book, a deposit is required for a confirmed reservation. Guests are requested to please note arrival and departure dates carefully. The deposit will be forfeited if the guest arrives after the date specified or departs before the final date of the reservation. Refunds will generally be made only if the reservation is canceled 7 to 14 days in advance of the arrival date, depending upon the policy of the individual inn, and a service charge will be deducted from the deposit.

It must be understood that a deposit ensures that your accommodations will be available as confirmed and also assures the inn that the accommodations are sold as confirmed. Therefore, when situations arise necessitating your cancellation on short notice, your deposit will not be refunded.

FOR FOREIGN TRAVELLERS

Welcome to North America! Many of you are making your first visit, and we're delighted that you'll be experiencing some of the *real* United States and Canada by visiting these country inns. Incidentally, all of them will be very happy to help you make arrangements and reservations at other inns listed in the book.

AUTHOR'S BACKGROUND

Most writers of inn guidebooks have never had the experience of actually owning and operating an inn. I presently own the award winning Inn at Sunrise Point near Camden, Maine, a three-room, four-cottage B&B that is on the ocean's edge. In addition, I owned and operated an urban inn in San Francisco for five years, and I've run a consulting business for innkeepers. In the summer you will find me either visiting Inns for the books or at my Inn in Camden, Maine.

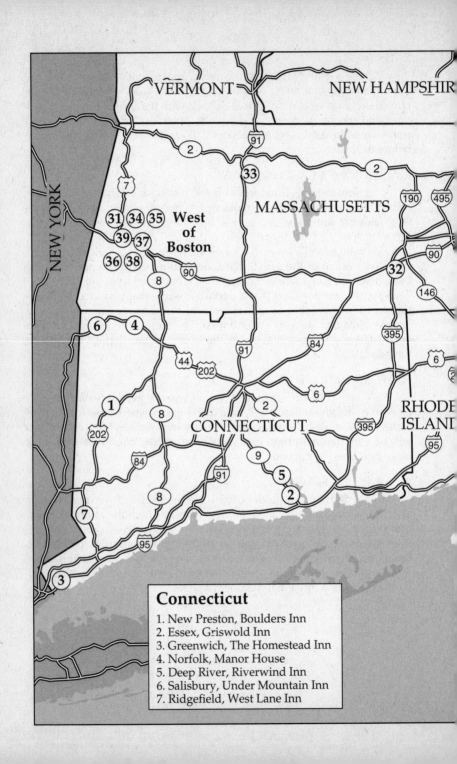

VERMONT   NEW HAMPSHIRE

MASSACHUSETTS

NEW YORK

West of Boston

CONNECTICUT

RHODE ISLAND

Connecticut

1. New Preston, Boulders Inn
2. Essex, Griswold Inn
3. Greenwich, The Homestead Inn
4. Norfolk, Manor House
5. Deep River, Riverwind Inn
6. Salisbury, Under Mountain Inn
7. Ridgefield, West Lane Inn

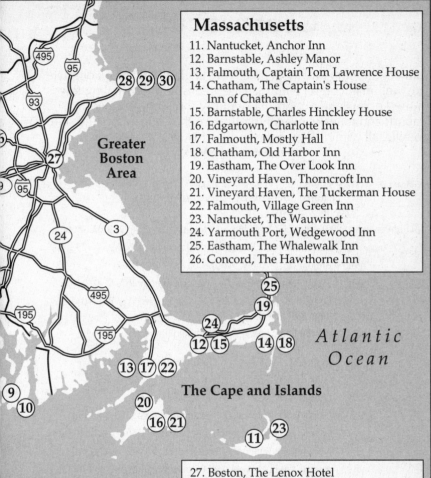

Massachusetts

11. Nantucket, Anchor Inn
12. Barnstable, Ashley Manor
13. Falmouth, Captain Tom Lawrence House
14. Chatham, The Captain's House Inn of Chatham
15. Barnstable, Charles Hinckley House
16. Edgartown, Charlotte Inn
17. Falmouth, Mostly Hall
18. Chatham, Old Harbor Inn
19. Eastham, The Over Look Inn
20. Vineyard Haven, Thorncroft Inn
21. Vineyard Haven, The Tuckerman House
22. Falmouth, Village Green Inn
23. Nantucket, The Wauwinet
24. Yarmouth Port, Wedgewood Inn
25. Eastham, The Whalewalk Inn
26. Concord, The Hawthorne Inn

Greater Boston Area

Atlantic Ocean

The Cape and Islands

0 —— 10 Miles
0 —— 10 Kilometers

27. Boston, The Lenox Hotel
28. Rockport, Linden Tree Inn
29. Rockport, Old Farm Inn
30. Rockport, Seacrest Manor
31. Lenox, Blantyre
32. Auburn, Captain Samuel Eddy House Country Inn
33. Deerfield, Deerfield Inn
34. Lenox, The Gables Inn
35. Lenox, Garden Gables Inn
36. Stockbridge, The Inn at Stockbridge
37. South Lee, Merrell Tavern Inn
38. Stockbridge, The Red Lion Inn
39. Lenox, The Village Inn

Rhode Island

8. Wakefield, Larchwood Inn
9. Newport, The Melville House
10. Newport, Wayside

Connecticut

Connecticut offers many classic New England villages, complete with well-manicured central village greens; former whaling towns on the Long Island Sound, particularly the reconstructed Mystic Seaport; and miles of peaceful rolling countryside in the Berkshire foothills, all within a few hours' drive of New York or Boston.

EVENTS

DECEMBER–MARCH	Warm Up to Winter, Farmington Valley: Early American Hearths Tours, discount passes to attractions (info: 203-674-1035)
MARCH–DECEMBER	Goodspeed Opera House, East Haddam (info: 203-873-8668)
APRIL–JUNE	statewide Spring Blossom Celebration (info: 203-258-4293)
APRIL	Annual Horse Show, Westbrook (info: 399-6317)
APRIL	Steam Train Ride from Groton to Putnam (info: 767-0103)
MAY	Deep River Junior Fife & Drum Corps' Civil War Weekend (info: 203-767-0103)
MAY	Annual Dogwood Festival, Fairfield (info: 203-259-5596)
MAY (MEMORIAL DAY WEEKEND)	Annual Toyota Trucks Grand Prix, Lakeville (info: 203-435-2571)
SUMMER THEATER	Charles Ives Center for the Arts, Danbury
	Candlewood Playhouse, New Fairfield (info: 203-746-6531)
	Croadway Theatre, Darien (info: 203-655-7667)
	Ivorton River Reperatory Theater (info: 203-767-0422)
JUNE	Annual Antiques Weekend, Farmington (info: 508-839-9735)
JULY, EARLY	Annual Deep River Fife & Drum Muster and Parade (info: 203-873-9614)
JULY 4	12th Annual Riverfest, Hartford (info: 203-728-3089)
JULY 4	Chester road race (info-203-663-1659)
JULY, MIDDLE	45th Annual Open House Day Tour, Litchfield (info: 203-567-9423)
JULY	120th Ancient Fife & Drum Corps Parade, Deep River (info: 203-527-4317)
JULY, LATE–AUGUST	PGA tour, Cromwell (info: 203-522-4171)
AUGUST, EARLY	16th Annual SoNo Arts Celebration, South Norwalk (info: 203-849-9366)
AUGUST, MIDDLE	18th Annual Oyster Festival, Milford (info: 203-878-0681)

AUGUST	Middlesex Triathlon
AUGUST	33rd Annual Westbrook Fife & Drum Muster (info: 203-399-6436)
AUGUST	81st Annual Haddam Neck Agricultural Fair (info: 203-267-2848)
AUGUST	Volvo International Tennis, New Haven (info: 203-776-7331)
AUGUST	8th Annual Quinnehtukqut Rendezvous & Native American Festival, Haddam (info: 203-282-1404)
SEPTEMBER 18–20	55th Annual Fall New Haven Antiques Show (info: 203-387-7006)
SEPTEMBER, LATE	72nd Annual Durham Fair
SEPTEMBER, LATE	Patriot's Weekend, Redding: a re-creation of life during the American Revolution, with military regiments, drills, camp life (for info, write: 6870 Brooks St., Bridgeport CT 06608)
SEPTEMBER–OCTOBER	Bristol Mum Festival (info: 203-589-4111)
OCTOBER, EARLY–MIDDLE	24th Annual Apple Harvest Festival, Southington (info: 203-628-8036)
NOVEMBER, LATE– DECEMBER, LATE	10th Annual Victorian Christmas at Gillette Castle, Hadlyme (info: 203-526-2336)
DECEMBER, EARLY	Christmas in Riverton (info: 203-489-2274)
DECEMBER (THROUGHOUT)	Christmas at Mystic Seaport (info: 203-572-0711)
DECEMBER	21st Annual Torchlight Parade, Old Saybrook (info: 203-388-3401)
DECEMBER	Victorian Christmas, Hotchkiss Tyler House (info: 203-482-8260)
DECEMBER	Bethlehem Christmas Town Festival (info: 203-266-7510)

SIGHTS

Aldrich Museum

American Clock and Watch Museum

Audubon Center

Blardslely Park Zoo

Bruce Museum

Bush Hollow House

Connecticut River Museum (info: 203-767-8269)

Essex Steam Train & Riverboat Ride (info: 203-767-0103)

Gillette Castle State Park (info: 203-526-2336)

Hillside Gardens

Hitchcock Museum

Indian Archaeological Museum, Washington

Johnsonville

Keeler Museum

Kent Falls, Kent

Lock Museum

Mystic Seaport Marine Museum (info: 203-572-0711)

N.E. Audubon Center

New England Carousel Museum, Bristol

New England Steamboat Line (info: 203-345-4507)

Norfolk Artisan's Guild

Putnam Cottage

Sloane-Stanley Museum

Stamford Town Center

Sundial Herb Garden

Tapping Reeve House

BOULDERS INN

New Preston, Connecticut

At the foot of the Pinnacle Mountains, on the shore of Lake Waramaug is the location of the Boulders Inn, a lovely nineteenth-century summer home renovated into an inn of warmth and charm. The inn is tucked in the Berkshire Hills of northwestern Connecticut overlooking the wooded shores of Lake Waramaug. Built in 1895 of huge granite boulders, the inn was used as a summer retreat for the wealthy. In 1987, Ulla and Kees Adema purchased Boulder and now, besides the spectacular view, the inn offers the best in cuisine.

A handsome Russian samovar dominates the expansive living room with its unrestricted views of the lake and surrounding hills. Wing chairs and sofas are grouped with small tables around a fireplace to provide a cozy atmosphere for late-afternoon tea and conversation. A library nook is stocked with a rich selection of reading materials.

Two comfortable country-style dining rooms overlooking the water provide a restful environment in which to enjoy an exceptional meal. Or, in the summer, you may be seated under a giant maple on one of the inn's open-air terraces.

Breakfast is hearty, and includes a buffet table of fresh fruits, yogurt, juices, cereals, and coffee cake. A hot item, such as French toast or a fluffy omelet, follows.

Dinner begins with a selection of appetizers that can include a spicy, thick, Cuban black bean soup with bourbon, or Belgian endive leaf "boats" filled with a blend of chopped walnuts, crumbled blue cheese, and watercress in a light vinaigrette. I ordered beef creole with andouille sausage from the numerous choices on the menu. The flavorful Cajun sausage was garlicky, and was a perfect complement to the

tender beef chunks, onions, green pepper, and fresh tomatoes that were
artistically served on a bed of wild and white rice. Just as I took my last
bite of the brandy-rich orange nut cake I had for dessert, the great orb
of a sun sank into the lake.

The five upstairs guest rooms are furnished in antiques and have
sitting areas that overlook the lake. The rooms' brass beds are covered
with century-old quilts that enhance the Victorian antique walnut
armoires and Ulla's handmade painted lampshades. Eight additional
rooms are located in cottages behind the inn and feature fireplaces and
lake views from private porches. All seventeen rooms have private
baths with tubs and showers.

If you're a ping-pong fanatic like I am, the game room in the base-
ment will satisfy your paddle itch. There are darts and other assorted
games for your enjoyment also. If you prefer outdoor sports, it's only a
short hike to the private beach with its sailboats, canoes, windsurfer,
paddleboats and rowboats. For those who would rather relax and
watch, the beach house has a hanging wicker swing where a lazy afternoon can be spent with Fred, the inn's friendly cat.

Nearby 18th-century villages such as Litchfield and Washington
offer antique shops and local crafts, and summer theaters and concerts
are active from the first of July to the last of August. The hiking and
biking paths of Litchfield's White Memorial Foundation also afford
trails for cross-country skiing in the winter.

BOULDERS INN, Route 45, New Preston, CT 06777; 203-868-0541.

A 17-guestroom (private baths) 19th-century granite inn, located at the foot of the
Pinnacle Mountains on Lake Waramaug. 4 rooms and 2 suites in main house, 8 guest-
houses, 3 rooms in carriage house. King, queen and twin beds available. Open all
year except the two weeks after Thanksgiving. Modified American plan. Close to lake
sports, antique shops, theater, concerts, hiking, and biking. No pets. Two cats in residence. Ulla and Kees Adema, owners/hosts.

DIRECTIONS: From Rte. 684 north, take Rte. 84 east to Exit 7, then to Rte. 7, then to
New Milford Rte. 202 (formerly Rte. 25), then to New Preston. Turn left on Rte. 45 to
Lake Waramaug and Boulder Inn.

INN EVENTS: DECEMBER, THIRD MONDAY—Christmas Dinner with madrigal singers

GRISWOLD INN
Essex, Connecticut

Among all the things that are special about the town of Essex, perhaps
foremost is its community feeling, with parades and special events on
holidays, such as Memorial Day and Halloween, and its wonderful
Christmas festivities. The Griswold Inn, affectionately known as "the

Gris," plays a very active role in these events, which invariably occur in and around the square in front of the inn.

The Memorial Day parade was especially affecting, with paraders in uniforms from bygone wars and campaigns, a fife-and-drum corps, the school band, Boy and Girl Scouts, the fire fighters on their red fire engines, the ambulance corps, and many others. A wreath is thrown into the water to commemorate all those who died at sea, and then the parade continues to the cemeteries in the three villages of Essex township.

Bill Winterer had wheeled out the antique popcorn machine, as he has done for years, dispensing popcorn to delighted children (and some adults). The Gris wore a festive air, with windowboxes planted with geraniums and petunias. Bill and his wife, Vicky, organize all sorts of special celebrations for the holidays—they even had a splendid sendoff on Groundhog Day, for which Bill served as grand marshal, complete with a great feast, song and dance, a magician, and costumes. Their Game Festival has become a December tradition, with pheasant, goose, wild turkey, vension, hare, and dishes made from Colonial recipes. In summer, Essex is a port of call for sailors the world over, who dock at the end of the street and troupe into town in their faded jeans and sneakers for lunch at the Griswold.

Stepping inside the inn brings back a couple of centuries of history. The Tap Room, built originally in 1738 as the first schoolhouse in

Essex, was later rolled on logs drawn by a team of oxen to its present location. The pot-bellied stove and all of the marine paintings, ships' artifacts, and steamboat memorabilia are nostalgic reminders of early life in this busy little seaport town on the Connecticut River.

Within its several dining rooms and parlors, the inn has many remarkable marine paintings, including some by Antonio Jacobsen. There is an extensive collection of ship models, firearms, binnacles, ships' clocks, and humorous posters and prints.

There are different kinds of entertainment almost every evening.

All of the guest rooms, furnished in "early Essex," have private baths and telephones. There are two additional buildings providing suites with living rooms and fireplaces.

Ask the innkeeper what the British commandeer said about the Inn when the British commandeered it during the war of 1812.

———

GRISWOLD INN, Main St., Essex, CT 06426; 203-767-1812.

A 23-guestroom (private baths) inn in a waterside town, steps away from the Connecticut River. European plan. Complimentary continental breakfast served daily to inn guests. Lunch and dinner served daily to travelers. Hunt breakfast served Sun. Closed Christmas Eve and Christmas Day. Near the Eugene O'Neill Theatre, Goodspeed Opera House, Ivoryton Playhouse, Gillette Castle, Mystic Village, Valley Railroad, and Hammonasset State Beach. Day sailing on inn's 44-foot ketch by appointment. Bicycles, tennis, and boating nearby. Marmalade the cat is in residence. Victoria and William G. Winterer, owners/hosts.

DIRECTIONS: From I-95 take Exit 69 and travel north on Rte. 9 to Exit 3, Essex. Turn right at stoplight and follow West Ave. to center of town. Turn right onto Main St. and proceed down to water and inn.

INN EVENTS: JANUARY—Connecticut Bounty Festival
FEBRUARY 2—Ground Hog Festival
FEBRUARY 14—Valentine Dinner
MARCH 17—St. Patrick's Day Dinner
APRIL—Baby Back Rib Festival
APRIL—Shad Festival
MAY—Mother's Day Dinner
OCTOBER—October Festival
OCTOBER 31—Halloween Parade & Party
DECEMBER—Game Festival
DECEMBER 31—New Year's Eve Gala

THE HOMESTEAD INN
Greenwich, Connecticut

I'm always delightfully re-surprised at the truly residential nature of its location, although it is only moments away from I-95. There has been

an inn here for a very long time, with a long succession of different innkeepers and many different types of accommodations; now, however, I believe the Homestead has reached the pinnacle of its success.

Today, the inn reflects the sensitivities and tastes of Lessie Davison and Nancy Smith, two attractive and talented women who literally saved this 185-year-old farmhouse from the wrecker's ball. They are very proud of the historic plaque that was awarded to the inn in 1988 by the Historical Society of Greenwich.

The inn began its life as a farmhouse, built in 1799. In 1859 it was sold to innkeepers who completely remodeled it in the distinctive Carpenter Gothic architecture of the Victorian era.

The inn is set back from the road in a lovely old orchard and gardens, and the sloping lawn is highlighted by handsome hydrangea bushes. There are now twenty-three guest rooms, all with different decorative themes. They are handsomely furnished, including many antiques and such comforts as clock radios, electric blankets, two pillows for every head, lots of books and magazines, and very modern bathrooms. In many ways, the guest rooms resemble those at Rothay Manor in the Lake Country of England.

Although many of the guest rooms are in the main house, some very careful attention has been given recently to the remodeling of other buildings on the property, and guests may now enjoy a variety of rooms, some with queen-sized beds and balconies or porches, as well as a queen-bedded suite, with a lovely, large, cathedral-ceilinged bedroom and a front porch overlooking the neighbor's apple orchard.

The Homestead is the perfect alternative to the busy, noisy New York hotels, and provides a very pleasant country-type atmosphere for city dwellers who want to leave the canyons of steel for the peaceful lanes of Greenwich.

The menu offerings include French country pâté, many marvelous soups, especially the mussel bisque, called Billi-Bi, tender sweetbreads of veal, lobster done several ways and duck with cassis sauce. Desserts made by the inn's pastry chef often include fresh fruit tarts, triple chocolate layer cake, or Linzer torte.

THE HOMESTEAD INN, 420 Field Point Rd., Greenwich, CT 06830; 203-869-7500.

A 23-guestroom (private baths) inn located in the residential area of a suburb, 45 min. north of New York City. Queen and twin size beds available. Lunch served Mon. thru Fri.; dinner served daily except Labor Day, Christmas, New Year's. Wheelchair facilities for restaurant. Located a short distance from Conn. countryside and shore. Accessible by train from New York City. No pets. Lessie Davison and Nancy Smith, owners/hosts.

DIRECTIONS: The inn is 3 mi. from Rte. I-95. Take Exit 3 in Greenwich; from NYC, turn left; from New Haven, turn right off ramp. Turn left onto Horseneck Ln. at light, just before railroad overpass. Go to next traffic light; turn left onto Field Point Rd., and continue approx.1/4 mi. to inn on the right.

MANOR HOUSE
Norfolk, Connecticut

Probably most remarkable among many unusual features in this baronial-looking mansion is the amazing fireplace with a huge raised stonework hearth and a curious roughened plaster wall in which a Roman frieze is embedded. Diane Tremblay, who with her husband, Hank, is the innkeeper, told me that sometimes guests can get into rather lively conversations about the origins of that frieze.

It's hard to know just where to start in describing this 1898 house—its builder, Charles Spofford, clearly had eclectic and aesthetic tastes, as can be seen in the many Tiffany and leaded-glass windows, intricate moldings, rich, hand-carved woods, ornate fixtures, and Moorish arches. Although the surroundings are imposing and elegantly Victorian, there is a casual air of easygoing informality in this spacious house.

There's a wide variety in the nine guest rooms—from a palatial master bedroom with a huge working fireplace and king-sized bed with antique lace canopy, as well as one with a private elevator and balcony, to the suite with a bedroom and sitting room on the third floor. All are furnished with interesting antique pieces and down comforters.

Breakfast might be blueberry pancakes, poached eggs with lemon-chive sauce, scrambled eggs and bacon, orange-spice waffles, or French toast. The honey comes from their own bees, and the maple syrup is local. Breakfast can be served almost anywhere—in bed, in the formal

Manor House
The Inn at Norfolk

dining room, in the small breakfast nook, on the sun porch, in the living room in front of the fire—take your choice.

MANOR HOUSE, P.O. Box 447, Maple Ave., Norfolk, CT 06058; 203-542-5690.

An 9-guestroom (private baths) Victorian baronial manor in the picturesque village of Norfolk in northwestern Conn. King, queen and double beds. Complimentary full breakfast. Open year-round. Summer weekends and holidays, 2-night minimum stay. Summer concerts at Yale Summer School and Music Mountain nearby. Tennis, golf, lake swimming, canoeing, horseback riding, biking, carriage and sleigh rides, skiing, antiques, shopping, nearby. Kennel facilities nearby. One cat in residence. Smoking in restricted areas. CCs: Visa, MC, AE. Diane and Henry Tremblay, owners/hosts.

DIRECTIONS: From NYC: Take I-84 to exit for Rte. 8 north (Waterbury, Conn.). At Winsted, turn right to Rte. 44 west. In Norfolk, look for Maple Ave. on right opposite village green. From north: Take Rte. 7 to Canaan, Conn., then Rte. 44 east to Norfolk. Rte. 44 takes a sharp left turn in front of village green; look for Maple Ave. on left.

INN EVENTS: Countryside tour by horse and carriage, or sleigh ride through the woods followed by hot mulled cider in farmhouse.

Two nights free with purchase of harpsichord by local craftsman Carl Dudash; visit his studio and master classes.

RIVERWIND INN

Deep River, Connecticut

Riverwind Inn is one of my favorite B&Bs: I can't remember where I've seen a better collection of museum-quality American folk art. Barbara Barlow's informal old (circa 1850) rose-beige clapboard is a reflection of her fun-loving ingenuity. And well it should be. Ever since

1984, when Barbara migrated from a teaching job and her home state of Virginia, she has been skillfully molding Riverwind into her own eclectic work of art.

But before I go on, I must divulge one of Barbara's not-so-well-kept secrets, since I found it so endearingly quirky: her love of pigs. Pigs appear throughout the inn in every imaginable form—patchwork pillows, a cookie jar, as little ceramic ornaments hung from the doors of her old Virginia pie safe, and as perfect porcine-shaped flaky Southern breakfast biscuits.

I really haven't room here to do justice to the amazing aspects of this inn, so I'll give you the bare-bones minimum and let *you* have the exciting pleasure of discovery.

Riverwind's common rooms offer guests the opportunity to mingle in spirited conversation or retreat to thoughtful contemplation. Numerous fireplaces maintain a cozy warmth room-to-room during cooler days. The front parlor is a comfy setting in which to sip sherry and read. You may even want to play a tune on the piano, whose keys once enjoyed Dave Brubeck's touch.

The glassed-in porch is one of Barbara's favorite spots. White wicker and ceiling fans make this an airy retreat during summer. If you're lucky the heavens will bless you with a spectacular thunderstorm.

I had an almost excruciating time deciding which guest room to choose: all eight are characteristically unique. I finally settled on the Smithfield room with its all-American color scheme and high maple rope bed. And while all rooms have private baths, I did envy the honeymoon couple who had the romantic suite with the Japanese steeping bath.

One evening, Barbara and I visited over cups of mulled cider near the cheerful kitchen cooking hearth. We both smiled as the inn's cat, Miss Hickory, "worked the room," begging attention from other guests. I teased Barbara about her pig obsession, but she laughed and said, "Just wait until breakfast, you'll love the Smithfield ham!"

RIVERWIND INN, 209 Main St., Deep River, CT 06417; 203-526-2014.

A one-of-a-kind, informal 8-guestroom (private baths) inn filled with American folk art. Southern buffet breakfast. Open all year. Central to all activities in the Connecticut River Valley. No pets. CCs: Visa, MC, AE. Barbara Barlow and Bob Bucknall, owners/hosts.

DIRECTIONS: Take Exit 69 from I-95 to Rte. 9 then to Exit 4. Turn left on Rte. 154. Inn is 1/2 mi. on right.

UNDER MOUNTAIN INN
Salisbury, Connecticut

I have always been charmed by everything English, and as a young man read as much of Charles Dickens' work as I could lug home from the library every month. So it was with "great expectations" (pun intended) that I drove to the great white farmhouse called Under Mountain Inn. I had recently read an article in the food section of a major national newspaper praising this inn's English Christmas dinner, and even though it was the middle of summer, I decided to visit for a weekend.

Salisbury is nestled in a rural valley beneath the Appalachian Trail, an area that offers unlimited walking opportunities, and is close to

lakes, streams, skiing, and cultural festivals. The Under Mountain Inn sits on 3 acres that are bordered by a 7,500-acre state park and a 50-acre horse farm. The lovely old two-story home has black shutters and is surrounded by huge shade trees. The area must be just as beautiful during the winter.

Innkeepers Peter and Marged Higginson have operated the inn since 1985. The early 18th-century home has wide plank flooring, and almost every common room has a cozy fireplace. The large attractive living room is the center of activity. Many comfortable sofas and chairs are grouped for conversation. A piano is available for after-dinner sing-alongs, the library is well stocked with English literature, and game tables await a round of whist. The parlor is a bit more intimate.

The guest rooms are large and done in a color scheme of Wedgwood blue, rose, and cream. To create an 18th-century ambience, Williamsburg reproduction wallpapers and a mixture of American antiques and reproduction pieces have been used. Each room has its own bath, some of them wonderfully large.

Peter is English, and the chef, so it's no wonder that the inn's cuisine features a number of English specialties. Although I wasn't going to have the gourmet pleasure of the Christmas feast, he did invite me into the kitchen to keep him company. "We usually begin with an appetizer of imported Scotch salmon, then follow that with roast goose. I like to use a traditional prune stuffing," he explained. "Then, we serve mince pie and petit fours for dessert!" For a bit of fun, an English Christmas cracker—a tissue-wrapped "firecracker" with a pop-out trinket and hat—is placed next to each plate.

Both dinner and breakfast are included with your room. Breakfast is a full-English affair, including the special treats of sautéed mushrooms and tomatoes, and fried bread. Thursdays and Sundays, through the summer, authentic fish and chips are served for dinner. A full menu of five or six choices of appetizers, entrées, and desserts is served the other evenings. For those guests attending the Tanglewood music festival, Marged will make up a scrumptious picnic supper. The inn has a full liquor license.

Sugar and Cocoa, the inn's resident canines, escorted me to the top of the stairs when I went to bed. I took some time to choose a book from the extensive second-floor library in the hall, and after skipping over title upon title, was pleased to find what I was looking for—*Great Expectations*. As I climbed into bed to get reacquainted with some old literary friends, I decided I had to come back for some of that Christmas goose next year.

UNDER MOUNTAIN INN, Under Mountain Rd. (Rte. 41), Salisbury, CT 06068; 203-435-0242.

A 7-guestroom (private baths), English-style, 18th-century farmhouse. All-size beds. Closed 2 weeks in Dec., and mid-March to mid-April. Modified American plan, with traditional English fare. Skiing, boating, hiking. Thirty min. to Tanglewood and Berkshire Theater Festival. No pets. Two dogs and three cats in residence. Smoking restricted. Marged and Peter Higginson, owners/hosts.

DIRECTIONS: Travel to Egremont, Mass. From New York City or N.J., go north on Rte. 41 for 4 mi. to Salisbury. From Albany or Boston, go south on Rte. 41 for 8 mi. to Salisbury. The inn is 4 mi. north of the Salisbury village center on Rte. 41 (Undermountain Rd.).

WEST LANE INN
Ridgefield, Connecticut

"Basically, I think that we have three different types of guests that find their way to our little inn." Maureen Mayer and I were seated on the broad front porch of the West Lane Inn enjoying a generous continental breakfast. "By the way," she added, "if you'd like a bigger breakfast, we have an à la carte breakfast menu that offers, among other things, grapefruit, sliced bananas, berries, yogurt, corn flakes, and poached eggs."

I might add that this breakfast was served at a table with real linen tablecloths and napkins, and there is a fine gourmet restaurant next door.

One of the things that sets West Lane Inn apart is the many additional amenities this attractive innkeeper provides for her guests. For example, there is a clock in every guest room, as well as a computerized phone system, a radio-TV, individual heating and air conditioning controls, and one-day laundry and dry-cleaning service; a basket of fruit, cheese, and crackers is presented to newly arrived guests.

"Among our guests are families being relocated to the Ridgefield-Fairfield-Danbury area who need a comfortable, roomy place in which to stay while they look for a new home. Many come and stay for a week or two. I decided that they would be much more comfortable if we had accommodations that reflected the feeling of the area, so we have rooms with decks overlooking our lawn and the forest in the rear. Some of these have fireplaces and kitchen facilities. You see, guests can literally establish a little home for a short time. One of our bathrooms is designed for the handicapped, similar to the one at the West Mountain Inn in Vermont."

West Lane Inn is set back from the village street with a broad lawn enhanced by azaleas, tulips, roses and maple and oak trees. It was originally built as a mansion in the early 1800s and the guest rooms are unusually commodious.

The other types of guests are commercial travelers, both men and women, and vacationers who enjoy country-inn hospitality. "I think we understand commercial travelers very well and we've done everything possible to have them feel that this is really a 'home away from home.'

"As far as the country-inn travelers are concerned, we're at sort of a crossroads for north-south, east-west travel, and many couples on their way to or from New England come back and stay every year."

The West Lane could well be a model for other bed-and-breakfast inns everywhere. Every lodging room is spotless and the furnishings and decorating are all part of a harmonious color scheme. Overnight guests are coddled even further with heated towel racks and wonderfully fluffy bath sheets.

WEST LANE INN, 22 West Lane, Ridgefield, CT 06877; 203-438-7323.

A 20-guestroom (private baths; several suites with kitchens) inn approx 1 hr. from N.Y.C., in a quiet residential village in southwest Connecticut. King and queen beds. Open every day in the year. Breakfast and light snacks available until 10:30 P.M. Restaurant within walking distance. Wheelchair access. Convenient to many museums and antique shops. Golf, tennis, swimming, and xc skiing and other outdoor recreation available nearby. No pets. Maureen Mayer, owner/host.

DIRECTIONS: From New York City: Westside Hwy. to Sawmill River Pkwy. Take Exit 6, going right on Rte. 35, 12 mi. to Ridgefield. Inn is on left. From Hartford: Exit I-84 on Rte. 7 south and follow Rte. 35 to Ridgefield.

Rhode Island

Historically, Rhode Island's fortunes were built on shipping and whaling (you can see how those fortunes grew by visiting the opulent mansions of Newport and Watch Hill). Water is still this small state's prime attraction: the sandy shores of the Rhode Island Sound hosts boaters, fishers and swimmers.

EVENTS

JANUARY	Twelfth Night Celebration, Westerly: full-scale medieval Christmas production with music, boar's head procession and peasant's feast (info: 401-596-8663)
JANUARY, LATE– FEBRUARY, EARLY	Newport Winter Festival (info: 401-849-8048)
MARCH	Irish Heritage Month, Newport (info: 401-849-8098)
APRIL	Southeastern New England Home Show, Providence (info: 401-331-6700)
APRIL–MAY	Blithewold Gardens & Arboretum Annual Spring Bulb Display, Bristol (info: 401-253-2707)
MAY (THROUGHOUT)	May Breakfasts: a state-wide tradition since 1867. Rhode Island jonnycakes and other native dishes are served in varied settings, from bird sanctuaries and church halls to yacht clubs and veterans' posts (info: 401-277-2601)
MAY	North American Small Boat Show, Newport (info: 401-846-1600)
JUNE	Festival of Historic Houses, Providence (info: 401-831-7440)
JULY 4	Nation's oldest Independence Day parade (info: 401-253-8397)
JULY 4	Ancient & Horribles Parade, Chepachet (info: 401-596-6691)
JULY, MIDDLE	Newport Music Festival: a world-renowned event (info: 401-846-1133)
JULY	Wickford Art Festival (info: 401-295-5566)
JULY	International Charity Air Show, Quonset (info: 401-295-0554)
AUGUST	Craft and food fair, Narragansett (info: 401-783-7121)
AUGUST, EARLY	Ben & Jerry's Newport Folk Festival (info: 401-847-3709)
AUGUST, MIDDLE	Newport Jazz Festival (info: 401-847-3700)
AUGUST	Cajun & Bluegrass Music, West Greenwich (info: 401-351-6312)
AUGUST	Annual Tuna Tournament, Narragansett (info: 401-737-8845)
SEPTEMBER, MIDDLE	International Sailboat Show, Newport (info: 401-846-1600)

SEPTEMBER	Providence Pasta Challenge (info: 401-351-6440)
SEPTEMBER, LATE	Octoberfest, Pawtucket (info: 401-728-0500)
OCTOBER, EARLY	International Quahog Festival, North Kingstown: in honor of the famous local shellfish (info: 401-885-6061)
OCTOBER-NOVEMBER	Haunted Monastery, Cumberland (info: 401-333-9000)
DECEMBER (THROUGHOUT)	Christmas in Newport: famed mansions and homes open to display holiday splendor (info: 401-847-1000)
DECEMBER	Christmas at Blithewold, Bristol: unique period decor and vignettes in turn-of-the-century mansion (info: 401-253-2707)
DECEMBER	Holidays at Slater Mill, Pawtucket: hand-crafted textiles and fiber arts (info: 401-725-8638)

SIGHTS

Astor's Beechwood

Cliff Walk

Hammersmith Farm

Museum of Yachting

Newport Preservation Society Mansions

Ochre Court

Tennis Hall of Fame

Redwood Library

Touro Synagogue

Trinty Church

LARCHWOOD INN

Wakefield, Rhode Island

Frank Browning and I were talking about lobsters, a subject that is near and dear to the hearts of those who are fortunate enough to live near New England's coastal waters. The Larchwood Inn certainly qualifies in this respect, since it's just a few minutes from the great beaches of southern Rhode Island.

"We buy from one source, and we know we're getting the best," he told me. "On Monday, we have special dinners of either twin lobsters or prime rib, and it is one of our most popular nights in the week. We always have a full-sized lobster every night and twin lobsters on Monday. I hope your readers will reserve ahead for lobsters because there's always a great demand. By the way, on Mondays in the summertime we have a cabaret performer and a piano player. It really livens things up."

I wandered into one of the dining rooms, where there is a mural

depicting the southern Rhode Island beaches. The tables were very attractively set for the next meal with green tablecloths. I noticed the living room had been redecorated since my last visit. It was very pleasant, with comfortable chairs and a fireplace with a very impressive ship's model on the mantel. There was also an exotic bird in a cage.

At this point, Frank returned, and I asked him about the ship's model. "That is a three-masted schooner, called *L'Astrolabe*, and everything was built to scale by a friend of mine. See the little boys on the deck—he thought of everything."

The Larchwood is a large mansion, dating back to 1831, in the village of Wakefield, set in the middle of a large parklike milieu with copper, beech, ginkgo, pin oak, spruce, mountain ash, maple, Japanese cherry trees, evergreens, dogwoods, and a very old mulberry tree. In all, there are three acres of trees and lawn.

The interior has many Scottish touches, including quotations from Robert Burns and Sir Walter Scott, and photographs and prints of Scottish historical and literary figures.

The conversation naturally turned once again to menu items, since Frank was the chef here for many years and is now carefully supervising the kitchen and dining room.

"We're in the process right now of working with the South County Hospital. They are coming out with low-cholesterol items, and they came to us to ask if we could cooperate with them. We're working on seven or eight items in our restaurant for their program. There will be lighter things, including different ways to serve chicken and fish."

I asked him about breakfasts, and I'm very glad I did. "We make the French toast with our own bread and offer it with either sour cream or whipped cream and warm strawberries. The strawberries make it absolutely fantastic. It's something that our guests really appreciate, along with our selection of different omelets."

Besides guest rooms in the main inn, there are additional attractively furnished guest rooms in the Holly House, a 150-year-old building across the street from the inn. Guests at the Holly House can enjoy breakfast, lunch, and dinner at the Larchwood Inn dining room.

My eye caught a card on the table that had a Catholic, Jewish, and Protestant grace, and also one from Robert Burns.

LARCHWOOD INN, 176 Main St., Wakefield, RI 02879; 401-783-5454.

A 19-guestroom (13 private baths) village inn just 3 mi. from the famous southern RI beaches. Queen, double and twin beds. European plan. Breakfast, lunch, dinner served every day of the year. Swimming, boating, surfing, fishing, xc skiing, and bicycles nearby. One cat in residence. Francis Browning, owner/host.

DIRECTIONS: From Rte. 1, take Pond St. exit and proceed 1/2 mi. directly to inn.

THE MELVILLE HOUSE
Newport, Rhode Island

The Melville House is a lovely old Colonial with a fascinating past. The French general Rochambeau quartered some of his troops at the 39 Clarke Street address when they fought in the Revolutionary War under President George Washington. The Melvilles purchased the property during the 1800s and tore down the original home, moving the Frank Street house to the site. Because of alterations, the current structure is more of an 18th-century design.

Located in a quiet part of Newport's Historic District, the home is within walking distance of the Brick Market boutiques, the wharf, and excellent restaurants. Innkeepers Rita and Sam Rogers have been true to their motto, "Where the past is present," by decorating with Colonial and early American furnishings, yet modernizing where updating was needed.

The inn's interior is charming. While the sitting room is small, comfortable wing chairs frame the fireplace, inviting intimate conversation over complimentary afternoon sherry. It is here, also, that Sam's collection of old appliances is displayed. Formerly a small appliance designer, Sam will enthusiastically demonstrate cherry pitters, dough makers, coffee grinders, and mincers. In the adjacent sunny breakfast room, guests are encouraged to help themselves to a homemade breakfast served buffet-style at polished pub tables.

The corridor leading to the guest rooms is stocked with games and books for rainy days. Braided rugs, Colonial pineapple-post beds, hand-

made afghans, and bureaus restored by Sam decorate the guest rooms. The original low ceilings, which might be uncomfortable in another environment, create a secluded, homey feeling here.

THE MELVILLE HOUSE, 39 Clarke St., Newport, RI 02840; 401-847-0640.

A 7-guestroom (5 private baths) Colonial located in Newport's Historic District. Breakfast included. Double & twin beds. Open March 1 to January 1. Within walking distance to boutiques, restaurants and the wharf. Newport Jazz Festival and other special events throughout the year. No pets. Off-street parking. CCs: Visa, MC, AE. Rita and Sam Rogers, owners/hosts.

DIRECTIONS: A 1-1/2 hour drive from Boston, and a 3-1/2 hour drive from New York. From the south, make a U turn around the square after exiting Rte. 114. Take a right on Clarke St. From NY, turn right when you come off the Newport Bridge. Go through first light, bear left at second light, then left at third light. Turn right on Clarke St.

WAYSIDE
Newport, Rhode Island

Part of the fun in visiting the "cottages" of the very rich is imagining how it would be to spend the night in such opulence. Now, if you have made reservations well in advance, you can turn into the circular driveway almost opposite the Elms and play houseguest for a night or more at the Wayside.

Among your neighbors: The Elms is across the street; down the block is Chateau-sur-Mer, Rosecliff (where *The Great Gatsby* was

filmed), Mrs. Astor's Beechwood, Marble House, and Belcourt Castle. Tour guides will tell you all about the scandals as well as the costs of living it up in the Gilded Age.

This Georgian-style, 1890s mansion has several bedrooms so large that they are sitting rooms as well, and each is individually decorated. Alas, the retinue of servants is gone, and you must serve yourself a simple continental breakfast from a buffet in the lobby before starting out on foot to pay calls at the museum palaces of the neighbors.

After a day's walking, it's especially nice to be able to take a dip in the house swimming pool before heading out for dinner in one of the fine restaurants of Newport.

Oh yes, the servants' quarters are also available.

WAYSIDE, Bellevue Ave., Newport, RI 02840; 401-847-0302.

A 10-guestroom (private baths) guest house on famous and fabulous Bellevue Avenue. Black and white television in every room. All size beds. Open year-round. Swimming pool, ocean beach, mansions, restaurants, shops nearby. No pets. No credit cards. Off-street parking. Reservations should be made well in advance. Al and Dorothy Post, owners/hosts.

DIRECTIONS: Bellevue Avenue is probably Newport's most famous street. As you drive toward Ocean Avenue, the Elms will be on your right. Watch for driveway on left marked Wayside (nothing so crass as house numbers in this neighborhood) and turn in.

Massachusetts

The Bay Colony, as every schoolchild knows, played a major role in early American history: who can forget Plymouth Rock, the Boston Tea Party, or Paul Revere's ride? The birthplace of an impressive number of important colonial figures, many well-preserved historical sites can be found in the greater Boston area. Cape Cod and the islands of Martha's Vineyard and Nantucket are summer playgrounds that offer miles of ocean and bay beaches, quaint seaside villages, and wonderful antique and craft stores. The area to the west of Boston includes the Berkshire Mountains, a mecca for music and dance lovers every summer, and the historic re-creation at Old Sturbridge Village.

Cape Cod and the Islands

On my last visit to Cape Cod, Martha's Vineyard and Nantucket I decided to fly on Cape Air. I found it very convenient. They always left on time and the price is very low when you consider the trips from Boston to Provincetown or Hyannis or Hyannis to the Islands take approximately 15-25 minutes. The planes are small. The air vents and lights didn't work, my luggage from the Islands to San Francisco was delayed and putting the label fragile on the luggage wasn't read by the workman, but don't major airlines have the same problems?. On Martha's Vineyard I rented a convertible from Budget-Rent a Car. The only way to go.

EVENTS

FEBRUARY	seal watching, Cape Cod (info: 508-349-2615)
MARCH	Annual Hat Parade, Falmouth
APRIL–OCTOBER	whale watching, Provincetown (info: 1-800-826-9300)
APRIL	Patriot's Day Weekend Celebration, Falmouth
APRIL	Daffodil Festival, Nantucket: annual spring celebration with antique car parade and house tours (info: 508-228-1700)
APRIL	Patriots Day, Nantucket (info: 508-228-1700)
APRIL	Annual Dart Tournament, Martha's Vineyard (info: 508-693-0085)
APRIL	Comsog Spring Concert, Oak Bluffs (info: 508-693-0085)
MAY	Winthrop Challenge Biathlon, Nantucket (info: 508-228-1700)

JUNE	Annual Cranberry Classic Road Race, Nantucket (info: 508-228-1700)
JUNE	Winthrop Challenge Triathlon, Nantucket (info: 508-228-1700)
JUNE	Edaville Civil War Reenactment, South Carver (info: 508-866-4526)
JUNE–AUGUST	Monomoy Theater, Cape Cod (info: 508-945-1589)
JULY 4	Parade and Blessing of the Fleet, Falmouth
JULY 4	Parade, Chatham
JULY, EARLY	Tisbury Street Fair, Vineyard Haven (info: 508-693-0085)
JULY, MIDDLE	Edgartown Regatta (info: 508-693-0085)
JULY, MIDDLE	Scottish Festival, Eastham
JULY	Annual Homestead Summer Fair & Tea, Nantucket (info: 508-228-1700)
JULY	Celebrity Tennis Tournament, Martha's Vineyard (info: 508-693-0085)
JULY–AUGUST	open-air Thursday night bank concerts, Falmouth
JULY–AUGUST	Friday night bank concerts, Chatham
JULY–AUGUST	Cape Playhouse (info: 508-385-3911)
JULY–AUGUST	Designer Showcase, Nantucket (info: 508-228-1700)
JULY–AUGUST	Melody Tent, Hyannis (info: 508-385-3911)
AUGUST, EARLY	Possible Dreams Auction, Edgartown (info: 508-693-0085)
AUGUST, MIDDLE	Arts & Crafts Festival, Eastham
AUGUST, MIDDLE	Illumination Night, Oak Bluffs (info: 508-693-0085)
AUGUST, MIDDLE	Agricultural Fair, West Tisbury (info: 508-693-0085)
AUGUST, MIDDLE	Falmouth Road Race (info: 508-540-7000)
AUGUST, MIDDLE	Fireworks, Oak Bluffs (info: 508-693-0085)
AUGUST	Fall River festival: tall ships, boat races, concerts, crafts, parade (info: 508-676-8226)
SEPTEMBER, MIDDLE	Tivoli Bike Race, Oak Bluffs (info: 508-693-0085)
SEPTEMBER, MIDDLE	Windmill Weekend, Eastham
SEPTEMBER–OCTOBER	Bluefish Derby, Edgartown (info: 508-693-0085)
OCTOBER, MIDDLE	Cranberry Harvest, Nantucket Island (info: 508-228-1700)
OCTOBER	Cape Cod Marathon, Falmouth (548-0348)
NOVEMBER, LATE	Plymouth Plantation, Plymouth: colonists prepare for winter, serve 17th-century dinners to visitors (info: 508-746-1622)
NOVEMBER, LATE	Festival of Lights, Eastham
DECEMBER, EARLY	Nantucket Christmas Stroll (info: 508-228-1700)

DECEMBER, MIDDLE	Whale of a Christmas Celebration, Edgartown and Vineyard Haven (info: 508-693-2725)
DECEMBER, MIDDLE	Twelve Days of Christmas, Tisbury (info: 508-693-0085)
DECEMBER	Christmas by the Sea, Falmouth (548-8500)
DECEMBER	La Salette Shrine Christmas Festival of Lights, Attleboro: largest religious-themed outdoor Christmas display in the U.S. (info: 508-222-5410)
DECEMBER	Old-Fashioned Christmas in Edgartown (info: 508-693-0085)
DECEMBER 31ST	1st night Celebration, Falmouth (362-3225)

SIGHTS

Cape Cod National Seashore & Nature Trails

Chicama Vineyards Winery, Martha's Vineyard

Dukes County Historical Society, Martha's Vineyard

Felix Neck Wildlife Sanctuary, Martha's Vineyard

Fish Pier, Chatham

Gingerbread Cottages, Martha's Vineyard

Heritage Planation, Sandwich

Lighthouse & Coast Guard Station, Chatham

Old Atwood House, Chatham

Old Grist Mill, Chatham

Provincetown Heritage Museum

Railroad Museum, Chatham

State Lobster Hatchery, Martha's Vineyard

Vineyard Playhouse, Martha's Vineyard

ANCHOR INN
Nantucket, Massachusetts

"We don't put chocolates on the pillow," Ann said. "We put a tray of them in the parlor." Ann and Charles Balas also own Nantucket Fine Chocolates a few blocks away, leading to a lot of guest puns about "what a sweet place this is."

It is, too, from the individually styled and decorated guest rooms, each named after a whaling ship, to Charles's freshly baked bran-and-fruit muffins served with juice and coffee or tea in the pretty, enclosed side porch turned breakfast room.

Anchor Inn was built in 1806 by the Nantucket whaling captain who gained recognition by being first to harpoon a whale in the far-off Pacific Ocean. More recent celebrity note: this is the place Frank

Gilbreth (of the *Cheaper by the Dozen* clan) wrote about in *Innside Nantucket*. A well-worn copy of the popular 1950s account of guest house tribulations can be found in the common room.

When Ann and Charles bought the Anchor Inn it had "a lot of history, but not nearly enough bathrooms." However, the couple from Connecticut was undaunted by details.

"Nantucket was clearly perfect," Charles muses. "But it is an expensive place to live. Then a friend suggested we look into running a bed and breakfast, and the next thing we knew we found the Anchor. It needed work, but doesn't everything?"

Charles and Ann did it all themselves. Today all the rooms have private baths, antique and period furnishings including some canopy beds, and, downstairs, such nice pluses as a separate refrigerator for guest use, current menus for all the nearby restaurants, and good maps, which Ann cheerfully marks for those of us who get easily lost.

Since the inn is strategically located next to Nantucket's Old North Church and within walking distance of everything in town, from ferry docks, harbor beaches, and tennis courts to shops, theaters, and museums, it is not necessary to bring your car. Leave it on the mainland along with your cares.

ANCHOR INN, 66 Centre St., Nantucket, MA 02554; 508-228-0072.

An intown B&B on Nantucket Island. 11 guestrooms (private baths); queen, double, twin beds. Open late April to mid-December. Continental breakfast. Many special rates. No pets. CCs: Visa, MC. Charles and Ann Balas, owners/hosts.

DIRECTIONS: From Steamship Authority, go 2 blocks up Broad St. to Centre; turn right; Anchor Inn on left just past church. From Hy-line dock, straight up Main St. 2 blocks to Centre; turn right, walk 2 blocks; Anchor Inn on left just past church. You can also come by plane.

ASHLEY MANOR
Barnstable, Massachusetts

Ashley Manor is a graceful gabled inn whose cedar shingles have weathered to a soft dove-gray. At the end of a curving drive, the estate sits on two lush acres of manicured lawns that are peppered here and there by apple and cherry trees. This gracious inn exhibits architectural signatures from the late 1600s, like enormous open-hearth fireplaces with beehive ovens, and unusual Nantucket spackled, and wideboard, flooring.

Other exceptional stylistic features make this inn very special. The downstairs parlor and, as innkeeper Fay Bain charmingly calls them, the *keeping rooms*, have wainscotted walls that are hand-rubbed with an antique glaze. Blown glass six-over-six windows filter sun into rooms that open onto a lovely brick terrace. Oriental rugs, antiques and country furnishings accent the rooms' easy comfort, and a grand piano awaits, sheet music at the ready.

Shuttered windows create an intimate environment in the romantic guest rooms. Of the six rooms, all but one have working fireplaces. Distinctive wallpapers, American antiques, beautiful private baths, and queen-sized pencil post beds complete the mood. Fresh flowers, fragrant soaps, body lotions, and individual coffee and tea service make guests feel coddled.

On chilly mornings, a fire warms the dining room where guests enjoy a full gourmet breakfast including Donald Bain's special home-made granola. The room's corners are highlighted by cupboards filled with a fine collection of porcelain plates, most of which are antiques.

Ashley Manor is centrally located to practically everything. Being in the heart of Cape Cod's historic district, the inn is within walking distance of Barnstable Village and the Harbor, which is known for whale watching cruises and sportfishing. Antique shops and museums are also close by for those landlubbers without sea legs.

Even though I'd like to keep this to myself, I really would be remiss not to mention a unique aspect of Ashley Manor—the inn's secret passageway connecting the upstairs and downstairs. Rumor suggests that the passageway was a clandestine hiding place for Tories during the Revolutionary War. This is the kind of colorful tidbit that makes vacations memorable.

ASHLEY MANOR, P.O. Box 856, 3660 Old Kings Highway (Rte. 6A), Barnstable, MA 02630; 508-362-8044.

A 6-guestroom (private baths) romantic pre-Colonial inn in the heart of Cape Cod's historic district. Double, queen and king beds. Full breakfast included. Open all year. Tennis court on premises. Near Barnstable Village, the Harbor, the beach, and all Cape Cod activities. No pets. CCs: Visa, MC, AE. Donald and Fay Bain, owner/hosts.

DIRECTIONS: Rte. 6 East to exit 6. Turn left onto 132 North to end. Turn Right onto 6A East. Go 3 mi. through the village of Barnstable to the traffic light. Go straight for 6/10 mi. Ashley Manor is on the left.

CAPTAIN TOM LAWRENCE HOUSE
Falmouth, Massachusetts

When a prosperous whaleboat captain builds a town residence for his family and uses a ship's carpenter for the job, it is four-square, hip-roofed, cupola-topped, and made to last.

Today's owner, Barbara Sabo-Feller, enjoys pointing out the continuing soundness of the historic house that is now her inn, as well as telling visitors about the days of sail. Captain Tom first shipped aboard Captain Jared Coffin's Nantucket whaler at the age of 17; he took his wife along on voyages of up to five years, and one of his daughters was a survivor of the famous "mutiny on the Bounty."

The 1861 house is set back from the road and shaded by two giant maple trees. It features a circular staircase that took three years to build, high ceilings and hardwood floors. The rooms are furnished with 19th-centry antiques, and there is a Steinway piano ("Go on, sit down

and play!" Barbara urges) as well as an Oriental carpet and a working fireplace in the Victorian sitting room.

The Captain's Room has a lace coronet canopy above a king-size bed. Other bedrooms have four-poster beds, and all have two present-day essentials: good reading lights and firm mattresses.

Barbara has added a distinctive continental touch from her German heritage, both in her decor and in her breakfast. Quiche Gisela, seafood crepes, or Belgain waffles with warm strawberry sauce may be the morning choice, and there are always freshly baked muffins and breads as well as eggs any way you like. Barbara even grinds her own flour, using organically grown grain, "to give the baking extra freshness."

The inn is just a few blocks from Falmouth village with its shops and restaurants. The beach is half a mile away, and you can walk to both Buzzards Bay and Nantucket Sound. Down the road at Woods Hole is the National Marine Fisheries Service Aquarium and the ferry dock for Martha's Vineyard. A trip to the island takes 45 minutes.

CAPTAIN TOM LAWRENCE HOUSE, 75 Locust St., Falmouth, MA 02540; 508-540-1445.

A 6-guestroom (private baths) inn on the southwest tip of Cape Cod. King, queen and single beds. Ceiling fans. Full breakfast. Closed Dec. 4th to Mar. 4th. No smoking or pets. CCs: Visa, MC. Barbara Sabo-Feller, owner/host.

DIRECTIONS: Cross Cape Cod Canal on Bourne Bridge. Drive south on Rte. 28 for 16 mi. to Falmouth Center and follow signs towards Woods Hole. Locust St. is the Woods Hole road; inn is on your right.

THE CAPTAIN'S HOUSE INN OF CHATHAM

Chatham, Massachusetts

Dave and Cathy Eakin are typical of many people who have fled the so-called corporate life and sought out a new career in innkeeping. They were indeed fortunate to find an exceptional house with over two acres in Chatham, one of Cape Cod's most picturesque villages.

The site was chosen in 1839 by Captain Harding for his home, and the antiques that the Eakins had been collecting for years, including many family heirlooms from their home in Yardley, Pennsylvania, found a most appropriate setting.

The bedrooms are named after the ships in which the good captain sailed, and they are now adorned with handsome flowered wallpapers and even some pictures of the captain's ships.

Besides comfortable bedrooms in the main house, there are additional accommodations in the Carriage House and in the Captain's Cottage.

Cathy does all the baking for breakfast and she explains that she puts out two or three sweet breads every morning, including Dutch Apple Loaf. She also makes homemade blueberry muffins. Breakfast is taken in the dining room, which has a splendid view of the lovely garden.

Dave and Cathy are both sailors but they own a 23-foot Seacraft Powerboat to take their guests out on when time permits.

The Captain's House is a real home-away-from-home and either Dave or Cathy are always on hand to attend to guests' special needs.

———

THE CAPTAIN'S HOUSE INN OF CHATHAM, 371 Old Harbor Rd., Chatham, MA 02633;508-945-0127.

A 16-guestroom (all private baths) Cape Cod bed-and-breakfast inn. King, queen and double beds. Open all year but Dec. 1 to Feb. 1. Breakfast and afternoon tea included in room rate. All of the historic, cultural, and scenic attractions of Cape Cod are most convenient. Beaches, golf, tennis courts, antiquing are nearby. No pets. Two schnauzers in residence. CCs: Visa, MC, AE. Dave and Cathy Eakin, owners/hosts.

DIRECTIONS: Follow the Mid-Cape Hwy. (Rte. 6) to Exit 11 and follow Rte. 137 for 3 mi. until it intersects with Rte. 28, at which point take a left, heading toward Chatham for 2 or 3 mi. At the rotary (traffic circle) with the Mobil and BP stations, look for a sign that says Orleans-Rte. 28 south. The inn is 1/2 mi. farther on the left.

CHARLES HINCKLEY HOUSE

Barnstable, Massachusetts

———

"What is that wonderful fragrance?" I asked Miya Patrick as we strolled down the little stone path through her wonderful wildflower garden. "Oh, that's thyme," she answered. "I've planted herbs all along the walk, so when anyone comes down the path they'll be surrounded by lovely scents."

Miya and Les Patrick have extended the naturalness and beauty of the gardens throughout this four-square, hip-roofed Colonial Federal house. As practiced "restorationists," doing most of the work themselves, they stripped, sanded, painted, and polished until the neglected house looked as bright as the proverbial penny.

The Charles Hinkley House is listed on the National Register of Historic Places, and they have kept a feeling of historical integrity in the furnishings and decorations of the inn, with Colonial paint colors, clay pots, hand-dipped candles, and dried-flower wreaths.

The three guest rooms in the house, all with fireplaces and baths, are refreshingly and simply decorated with pencil-post, curtained beds, shuttered windows, Oriental scatter rugs, and lovely fresh flowers. Another guest room in the separate summer kitchen is delightful and cozy with a brass bed and fascinating original brick cooking fireplace, painted pristine white.

Miya runs a catering service, in addition to preparing incredibly beautiful breakfast dishes—and I mean beautiful! The sun streaming through the dining room windows made the silver and glass sparkle on the polished cherry table, laid with white placemats, blue napkins, and fresh flowers, as I pulled up my chair. "I bake all the breads and pastries, and I usually serve scrambled eggs with smoked salmon or pecan waffles," Miya said. Pineapple with raspberries, choice of juice, and coffee or tea complete the menu.

Les and Miya are a winsome and hospitable couple. I wish I could have stayed longer.

CHARLES HINKLEY HOUSE, Olde Kings Highway, Box 723, Barnstable, MA 02630; 508-362-9924.

A 4-guestroom (private baths) Federal Colonial circa 1809 inn in the historic district of Barnstable. Queen and double beds. Breakfast included; dinner available weekends by reservation. Open year-round. Cape Cod Bay 5 min. walk away. Indoor dog and cat. No pets. No smoking. No CCs. Two-night minimum May-Nov. Les and Miya Patrick, owners/hosts.

DIRECTIONS: From Rte. 6, take Exit 6, turning left at stop sign, and go 1/2 mi. to Rte. 6A. Turn right and continue 1-1/2 mi. to inn.

CHARLOTTE INN
Edgartown, Massachusetts

This inn is located on South Summer Street in Edgartown on Martha's Vineyard Island, off the southern coast of Cape Cod. The main house, like many other Edgartown houses, is a classic three-story white clapboard with a widow's walk on the top. It is the former home of a Martha's Vineyard sea captain. The guest rooms are highly individual. There are pineapple bedposts, brass beds, carved antique headboards, beautiful chests, handsome silver, and positively scrumptious bathrooms. One has a tub from 1912 that weighs about a thousand pounds and had to be lifted through the window by a crane. Several rooms

have working fireplaces, and many have four-poster beds. There are lots of fresh flowers, books, magazines, good reading lamps, and perhaps most important of all, a very romantic atmosphere.

The main house has two areas for sitting with an overabundance of paintings for sale on the walls. I would have prefered not so many.

Besides the main house, there is the Carriage House, with a cathedral ceiling and unusual adornments as well as the Garden House, across the street from the main inn. This has been decorated with a French country look, and as is the case with the other guest rooms throughout the inn and annex, the furnishings and decorations have been done with great care and taste. This house also provides houseguests with a private lounge of their own, where they may enjoy the fireplace, play games, watch TV, and get acquainted.

There are two suites. I stayed in the Coach House. I should say I got lost in the Coach House since it has to be over 1200 sq. feet. Entering through the downstairs tack room, I immediately felt as if I were in a British stable. Here you will find a surrey with a fringe on top, two beautifully restored antique cars, antique oil cans and auto tools. Upstairs is a sumptuous two-room suite with a Palladian window and central air conditioning. It is luxuriously decorated with English antiques. You feel you are in a museum. Antique sports equipment are everywhere. A croquet mallet, a gold club, tennis clubs. Original paintings one depicting two horses. Four poster bed with lace bedspread, and a wonderful old dressing table. Old hat boxes, thick wall to wall carpeting, and many more items and not speck of dust on any of them. Remarkable.

The outside grounds are just as impressive with brick walkways, shaped carved English boxwood. When you stroll, look for the water pump with the old water cans around it, or the gardener's tool house.

You will most likely find the owner Gery Conover sweeping in front of one of the Inn's houses in the early morning or if you're a late sleeper, meet his wife while she serves you coffee in the open-air terrace or bow-windowed conservatory. By night this room becomes the candlelit dining area.

Gery Conover and his wife have lived in the Inn for over 20 years raising several children, some joining them in the business. They fantasize the time between 1870 and 1920 and that is why there will never be a computer at the Inn. The telephones in the rooms are not push button. He strives for a quiet experience and refuses accommodations to more than two guest parties that know each other. This is not an Inn where there is much interaction between the owners and the guests, but the service is extremely attentive. In fact this is not an Inn in the sense that I use the term in this book. This is really a very luxrious small hotel with all the amenties you would expect from a hotel except room service.

The dining room is not run by the Conovers, but is leased to Mike Brisson, the chef and is called L'Etoile. This allows the Conovers to spend all their time satisfying the Hotel guests.

Among the entrées on the prix-fixe dinner are chilled terrine of lobster, scallops and smoked salmon, with wasabi mayonaise sauce, pan roasted sirloin with greenpepper corns, fresh sauteed softshell crab in black & white sesame sauce, a green salad and dessert. The waiters wear black vests and bow ties. For the price I found the dinner not up to expectation.

October is an ideal time to be at Martha's Vineyard. The weather is usually pleasantly chilly in the morning and warms up as the hours go by. The island and the ferries are not crowded, and it's possible to enjoy the Vineyard as a place with its own personality.

CHARLOTTE INN, So. Summer St., Edgartown, MA 02539; 508-627-4751.

A 25-guestroom (23 private baths) combination inn-art gallery and restaurant on a side street, a few steps from the harbor. Queen, double, and twin beds available. European plan. Continental breakfast served to inn guests except Sun. Open year-round. L'étoile restaurant is open for dinner from mid-March thru New Year's Day, also winter weekends. Boating, swimming, beaches, fishing, tennis, riding, golf, sailing, and biking nearby. No pets. Not suitable for children under 15. Gery and Paula Conover, owners-hosts.

DIRECTIONS: The Woods Hole/Vineyard Haven Ferry runs year-round and automobiles may be left in the parking lot at Woods Hole. Taxis may be obtained from Vineyard Haven to Edgartown (8 mi.). Check with inn for ferry schedules for all seasons of the year. Accessible by air from Boston and New York.

MOSTLY HALL
Falmouth, Massachusetts

Although Mostly Hall was built in 1849 by a Yankee ship captain for his New Orleans bride, there is an English country house feeling to the place. It may be the beautifully restored and maintained front garden with its rolling lawn and dogwood. Few Cape Cod houses are set so majestically back from the road. Since the interior hallways dominate the house, it got its name early on from a young child who, when entering the house, gaped and exclaimed "why, it's mostly hall!"

In warm weather, breakfast is served on the spacious wraparound veranda, overlooking the gazebo. There is usually something special, like stuffed French toast or cheese blintz muffins with warm blueberry sauce, favorite recipes featured in the inn's popular breakfast cookbook.

There is much to do in this corner of the Cape: warm water beaches, a four-mile ocean bike path, and the ferries to Martha's Vineyard (a wonderful day trip). Mostly Hall is right on the historic village green with the shops, galleries, and summer theater of Falmouth close at hand. Of course, you can also spend the day reading or visiting with other guests on the veranda in the gazebo or high up in the many-windowed widow's walk, which has been converted into a sitting room.

There are six spacious corner guest rooms furnished with queen-sized canopied beds, a variety of antiques, Oriental rugs, and comfortable chairs.

MOSTLY HALL, 27 Main St., Falmouth, MA 02540; 1-800-682-0565; 508-548-3786.
A 6-guestroom inn (private baths) on the village green in Falmouth, Cape Cod. Queen beds. Approx. 90 min. from Boston, Newport, or Provincetown. Air conditioned. Open year-round except for a few weeks in Jan. or Feb. Full breakfast included

in rate. Located in a historic and scenic area convenient to Woods Hole and ferries to Martha's Vineyard. Complimentary use of bicycles. Air-conditioning. No pets or smoking. CCs; Visa, MC. Caroline and Jim Lloyd, owners/hosts.

DIRECTIONS: As you approach the Cape, follow signs that say Falmouth and the Islands. Cross the Bourne bridge to Cape Cod and follow Rt. 28 to Falmouth. Mostly Hall is 14 mi. from the bridge. Turn left at sign for Falmouth Village Center, take first right on Hewins St. at village green, turn right at next corner. Inn on left, off street parking in rear.

OLD HARBOR INN
Chatham, Massachusetts

No amount of homey charm, designer bed linens, or scrumptious muffins can make up for an innkeeper who is brusque or inattentive. I believe that a B&B offers the exact opposite possibility: a chance for guests to get to know their hosts in a warm, personal way.

Sharon Ferguson apparently agrees with me. From the moment I walked into the Old Harbor Inn I felt as if I were at the home of a very dear friend. When the Fergusons "put out their welcome mat," they really mean it. "Tom and I want guests to feel honored," she told me.

The gray clapboard was originally the home of Chatham's Doc Keene (who delivered nearly 2,000 of Chatham's residents!), and wasn't turned into an inn until 1987 when it was renovated. The six-over-six windows were trimmed in white, a back deck was built, and beautiful terraced landscaping was added.

Sharon has shaped the inn's spacious interior into a very intimate and restful environment. Green and pink floral chintz window treatments appear in both the common room and the cheery sunroom, creating a sense of unity. This fresh garden theme is repeated in the botanical prints and oil seascapes and landscapes on the walls. The furnishings are both traditional and antique. Comfortable chairs and couches frame the walnut-mantled fireplace, and wicker accents the sunroom.

I had one of my best nights of sleep at Old Harbor. Every guest room has a firm queen-sized mattress. The headboards vary from wicker to a cherry four-poster. Laura Ashley coordinated wallpapers and linens, eyelet and Battenburg lace accessories, and piles of extra pillows made me feel like I was in an English country bedroom. The private baths are modern, but pedestal sinks with brass and porcelain faucets maintain the old-fashioned mood. After your bath you'll want to wrap yourself up in one of the oversized fluffy towels.

Breakfast is served in the sunroom or on the deck, and Sharon will happily make reservations for you at a nearby restaurant for dinner. The inn's location on the Cape's "elbow" assures lovely weather most of the year and also provides an excellent home base for touring.

OLD HARBOR INN, 22 Old Harbor Rd., Chatham, MA 02633; 508-945-4434.

A 6-guestroom (private baths) warm, comfortable inn on the "elbow" of the Cape. Queen beds. Open year-round. Walk to restaurants, the beach, shops and galleries. No pets. Smoking restricted. Sharon and Thomas Ferguson, owners/hosts.

DIRECTIONS: Take Rte. 28 to Chatham, and go 3.4 miles to the rotary (traffic circle); turn left. This is Old Harbor Rd. (Rte. 28S.) Inn is on right.

THE OVER LOOK INN

Eastham, Massachusetts

Walking up the gravel drive to The Over Look Inn, I was stopped in my tracks by the haunting drone of distant bagpipes. I set my bags down and wandered toward the sound, which seemed to originate at the barn behind the house. Seated in front of the barn door, a sleepy-eyed basset hound, whom I later found to be named Winnie, sat up to give a few short woofs, more in welcome than alarm. The door opened to reveal innkeeper Ian Aitchison with bagpipes draped around his shoulder. "Hi there," he said extending a well-calloused hand. "I guess Nan didn't hear you arrive. Don't mind Winnie, she's really my only fan and loves our guests."

Ian and Winnie escorted me around to the airy front porch and Ian explained that he and Nan had fallen in love with the Cape Cod area because it reminded them of their Scottish homeland. The cheerful

yellow-and-white Queen Anne sits directly across from the Cape Cod National Seashore. Nan and Ian purchased the inn because they wanted to restore a historic building, work together, and avoid what Ian calls "retirement crises." Their son Mark often acts as host and was pivotal in the restoration process.

Mark also writes short stories, which guests can find in their room's well-stocked bookcases. The romantic guest rooms have lace accents, brass beds, down comforters, and antiques. Each room has either air conditioning or a ceiling fan, and a private bath.

After a luscious afternoon tea served in front of the parlor's crackling fire, I spent two hours in the inn's library perusing Ian's collection of works by Winston Churchill. Sporting souls can chalk up cues in the Hemingway billiard room which, true to Hemingway's passion, is decorated with exotic hunting trophies.

Nan's excellent breakfasts are served in the large garden dining room. Calling on her Scottish heritage, Nan serves "Kedgeree," a dish of smoked cod, rice, onion, chopped egg and raisins, all sautéed in butter and finished with a dollop of tart mango chutney.

Besides the exploration of the seashore, guests can visit the Audubon Wildlife Sanctuary, ride bike paths, and study the educational exhibit at the Salt Pond Visitor Centre.

THE OVER LOOK INN, Rte. 6, 3085 County Rd., Eastham, MA 02642; 508-255-1886 or 1-800-356-1121.

A 10-guestroom (private baths) Victorian across from the Cape Cod National Seashore. Queen, full and twin beds. Wonderful breakfast. Open all year. No pets. One dog in residence. Smoking restricted. CCs: Visa, MC, AE. Nan and Ian Aitchison, owners/hosts.

DIRECTIONS: From Rte. 6 go 3 mi. past Orleans rotary (traffic circle). Take the third drive on left after traffic lights at Cape Cod National Seashore.

INN EVENTS: FEBRUARY—Valentine Weekend
MARCH—Easter special: eggs and flowers.
MAY—Mother's Day Weekend
JUNE—Father's Day Weekend
SPRING AND FALL—Biking Weekends
NOVEMBER—Thanksgiving Weekend
DECEMBER—Hogmanay: Scottish New Year's Dinner

THORNCROFT INN

Vineyard Haven, Massachusetts

"This house was built for guests," Karl Buder said. He gestured to the pillared gates across the street. "In 1918, it was the guest house for the estate of Chicago grain merchant John Herbert Ware I." The only object at Thorncroft left from that day is the mantle clock in the sitting room which has a country scene painted a century ago by Ware's mother.

However, the essence of such an auspiciously hospitable beginning has been more than carried forward by owners Lynn and Karl Buder. I felt as if I had been invited to stay in a sumptuous private home with a particularly caring staff. Even my need for a cup of tea was anticipated and appeared magically accompanied by nut bread and buttery cookies. Because it was an autumn day, a fire thoughtfully had been laid match-ready on the hearth in my room.

No two guest rooms are alike at Thorncroft, but all are large, handsomely furnished with antiques, and have comfortable chairs flanked by good reading lamps. Beds may be lace-canopied four-posters or simply have magnificent mahogany headboards, but all mattresses are firm and pillows fluffy. Nearly every room has a wood-burning fireplace.

My bath had a claw-foot tub, but some others have whirlpools big enough for two—sybaritism unheard of in its guest house days. Some rooms have private porches, and some are suites. Victorian dolls stand primly on tables and highboys; a wonderful 19th-century baby carriage sits on a landing.

When guests aren't out touring, shopping, biking, sailing, or watching the sun set over the sea, they mingle in the parlor, which has an old-fashioned standing phonograph or in the sunroom, with its refrigerator, icemaker and television.

Thorncroft is actually in two locations. The main and carriage houses are a mile north of the ferry dock at the quiet end of Main Street. "Greenwood House" consists of a vintage house within easy walking distance of the dock; the atmosphere is a tad less formal, with Buder sons Hans and Alex likely to be playing in the yard next door. Guests are transferred to the main house dining room for dinner (breakfast is served on the premises at Greenwood), but the central village location is especially good for those who want to get around the island on the summer shuttle bus rather than by car. All the buildings are linked by a sophisticated 24-hour telephone system. "We are always available," Karl says.

The two intimate dining rooms are open only to guests and a few lucky townspeople who must reserve in advance and on a space-available basis. The cuisine can be characterized as "New American," which means preparing fresh local products with a flair.

The chef receives approximately twelve varieties of lettuce and exotic corkscrew radishes from an adjacent farm. "We can create any dish to order," he explained. "We just did a chateaubriand with all the sauces for a honeymooning couple. One man wanted a four-pound lobster, and we found it. We also do wedding cakes."

My desires were quite satisfied with the menu (parsley crusted veal loin chop roasted with a ragout of smoked bacon, shiitake mushrooms and sun dried tomatoes. Dessert was a flourless chocolate torte with creme anglaise.

THORNCROFT INN, 278 Main Street, P.O.Box 1022, Vineyard Haven, MA 02508, 508-693-3333; fax 508-693-5419; 1-800-332-1236.

A romantic 19-room (private baths) country inn in four retored homes. The main house and carriage house are at the quiet end of Main street on the north side of the island, one mile from the ferry dock. Greenwood House (two restored homes) nearer town, free transfers provided. Queen, double and twin beds. Some rooms with Jacuzzis and wood-burning fireplaces, balconies. Full breakfast and afternnon tea included in rates. Tennis and harbor swimming nearby. Bicycles and boats available in village. Open all year. No pets. No smoking. CCs: Visa, MC, AE, Enroute. Lynn and Karl Buder, owners/hosts.

DIRECTIONS: Take Steamship Authority ferry from Woods Hole (you may leave your car at Woods Hole or bring it) or by passenger-only ferry in summer from New Bedford. From Vineyard Haven ferry dock, if you drive you will be directed left. Turn right at first stop sign then next right onto Main Street. Inn is one mile on your left. Accessible by air from Boston and New York.

THE TUCKERMAN HOUSE

Vineyard Haven, Massachusetts

"We call these 'Martha's Muffins' after the Vineyard," Joe Mahoney said. "Actually they are Carolyn's grandmother's recipe for Irish soda bread."

"Delicious," I said. "As good as in Ireland."

Joe, a former certified financial planner, and Carolyn, a school teacher who continues to teach third grade, had been coming to the Vineyard for fifteen years before they decided to buy the white clapboard house with the lath fretwork and the Greek Revival door frame

in the heart of the historic district. Restoration and redecoration are still underway.

The house is furnished with an eclectic mix of antiques and keep-sakes. As you enter, the cozy parlor with its fireplace and jumble of antique furniture and Mahoney memorabilia is on your left; the stair-way on your right. Upstairs, the bedrooms are one-of-a-kind. with handmade quilts and some four-poster beds. You can choose to look out over village rooftops or on the harbor. When I asked Joe about his hobbies he said, "Prior to becoming an innkeeper, we liked to travel and putter. Now I get a chance to do one of my hobbies full-time."

Breakfast is served on the veranda from Memorial Day through Labor Day ("sometimes longer, weather permitting"), then in the din-ing room family-style. Guests help themselves to juices, fresh fruit, gra-nola, and just-out-of-the-oven breads or ("Martha's") Irish muffins.

The house, built in 1836 by Thomas Tuckerman of New Bedford for his wife Eleanor, is an in-town inn. You can walk to the ferry dock, the bike rental shop, the galleries, boutiques, playhouse, and restau-rants of Vineyard Haven. Beach and tennis courts are nearby. In sum-mer, the cross-island shuttle bus leaves from just down the street.

As a special souvenir of your stay at the Tuckerman House, Joe will take your picture with his quadric-lens camera. You'll receive the three-dimensional color result after you return home. "For your mem-ory book," he says. Sure now, and who could forget an inn like this?

———

THE TUCKERMAN HOUSE, 45 William Street, Box 194, Vineyard Haven, MA 02568-0194; 508-693-0417.

A 5-guestroom, 1-suite (private baths) inn in the historic district. Queen and dou-ble beds. Some working fireplaces, air conditioning. Open all year. Continental-plus breakfast; afternoon tea or lemonade. Off-street parking. No smoking or pets. CCs: Visa, MC, AE. Carolyn and Joe Mahoney, owners/hosts.

DIRECTIONS: Walk straight up from the Vineyard Haven ferry to Main St. Turn left and go to Spring St.; right to William St., then left again. The inn is on your left, on the corner of William and Camp Sts.

VILLAGE GREEN INN
Falmouth, Massachusetts
———

Being right on a historic green may be the most advantageous possible location for a federal-style traditional white New England inn. You can dawdle over your morning coffee surrounded by pots of geraniums on the porch and watch the village come alive the old-fashioned way, without hustle or hassle.

Conversation before the fireplace in the blue and ivory guest parlor

is less likely to center on the business world than on Don Long's grandmother's platform rocker, which may be one-of-a-kind and is as comfortable as it is unique. All through the 1804 house are conversation-piece arrangements of dried flowers so appealing that guests buy them right off the cherry and mahogany tables.

Every room is different, too, with the upstairs more colonial and the downstairs more Victorian. The "Pineapple Room" was named for its bedposts, but it also has such late 19th-century touches as a colored glass window and an inlaid floor. The suite has twelve windows and views in three directions. Understandably, it is the first choice of homeymooners and return guests.

Don, a former sports coach and physical education teacher, made the most of his woodworking hobby by doing all of the restoration carpentry himself. His wife Linda, who previously taught elementary school, has been responsible for the authentic period decorating and the breakfast treats.

Breakfast is served family-style in the dining room. It may be the day for apple-plum crumble or blueberry almond bread in addition to a fruit dish, the main entrée, and freshly-ground coffee.

After a suitable interval, you can explore the shops and sights of Falmouth town, play golf on a nearby championship course, or head for the beaches or Woods Hole by way of the Shining Sea Bike Path. On another day, you can catch the bus to the island ferry and visit Martha's Vineyard. For jaunts or just relaxing, the Village Green makes a great base.

VILLAGE GREEN INN, 40 West Main St., Falmouth, MA 02540; 508-548-5621.
    A 5-guestroom, 1-suite (private baths) inn on the green. Queen beds. Ceiling fans.

Fireplaces. Full breakfast and afternoon tea or sherry. Closed January. No smoking or pets. CCs: Visa, MC, AE. Linda and Don Long, owners/hosts.

DIRECTIONS: Follow Rte. 28 south from the Bourne bridge to Falmouth. Turn left at Queen's Byway, right on Hewins St. and right on Main St. Inn is on the southwest corner of the Green with off-street parking from Main St.

THE WAUWINET
Nantucket, Massachusetts

The only thing left from the inside of the old Wauwinet is the fireplace mantel in the dining room, yet so true has been the striving towards keeping the spirit of this 19th century Nantucket landmark, I felt immediately in tune with both past and present country inns by the sea.

Actually, two seas—three if you count the Sound, which is visible beyond the sand bar that embraces Nantucket Harbor. The Wauwinet is situated on a neck of land between the Atlantic and Nantucket waters, the only inn on the island with such strategic placement. There are 26 miles of beaches to walk.

Bostonians Jill and Steve Karp loved the old place when they summered in the neighborhood, and when they heard the closed-down Wauwinet House was for sale, they bought it. Under their caring and personal supervision, the gray shingle exterior was restored, and the interior completely rebuilt.

This was a labor of love, and it shows. Jill selected the one-of-a-kind country antiques and worked with the decorators every step of the way. Steve, a builder of shopping malls rather than inns, says he was able to do something "just for us this time." Both the restuarant, Topper's, and the inn boat, *Topper's II*, are named for the Karp family terrier, whose portrait hangs in the main dinning room.

Though they live off-island, Jill and Steve are often at their inn. They bring it presents—like "Woody," the 1936 Ford station wagon that serves as a unique runabout and represents the inn at the annual Daffodil Weekend parade of vintage automobiles every April.

Each guest room is different, so let me tell you about mine, a standard double and one of the few with twin beds. The walls, ceiling and chintz are the same blue on cream flower pattern; the beds are white iron with brass trim; the tables and armoire, antique pine. A bouquet of fresh garden flowers sits beside two books about Nantucket. Nice extras include a basket of excellent toiletries, eyelet-trimmed cotton sheets, two big fluffy bed pillows per bed, good reading lights, a hair dryer, and a TV-VCR combination stowed out of sight until wanted.

There are larger, more country-elegant rooms with grander views in the inn, but none have more charm.

In the library/sitting room downstairs I found a wide selection of board games and books ranging from current best sellers to those popular when the Wauwinet advertised "Shore Dinners for 25 Cents." You can identify with your choice of decade. I was glad to see books and games for children as well.

The selection of videos also includes films for youngsters. This is another thing I like about the Wauwinet; the guests are a natural mix of ages. The cottages are expecially nice for families—the largest, "The Anchorage," has three bedrooms and is in great demand.

Outside there is croquet, and a wonderful creative 600 sq. ft. chess board with chess players that come to your waist to move around. Or you can walk the 26 miles of beaches. A 4-wheel drive will take you over the sand dunes and between mid-june and Labor Day, an old sea captain will boat you to a distance shore with your prepared picnic from the Hotel and pick you up later that day. There is a 14 foot Capri sailboat, row boats, tennis and bicycles for your use.

The general manager has had quiet a glorious past. He first managed the well known Salishan Lodge in Oregon, then the Inn at Williamsburg and now is happy pampering the guests at Wauwinet. He often takes guests on a history and nature walk. His wife can be found sitting you at dinner. (She's actually the food and beverage director. They met at Salishan.)

Topper's presents the New American Cuisine, which places great emphasis on just-picked locally grown vegetables, top quality meats, pastas, and such delicacies as Nantucket Bay scallops with Asian vetetables and ginger-garlic vinaigrette. I had the smoked blue fish pate and a scotch malt that even with my research on my book on Britain & Ireland hadn't come across it. It's called Michel Couvreur and is very smooth. Next came baby field greens with goat cheese. Grilled Arctic Char was wonderful. My partner had Grilled Medallions of beef with sweet & sour chutney. Make sure you take the Santa Fe Thunder Cloud for dessert. It consists of chantilly cream, baked cocoa meringuie, a scoop of chocolate moose and carmelized sugar.

A full breakfast of your choice is served as part of the room rate. Try the turkey hash. I know it sounds awful, but it was wonderful.

Although the Wauwinet is a peaceful eight miles from the village of Nantucket, there is no need to rent a car or bring your own the 30 miles across from the mainland. Complimentary jitney service from inn to town and back every hour is not only convenient but a delightful ride along the moors and cranberry bogs.

THE WAUWINET, P.O. Box 2580, Nantucket, MA 02584; 508-228-0145, fax 508-228-0712, toll free except Canada and MA 800-426-8718.

A full-service 40-guestroom (private baths) country inn with 5 cottages. King, queen and twin beds available. Private beach, Har-tru tennis courts, bicycles, sailboats and watersports. Free transfers to town 8 miles away. Open late April-Oct. No pets. Jill and Steve Karp, owners; Russell Cleveland, manager/host.

DIRECTIONS: From ferry, take Main St. to Orange, left to rotary (traffic circle), then Milestone Rd. to Polpis Rd; left to Wauwinet Rd., follow to inn. Without car, take taxi from airport to Wauwinet; from ferry, taxi or walk to information center on Federal St. where you can pick up the Inn jitney on one of its scheduled trips.

WEDGEWOOD INN
Yarmouth Port, Massachusetts

After staying a night or two at the Wedgewood Inn you may want to rush home and change your color scheme to blue. Wedgewood blue.

Blue or not, you won't be able to replicate the unusual built-in hall clock of this, Yarmouth Port's first house designed by a professional architect. Nor the pretty breakfast room with its tables for two or four, bow-back windsor chairs, and garden view. There are also unique pieces of furniture, such as the common room's coffee table, which was made from an enormous blacksmith bellows.

The symmetrical white clapboard house with black shutters, listed on the National Register of Historic Places, was built in 1812 for a well-to-do maritime lawyer. Today's owners, Gerrie and Milt Graham, have made sure it is as comfortable as it is handsome. Small rooms have been consolidated into large ones. Handcrafted cherrywood pencil-post beds have firm mattresses under the Appalachian quilts. Good

reading lights flank the wing chairs and the beds. In each guest room you'll find magazines, bowls of fresh fruit, and flowers, plus a wonderful collection of bath amenities.

My room had a working fireplace as well as a private screened porch. Both came in handy as a typical autumn day on the Cape went from midday warm to evening crisp. The breakfast menu changes daily, and there is always an additional buffet selection of cereals, fruit, and homemade muffins.

Gerrie, an elementary school teacher, and Milt, a onetime professional football player, summered on the Cape when they lived in Fairfield County, Connecticut. "We always wanted to return," Gerrie said.

WEDGEWOOD INN, 83 Main St., Yarmouth Port, MA 02675; 508-362-9178.

A 6-guestroom, 2-suite (private baths) inn on the north shore of Cape Cod. Queen beds. Working fireplaces. Private screened proches. Air conditioning. Off-street parking. Walk to beach. Open all year. Restricted smoking. No pets. One dog in residence. CCs: Visa, MC, AE, DC. Gerrie and Milt Graham, owners/hosts.

DIRECTIONS: Cross the Sagamore Bridge on Rte. 6. From Exit #7, Willow St., turn right. At stop sign, turn right onto Rte. 6A. Inn located 75 yards on right.

THE WHALEWALK INN
Eastham, Massachusetts

A potted geranium on the patio table, sea shell door knocker, fresh flowers spilling from vases, neatly placed throw pillows are just a few of the simple details which add to The Whalewalk Inn's appeal. As Louise and I stepped over the threshold of the front door, we were enveloped in a welcome atmosphere of softly colored walls, trimmed by clean, white wainscoting and muted water colors framed in gold. Our footsteps echoed on the pine floors.

"Well, you finally made it," greeted owner, Dick Smith, hand outstretched. The smiling face of his wife, Carolyn, appeared over his left shoulder.

"The other guests are enjoying hor d'oevres in the sitting room. I hope you remembered that bottle of famous Napa Valley wine you promised me. I've been waiting all day for it," she teased. Seeing my affirmative reply, she went off to find a corkscrew. Dick, relieving Louise of her bags, led the way to our room.

"Carolyn made sure you got the Salt Box Cottage, also known as the Honeymoon Cottage" he said, winking in my direction as he opened the door to the roomy studio suite. "Get settled, then join us in the living room and we'll sample some of that fine wine."

The welcome warmth that we had experienced as we entered the inn extended itself into our room, and it wasn't just the glowing fireplace. A pink and green wool blanket was draped over the white rattan chair. Matching green material provided a cornice effect over the window. Plump throw pillows lined the rattan sofa. Huge bouquets of fresh flowers spilled from wicker baskets. A fluffy, white comforter covered the brass bed. We had the added convenience of a small kitchen and private patio.

We found our way to the living room, similarly decorated in soft pastels, and logs crackling in the fireplace. When I complimented the Smiths on the inn decor, Dick handed the credit over to Carolyn.

"Well, we were both advertising executives before this venture, so we know how important service the little things are," she replied. "But wait till you sample Dick's cooking at breakfast tomorrow morning."

We followed Dick's advice and had dinner at a quaint restaurant in the village of Orleans, a short distance from the inn. Darkness was falling when we arrived back at the inn. Shadows crossed the white picket fence cutting a border around the inn's three acres. In the yellow glow of large porch lamps, we could still make out the dark shutters beside each window and the gingerbread trim along the roof line. What a welcome sight it must have been to the whale

master, who built the home in the 1830s, when he returned home from sea.

We sampled rich Grand Marnier French toast and a stack of Cranberry/blueberry pancakes the following morning before exploring the nearby shoreline to do a little whale watching.

THE WHALEWALK INN, 220 Bridge Road, Eastham, MA. 02642; 508-255-0167.

Twelve private guest rooms, including suites, in this wonderful Greek Revival home. All sized beds. Hearty breakfast included. Open April 1-Dec.15. Some minimum stays, call ahead for information. Not suitable for children under 12. Cape Cod bike trails, beaches, shopping and sightseeing within easy distance. Audubon wildlife preserve and whalewatching for the animal lovers. Bring your golf clubs as courses are nearby. No pets please. No credit cards accepted.

DIRECTIONS: Route 6 from Eastham to Rock Harbor Rd. Go right on Bridge Rd. and watch for the Inn.

Boston and Vicinity

EVENTS

FEBRUARY	Boston Festival: weekend hotel packages, music performances, art exhibits (info: 617-536-4100)
MARCH	St. Patrick's Day Parade, South Boston (info: 617-268-8525)
APRIL–MAY	Big Apple Circus, Boston (info: 617-423-6996)
APRIL	Annual Lantern Service, Boston: reenactment of the hanging of the two lanterns that signaled Paul Revere of the advance of British troops (info: 617-523-6676)
APRIL	Boston Marathon (info: 617-435-4303)
MAY	Museum of American Textile History Annual Sheep Shearing Festival, North Andover (info: 508-686-0191)
MAY–OCTOBER	Great Woods Center for the Performing Arts, Mansfield: summer home of the Pittsburgh Symphony (info: 508-339-2333)
APRIL–OCTOBER	whale watching, Boston (info: 617-727-3201)
JUNE, WEEKENDS	Rockport Chamber Music Festival (info: 508-546-6575)
JUNE	Back Bay Festival, Boston
JUNE	Massachusetts Maritime Festival, Salem (info: 508-745-1470.)
JUNE, LATE	Gloucester New Fist Festival (1-800-321-0133)
JUNE, LATE	Gloucester St. Peter's Fiesta & Blessing of the Fleet (1-800-321-0133)
JULY 4	Boston Harborfest (info: 617-227-1528)
JULY 4	parade and bonfire, Rockport (info: 508-546-6575)
JULY	Boston Chowderfest: sample clam chowder from restaurants, cast your ballot for the best (info: 617-227-1528)
JULY, MIDDLE	Tall ships grand parade
JULY	Lowell Folk Festival (info: 508-459-1000)
AUGUST, MIDDLE	Rocky Neck Festival of Lights, Gloucester (1-800-321-0133)
AUGUST, LATE	Gloucester Waterfront Festival, Arts & Crafts (1-800-321-0133)
SEPTEMBER, EARLY	Waterfront Festival, Newburyport (info: 508-262-2424)
SEPTEMBER, EARLY	Faneuil Hall Birthday Celebration
OCTOBER, MIDDLE	Amateur Art Festival, Rockport (info: 508-546-6575)
OCTOBER, MIDDLE	Head of the Charles Regatta, Boston (info: 617-536-4100)
OCTOBER, LATE	Artists' Gallery walk and demonstrations, Rockport (info: 508-546-6575)
NOVEMBER, LATE	Plimoth Plantation, Plymouth: colonists prepare for winter, serve 17th-century dinners to visitors (info: 508-746-1622)
DECEMBER	La Salette Shrine Christmas Festival of Lights, Attleboro: largest

religious-themed outdoor Christmas display in the U.S. (info: 508-222-5410)

SIGHTS

Beauport & Hammond Castle, Gloucester

Boston Common

Faneuil Hall

Halibut Point State Park, Rockport

Marblehead

Museum Wharf

Newbury Street

Old Church

Portsmouth

Salem

THE HAWTHORNE INN

Concord, Massachusetts

First, there was Gregory Burch. No, I'm wrong there. First, there were men like Ralph Waldo Emerson, Bronson Alcott, Nathaniel Hawthorne, and others who sought out the quietude of Concord and established their homes here. Gregory Burch came along about 1976, looking for a place somewhere in New England that needed work and

would provide studio space along with some sort of income. In the year of the Bicentennial, he and the Hawthorne Inn were joined.

I think it's only fair to mention that I appeared just briefly on the scene when Gregory was working day and night to whip the inn into the kind of hospitable residence that he would be proud of. However, there are a few more persons to be accounted for in this informal history of the Hawthorne Inn. Next is Marilyn Mudry: "Having met and fallen madly in love, I, too, came to call the Hawthorne Inn my home. We are now a family of five, with Ariel Zoe, Ezra Avery, and Jasper Gardener having arrived on blessed wings from the heavens. Their angelic presence has filled our days with joy and our nights with peace."

The Hawthorne Inn is located in the historic zone of Concord just a short walk from the Alcott House on the road out of Concord toward Lexington. It is the very same road that was neatly named "Battle Road," after the events of April 1775, when the Minutemen routed the British and sent them in retreat toward Boston.

The inn is situated on land that once belonged to Emerson, the Alcotts, and Hawthorne. Here, Bronson Alcott planted his fruit trees and made pathways to the mill brook, and the Alcott family tended their crops of vegetables and herbs. Two of the original trees, which Hawthorne planted, are still standing and can be seen on the west side of the inn.

The guest rooms—in fact all of the rooms in the inn—have antique furnishings, handmade quilts, and Oriental and rag rugs. There are original artworks both ancient and modern, antique Japanese Ukiyo-ye prints, and sculpture by Gregory. There are floor-to-ceiling bookshelves in the Common Room, which is warmed by a cozy fire in the chilly season.

Breakfast, the only meal served, is taken in the dining room and features homemade baked breads, fruit juice, a selection of teas, or a special blend of freshly ground coffee. In season, there are fruits from the gardens and vines of the inn and honey from the inn's own beehives.

Henry David Thoreau, another resident of Concord, built a small cabin on the shores of Walden Pond during the 19th century and tried to find out what life was all about. Maybe he would have found a visit with Gregory and Marilyn at the Hawthorne Inn interesting and enlightening, because they would have been happy to share some of the truths that they have discovered.

THE HAWTHORNE INN, 462 Lexington Rd., Concord, MA 01742; 508-369-5610.
A 7-guestroom (private baths) bed-and-breakfast village inn approx. 19 mi. from Boston. Double and twin beds available. Breakfast to houseguests is the only meal

served. Open all year. Within walking distance of all of the historic and literary points of interest in Concord. Limited facilities for young children but ideal for young people who have an appreciation for history and literature. No pets. Three dogs and three cats in residence. No credit cards. Gregory Burch and Marilyn Mudry, owners-hosts.

DIRECTIONS: The Hawthorne Inn is in the historic zone of Concord, 3/4 mi. east of the town center. From Rte. 128-95 take Exit 30B west for 3-1/2 mi. Bear right at the single blinking light. The inn is 1 mi. farther on the left (south side), directly across from Wayside (home of Hawthorne and Alcott).

THE LENOX HOTEL
Boston, Massachusetts

I like Boston. It is truly a civilized city. To me the Lenox Hotel and Boston go hand-in-glove.

The time was 7:00 A.M. and the streaks of a mid-October dawn over the city were giving way to a full-fledged day. I was seated in the window of my corner room on the eighth floor of the Lenox, looking east. One by one, the street lamps were flickering out and the tail lights of the early morning traffic were becoming more obscure. There was a

potpourri of Boston architecture in front of me, with restrained 19th-century business buildings cheek-by-jowl with the single bell tower and spire of a church. The trees on Boylston Street still had a generous tinge of the fall colors. A seagull swooped by my window and perched on the very top of a modern building on the opposite corner. Through the other window I could look down the street toward the Charles River and Cambridge on the other side. The runners and joggers were already out. By the way, the Lenox provides a jogger's guide to Boston.

Now the sun poked its way up over the harbor and I glanced around this most "unhotel" of all hotel rooms. The sleeping rooms are well appointed with French Provincial, Oriental and Ethan Allen decor.

Perhaps most surprising and gratifying of all was a working fireplace. "This took a lot of doing and designing," Gary Saunders told me. "But we comply with all of the Boston codes and many of our guests can enjoy the fun of actually having a wood fire in their fireplace at a hotel in the city. They should indicate their preference when making reservations; not all of the rooms have working fireplaces."

The Hotel, a turn-of-the-century establishment conveniently located in the Back Bay area of Boston (next door to Copley Square), is something of a rarity in these days of corporate ownership—a family-run hotel, whose owners are very visible. Gary Saunders and his father Roger, along with other members of the family, have owned the hotel for the past twenty-five years.

The Lenox has been completely restored with a new centralized heating and air conditioning system throughout the entire hotel, each room with self controlled thermostats.

Hearty New England fare is served in the Olde London Pub and Grille, for which the main paneling, posts, and tables were shipped over from England.

Diamond Jim's Piano Bar, which has recently been expanded, has become an institution after more than two decades of popularity, and is another reason people feel so at home at the Lenox. Everybody joins in and sings; anybody can get up and perform a solo, and several professionals and young hopefuls have been "discovered" there. The annual amateur singing competition is a big event. The feeling of camaraderie and friendliness makes going to Diamond Jim's a lot of fun.

There is one particular convenience that guests at the Lenox enjoy, which pleases me very much, and that's the airport and limousine service, available at a reasonable charge for guests arriving and departing. This is particularly handy for those of us who have to fly out of Logan Airport in Boston. Incidentally, I must admit that I also enjoyed the valet parking service that eliminates the hassle of finding a garage that isn't full. An exercise room is located on the premises and a wheelchair lift has just been installed, making entrance to the lobby, meeting and dining room area much easier for the handicapped.

I don't normally list hotels between the covers of this book unless the personnel are warm and friendly with an obvious desire to help guests feel comfortable. That is certainly the case at the Lenox.

In the event the hotel is full, the staff will refer you to the Copley Square across the street, which is run by Jeff Saunders, another of Roger's sons. Although it does not offer all of the amenities or services the Lenox does, it is conveniently located and features an interesting Hungarian restaurant in its cellar.

THE LENOX HOTEL, 710 Boylston St., Boston, MA 02116; 1-800-225-7676 (Mass.: 617-536-5300).

A 222-guestroom (private baths) conservative hotel in Boston's Back Bay area. Breakfast, lunch, and dinner served every day. Open all year. All contemporary hotel conveniences provided. Drive-in garage with valet parking service. Convenient to business, theaters, sightseeing, and shopping. All major CCs. The Saunders Family, owners-hosts; Michael Schweiger, general manager.

DIRECTIONS: If arriving by automobile, take Exit 22 from the Mass. Tpke., the Copley Square ramp, and turn left on Dartmouth St. for 2 blocks to Newbury St. Take a left on Newbury St. for 1 block to Exeter St., take a left on Exeter for 1 block and the hotel is ahead at the corner of Exeter and Boylston Sts. An airport limo service between Logan Airport and the Lenox is available for a fee.

INN EVENTS: FEBRUARY—Valentine's Day package

JANUARY–MAY (SECOND WED.)—Sing-off Competition

APRIL—Marathon Day special

MAY—Sing-off Finals

DECEMBER—tree trimming, caroling

DECEMBER 31—New Year's Eve Brunch

LINDEN TREE INN
Rockport, Massachusetts

"We wanted to come back home," was Larry Olson's answer when I inquired how he and his wife, Penny, had become innkeepers. Larry spent his childhood just down the street and Penny, a native of Providence, used to spend her summers here. Disillusioned with life in the larger city of Peabody, Larry left a career with General Electric; they packed up the kids and moved back to the small seaboard community of Rockport. They knew the previous owners of Linden Inn, and were first in line to purchase the Victorian in 1979. A guesthouse at the time of the sale, it was Penny's idea to convert the white structure with black-trimmed windows, marked by a towering linden tree in the front, to a bed and breakfast. Along with the conversion, she developed a new career: breakfast baker.

"I knew very little about baking when I married Larry," she said, a twinkle of amusement in her eyes. "But I perfected my own recipes right

here." Each morning a breakfast buffet reveals an assortment of breads and cakes baked the night before. Depending on Penny's mood, the variety may include mango bread, poppyseed bread, rhubarb cake, or raspberry muffins; on Sundays, you can count on sour cream chocolate chip coffee cake and lemon nut sour bread, a Linden Tree tradition.

These are just a few selections—Penny's breakfast repertoire seems endless. My plate piled high, I joined other guests in the informal dining room around a large table that had been passed down through Penny's family. A stenciled border divides walls and ceiling in this room, located just at the foot of the stairs. An original seascape hangs on one wall, a small overhead lamp enhancing the oil-brushed colors. This is just one of many original paintings that grace the inn. An Oriental rug of deep reds partially covers the refinished hardwood floors. As the dining room became full, guests took their plates to the living room or sun parlor.

The living room is a bit more formal, but still very cozy. The old marble fireplace has been converted to accommodate a more efficient wood-burning stove. Above it, resting on the mantle, is a large mahogany-trimmed mirror, which reflects the small replica of a ship, a gift from a satisfied guest. It's not unusual to spot gift items on display.

The bright sun parlor provides the perfect growing spot for the many flourishing houseplants which decorate the room. The inn has eighteen guest rooms, including four in the Carriage House. Typical of 1850 Victorian design, there are winding stairways, halls, and corners accessing each of the three floors, as well as nooks and crannies that provid wonderful storage space. There is also a cupola perched above the third floor providing a panoramic preview of sights I would later enjoy up close. The rooms in the Carriage House are more modern and have convenient, small efficiencies. My room in the main portion of the inn was simple in decor and furnishings and spotlessly immaculate. The large four-poster bed was covered by a chenille spread. The walls had pale yellow wallpaper with tiny flowers, and sheer Priscilla curtains hung over the windows. Wing-backed chairs provided an intimate sitting area near one window; a small table held a vase of fragrant, fresh flowers.

LINDEN TREE INN, 26 King St., Rockport, MA 01966; 508-546-2494.

Restored 18-guestroom 1850 Victorian; four rooms with small efficiencies. All sized beds. Delicious home-baked continental breakfast included. Restricted smoking. Fully open Apr.-Nov.; limited rooms Nov.-Apr. (Penny on vacation then). Two-day in-season minimum; 3-day minimum during holidays. Situated on one landscaped acre in residential area of Rockport, overlooking the Mill Pond. Walk to beaches, harbor or downtown. Short drive to Halibut State Park. Three cats in residence. No pets please. CCs: Visa, MC. Penny and Larry Olson, owners/hosts.

DIRECTIONS: Proceed on Rte. 95N to Rte. 128N in Peabody. At Gloucester you will come to stop lights. At lights, turn left onto Rte. 127 Rockport. Travel about 4 mi. to 5 Corners, turning left again, staying on Rte. 127. Go approximately 1/] mi. and turn right on King St. Watch for Inn on the left.

OLD FARM INN
Rockport, Massachusetts

"We are not a museum filled with delicate antiques, so we encourage you to kick off your shoes and relax for a quiet moment or a cozy chat with our other delightful guests," states the brochure on the Old Farm Inn. After following that advice on my own visit, I would urge you to do the same.

Built upon five acres sometime in the late 1700s, the old house has been connected to the Balzarini family since the early 1900s. Antone

Balzarini rented the farm for years, raising twelve children here. In 1964 his son, John, along with John's wife Mabel and their son William, purchased the place and refurbishing it to a nine-guest room inn. William—now known as Bill—and his wife Susan, often with Mabel's help, have been the family innkeepers for the past twenty years, inviting guests into the welcoming arms of this family home from April through November.

I had made the drive at dusk from busy Rockport and passed through the stone fence surrounding the inn just five minutes later. The farmhouse, painted in traditional barn shades of red and white, sits within a grove of tall trees. Green and red striped awnings shade the windows. The five-acre property borders the headlands of Halibut Point State Park. The newly-added two-bedroom cottage near the inn offers a full kitchen and can accommodate up to a seven people. The grounds surrounding the inn have neatly manicured lawns, and colorful flower beds extend outward to the surrounding natural environment.

"I'm very proud of this set," Susan said, pointing to the couch and matching chairs of dark wood with satin cushions. "It's a walnut Victorian parlor set from the early 1900s. It is very unusual to come across a complete set, but they were a mess. I stripped them and had to use a toothbrush to refinish them."

I complimented her on the delicious breakfast of fresh fruits, cereal, and homemade breads I had enjoyed that morning. Sunlight had streamed into the eating room through modern sliding glass doors, but the decor was country-kitchen yellow with pine tables and chairs, green house plants, and wall-hung quilts.

We wandered into the common room with its small adjoining library. Floral printed couches with bright reading lamps strategically placed makes this an excellent place to settle in and read. On cooler days, a fire adds warmth to the room. Magazines were spread upon an old refinished trunk. The adjoining small library has games and informational brochures explaining local sights and activities.

OLD FARM INN, 291 Granite St., Rockport, MA 01966; 508-546-3237.

Comfortable, cozy nine-guestroom farmhouse with cottage offering longer stays for larger parties. Open April-Nov. All sized beds. Breakfast included. Restricted smoking areas. Close to Rockport, Halibut Point State Park, and beaches. No pets. Resident cat named Winky. CCs: Visa, MC, AE. Susan and Bill Balzarini, owners/hosts.

DIRECTIONS: Rte. 128 to Cape Ann (Gloucester/Rockport). Follow signs to Rockport. Turn left at traffic lights onto Rte. 127. Follow Rte. 127 as it turns left at bottom of hill. About 5 minutes to inn.

SEACREST MANOR

Rockport, Massachusetts

The flag of Bermuda was flying with the American flag over the Yankee Brahmin mansion one sunny May morning. It turned out to be just one more way the innkeepers were signaling welcome to Bermudian guests, a nice gesture, though not surprising. There is a stately-home atmosphere of appropriate greeting for all who stop at Seacrest Manor. With its highly polished furniture and paneled walls, this is not Colo-

nial Rockport, but early 20th-century North Shore coupled with English country house, a tribute to living well.

Two acres of gardens and woodland, afternoon tea by the fire, and a library full of books almost make the delights of the area superfluous. Almost, but not quite. The views from the sundeck are too appealing—on a clear day you can see Maine.

Breakfast is the only full meal served, and it is an event. Fresh fruit cup, eggs and bacon are supplemented with such house specialties as blueberry-buttermilk, peach, and apple pancakes, Irish oatmeal with dates or corn fritters. However reluctant to leave the charming breakfast room with its garden view, even the most dedicated sightseer can last the morning on such fare.

"Decidedly small, intentionally quiet" is the motto of Seacrest. For guests who want to unwind, this is the right idea.

SEACREST MANOR, 131 Marmion Way, Rockport, MA 01966; 508-546-2211.

An 8-guestroom (6 with private bath; 2 rooms with private entrance to deck as well) inn in a residential section of Rockport. All size beds. Open mid-Feb. to mid-Dec. Full breakfast and afternoon tea included in rate. No other meals served. Located in a historic and scenic area approximately one hour from Boston. No pets. One dog in residence. No credit cards. Leighton T. Saville and Dwight B. MacCormack, Jr., owners/hosts.

DIRECTIONS: From the end of Rte. 128 (Boston's inner beltway) take Rte. 127A not quite 5 mi. to Rockport. Marmion Way is on your right.

INN EVENTS: DECEMBER 19—Christmas Pageant

West of Boston

EVENTS

JANUARY	Annual Jimmy Fund Charity Weekend, Holyoke: ski demonstrations, Giant Slalom race (info: 413-536-0416)
JANUARY	Mystic Valley Railway Society Snowflake Special (info: 617-361-4445)
FEBRUARY	Washington's Birthday Celebration, Old Sturbridge Village: demonstrations of 1830s fashions and dance (info: 508-347-3362)
MARCH	Spring Bulb Show, Northampton (info: 413-585-2740)
APRIL—MAY	Berkshires in Bloom (info: 800-237-5747)
MAY	Stockbridge Daffodil Festival (info: 413-298-5200)
MAY	Basketball Hall of Fame Enshrinement Events, Springfield (info: 413-781-6500)
JUNE, MIDDLE	Crafts Fair, Deerfield (info: 413-774-7476)
JUNE—SEPTEMBER	Jacob's Pillow Dance Festival, Becket (info: 413-243-0745)

JUNE–AUGUST	Tanglewood Music Festival, Lenox: summer home of the Boston Symphony Orchestra (info: 413-637-1940)
JUNE–AUGUST	Williamstown Theatre Festival (info: 413-597-3400)
JUNE	A.C.C. Craftfair, West Springfield: largest and most prestigious craft fair in America (info: 413-787-0131)
JULY 4	Old Sturbridge Village Independence Day Celebration (info: 508-347-3362)
JULY 4TH	Parade, Pittsfield (info: 800-237-5747)
JULY, MIDDLE	County Balloon Fair, Greenfield (info: 413-773-5463)
JULY–AUGUST	Berkshire Choral Institute (info: 800-237-5747)
JULY–AUGUST	Berkshire Opera (info: 800-237-5747)
JULY–AUGUST	Berkshire Public Theater (info: 800-237-5747)
JULY–AUGUST	Berkshire Theater Festival (info: 800-237-5747)
JULY–AUGUST	Mac Hayden Theater (info: 800-237-5747)
JULY–AUGUST	Shakespeare & Company (info: 800-237-5747)
AUGUST, EARLY	Annual Teddy Bear Rally, Amherst (info: 413-549-1252)
SEPTEMBER	The Big E, West Springfield: largest fair in New England (info: 413-737-BIGE)
SEPTEMBER	Crafts Fair, Deerfield (info: 413-774-7476)
DECEMBER	Winter Concert Series, Deerfield (info: 413-772-0157)

SIGHTS

Chesterwood: studio of Daniel Chester French

Clara Barton Homestead

Clark Art Institute

Deerfield historic village

Hancock Shaker Village

Herman Melville Home

Higgins Aviary

Mission House

The Mount: home of Edith Wharton (info: 413-637-1899)

Mount Greylock

Naumkeag: home of Ambassador Joseph Choate

Norman Rockwell Museum (info: 413-298-3822)

Nathaniel Hawthorne Cottage

Old Sturbridge Village

Willard Clock Museum

BLANTYRE
Lenox, Massachusetts

Winding up a tranquil gravel drive through stately trees and rolling acres of manicured green, I was unprepared for my first sight of the imposing Blantyre. Backed by the towering pewter clouds of a late spring storm, the Elizabethan-style manor, with its stone gargoyles, turrets and carved friezes, brought to mind the turn of the century, when the home was built as a "weekend cottage" patterned after the Tudor mansions of Scotland.

The mansion was purchased and rejuvenated to its original grand condition in 1980 by owner Jane Fitzpatrick. Britisher Roderick Anderson was hired as manager. His philosophy of innkeeping harkens back to a dignified tradition—to a time when guests were pampered with the ultimate in comfort; when staff looked on their work as a respected profession, not "just a job."

This pride is obvious from the moment you step into the Great Hall through the massive oak door. The Hall, with its lofty beamed ceiling, is furnished with heirloom Victorian antiques, as are many of the other rooms. While the mood is formal, it is also comfortable. A majestic fireplace is usually set with a blazing fire, warming the guests who gather there in the evening to enjoy a drink from the help-yourself bar.

The Music Room is quiet and intimate. Reminiscent of a 19th-century salon, the furnishings are museum-quality yet welcoming. We relaxed here late one night with discreetly delivered glasses of brandy. The French doors were opened to the covered terrace and the sweet scent of rain floated in from the formal croquet lawns beyond.

Twenty-foot-high leaded glass windows backlight the main house's grand staircase. Eight of the manor's twenty-four air-conditioned guest rooms await at the top. The rooms are luxurious, with four-poster beds, comfortable Victorian furnishings, and decorator fabrics. Here, and in the other rooms, accents like fresh flowers and satin hangers add elegance. A fruit basket, cheese tray and bottle of wine await your arrival.

Modern baths offer hooded terry robes, piles of plush towels, and complimentary toiletries and soaps.

Just down the hill from the main house, past the swimming pool and hot tub/sauna, the converted Carriage House is separated into additional rooms which are more contemporary in design. Some have lofts; others feature downstairs sitting rooms decorated with unusual frescoed walls and staircases spiralling to bedroom balconies.

Soft candlelight glints off silver, china and handcut glassware on the beautifully laid tables in the paneled dining room. The menu is classical and price-fixed. We decided to savor two appetizers: roulade of smoked salmon with avocado mousse, and a chilled soup of melon and champagne with crab. The flavors were subtle and the seafood very fresh. We followed with a shared entrée of roast boneless leg of lamb with fresh rosemary and orange sauce. The lamb was moist and enhanced by the unusual blend of rosemary and orange flavors. A selection of desserts, from rich to simple, completed the superb meal.

Breakfast moves guests into the airy glass-walled garden/conservatory. Here croissants and scones can be enjoyed with fresh juice, fruit and tea or coffee. Lunches, available on request, are also served in this cheerful room.

———

BLANTYRE, Route 20, Lenox, MA; 413-298-3806 before May 1, 413-637-3556 after May 1.

A 23-guestroom (private baths) country manor on 85 acres just 5 min. from Lenox. Open May 15-Nov. 1. Continental breakfast included; lunch and dinner available. Tennis, pool, tournament croquet courts, spa/sauna. CCs: Visa, MC, AE, DC. Ann Fitzpatrick, owner; Roderick Anderson, manager.

DIRECTIONS: From New York City, take the Taconic State Parkway north to Rte. 23, then east to Rte. 7, for Great Barrington, then follow Rte. 7 North five mi. to the second stoplight north of Stockbridge. Bear right onto Rte. 20 South, and go about a half-mile to Blantyre's drive, on your left.

CAPTAIN SAMUEL EDDY HOUSE COUNTRY INN

Auburn, Massachusetts

———

First of all, Carilyn and Jack O'Toole are born collectors, which is as it should be in this mid-Massachusetts area of famous flea markets and multiple antique shops. The Captain Samuel Eddy House is full of enchanting knickknacks and handcrafts, new and old. Many are for sale. "We thought of having a shop, too," Carilyn says, "but decided just to put things out and in use where people can see them and buy them if they like."

Carilyn is also mad about herbs, and once ran an herb farm. So of course there is an extensive herb garden, and the rooms (called "chambers," 18th-century style) are named for the herbs hung on each door: Rosemary, Spearmint, Santalena, Thyme, Scented Geranium. The latter is an enormous third-floor suite. Each guest room is color-coordinated to its namesake herb.

Herbs appear on the dinner menu, too, in such dishes as chicken with pesto, havarti, dill, and sundried tomatoes; stuffed sole with herbs and white wine sauce; tarragon and oregano butter; pesto bread; crab with fresh dill and chives, just to name a few. Carilyn also serves herbal luncheons June through October.

Dinner at Eddy House began as a meal served only to inn guests, but now the public is invited on a reservation-only and space-available basis. It is served by candlelight in the several rooms set aside for dining, including the keeping room and the south parlor.

Captain Samuel Eddy built the house for his family in 1765 on 125 acres by the shore of what is now called Eddy Pond. Eddy fought in the American Revolution, then later represented his district in the Boston Statehouse. The property remained in the family for a century, but a series of owners sold most of the land, and a lot of neglect brought the house to fixer-upper status when the O'Tooles appeared. They completely restored the old homestead—doing most of their own work—and turned it into a full-service inn.

Today's inn sits on three acres looking out on woods, swimming pool, lawn, flower and vegetable gardens in addition to the herbs. A new addition is a brick smokehouse modeled after the one at Old Sturbridge Village to smoke meat and fish for the inn dining room.

Captain Samuel's place is an idea house throughout. I must have murmured "What a good idea!" a hundred times during my visit. The day I arrived, the house was decorated inside and out for Halloween. Swaths of "spider web" hung around the front door; jack-o-lanterns were everywhere; the flag that snapped in the breeze was orange and pictured a witch riding her broomstick.

"I love holidays. Our Christmas Open House is spectacular, and every room has its own tree," Carilyn said. When I discovered nightly turndown service meant not only a chocolate but an O'Toole hand-craft, I decided Christmas lingered for 12 months here.

Breakfast is a genuine occasion any day, with such treats as French toast with strawberries, home-smoked bacon and eggs, fresh berry muffins, and homemade granola. In winter it is served in the keeping room before the original colonial fireplace with its beehive oven. It may, in fact, be cooked on the hearth. In summer, guests move to the solarium, where they can dawdle over their fresh raspberries while looking out on the gardens.

Carilyn is likely to appear wearing a pinafore and duster cap. She has researched the period of her house and can tell you the use of every curious tool hung on the keeping room wall ("Those Yankees were full of ingenuity," she says), the stories behind the quilt patterns (her mother makes the quilts)—all the whys and wherefores of life on a pre-revolutionary farm.

As each bedroom is different, so too are the rooms where guests gather. The North Parlor is proper colonial ideal for afternoon tea with homebaked goodies, and the Tavern Room has books, board games, television, an old-fashioned juke box, and a bar.

If you can tear yourself away from the inn, central Massachusetts is a prime place to sightsee. Old Sturbridge Village, a living museum of the early 1800s, is a short drive away. Worcester is the home of the New England Science Center, a 59-acre park and zoo; Higgins Armory Museum, a unique assembly of weapons and armor in a Gothic castle setting; and the Worcester Art Museum, with special exhibits as well as a notable permanent collection of pre-columbian art and artifacts.

CAPTAIN SAMUEL EDDY HOUSE COUNTRY INN, 609 Oxford Street South, Auburn, MA 01501; 508-832-5282.

A 5-guestroom (private baths) historic inn on a quiet residential street three miles southwest of Worcester in the heart of central Massachusetts. Queen beds. Open all year. Complimentary full country breakfast and afternoon tea. MAP also available. Guest dining room open to public by reservation only. Herb gardens. Swimming pool. Yard games, hiking trails, ice skating and sledding. No pets. No smoking. Carilyn and Jack O'Toole, owners/hosts.

DIRECTIONS: From Interstate 90 exit 10, follow Rte. 12/20 to end of ramp, bear right to Faith Ave. Turn left on Faith to end, then straight across highway. You will be on Oxford Street South. Inn is 1/8 mile on left.

INN EVENTS: JANUARY–MARCH—Murder Mystery Weekends

DEERFIELD INN
Deerfield, Massachusetts

Karl and Jane Sabo became enchanted with the wonderful lifestyle that innkeeping offers those who don't mind living where life is slower and time together has quality in quantity. As newlyweds they toured New England, a tour that resulted in their company called Innsitters, a service that allowed innkeepers to take a needed vacation, and inns in transition to be managed. The experience changed their lives and resulted in their move to the Deerfield Inn in 1987.

The Sabos both had successful careers in New York. Karl is a graduate of the Culinary Institute of New York, and has been a chef on an ocean liner and manager at New York's prestigious "21" Club. Jane, who is English, has been an editor with publishing houses in London and New York.

The Deerfield Inn is located in historic Deerfield, scene of attacks by the French and Indians during the 17th and 18th centuries. Historic Deerfield maintains twelve museum houses that line the mile-long Street, of which the Deerfield Inn is one. The homes are mirrors of the cultural history, art, and craftsmanship of the Pioneer Valley. The twenty-three-room Deerfield Inn was built in 1884 and modernized in 1977. All guest rooms have been named for people connected with the village's history, and some guests claim that they have seen the amiable spirit of at least one of these characters walking the halls.

All guest rooms are decorated individually. Greeff fabrics, charming print wallpapers, and period reproduction furniture are accented by old prints of the Deerfield area. Queen, double, and twin beds are available, and all rooms have private baths with combination shower and tub. A basket brimming with soaps, shampoo, and other luxury items is in each bathroom. The Sabos have also thoughtfully provided a hair dryer, an ironing board, a sewing kit, and extra toothbrushes and toothpaste, should you need them.

Two airy porches with rockers, a garden terrace, and a lovely herb garden are wonderful spots to spend time during summer evenings. The common rooms are elegant, yet relaxing. Two living rooms and a large fireplace in the main inn and one living room in the south wing are furnished with cozy sofas, well-stocked bookcases, card tables, and desks.

Morning begins with a country breakfast of French toast, eggs Benedict, pancakes, bacon and sausage, home-baked sweet breads, yogurt, and fresh fruit and juices. Weekend guests are served buffet style.

Evening brings a candlelight dinner in the inn's main dining room where you will enjoy regional specialities and local wines. I particularly enjoyed my entrée of cold poached salmon on a bed of sesame-sautéed spinach and sauce verte. Chef Louis Wynne uses the freshest local ingredients available, and often prepares recipes garnered from the old cookbooks in the village's archive library.

The area around Deerfield is fun to explore. History lives and breathes in almost any direction you look. In fact, farmers still unearth bones and ax heads from the Indian massacre of 1704. There are also country walks, nearby boating and fishing, golfing, skiing, buggy rides, and antiquing to occupy your time.

I made it a point to thank Chester Harding for the use of his four-poster bed as I crawled in that evening. I thought it wise, just in case he decided to walk the corridor.

DEERFIELD INN, The Street, Deerfield, MA 01342; 413-774-5581. 1-800-926-3865.

A 23-guestroom (private baths) historic 18th-century village inn. Queen and twin beds available. Open year-round. Modified American plan, or B&B plan including afternoon tea. Pets allowed with prior notice. Historical places of interest and outdoor sports nearby. CCs: Visa, MC. Karl and Jane Sabo, hosts.

DIRECTIONS: From New York City, take I-91 north, then Exit 24. The inn is on The Street, just off Rtes. 5 and 10. Take Exit 25 if going south on I-91.

THE GABLES INN
Lenox, Massachusetts

During the Gilded Age, when the Gables was a Berkshire "cottage" known as Pine Acres, Edith Wharton married the family scion and lived here while her mansion, The Mount, was being built nearby. You will see first editions of her books and the eight-sided library where she wrote many of her short stories. Edith's bedroom—call buttons no longer functioning—doubles as the bridal suite.

After rehabilitating brownstones in Manhattan, moving into the inn business seemed a logical next step, and hosts Mary and Frank Newton found the year-round cultural ferment of the Berkshires plus the regional beauty an irresistible combination.

For all its literary significance, paintings that span five centuries, the amazing assortment of antiques and collectibles, indoor swimming pool, and outdoor tennis courts, the house today has a predominately show biz theme. The past and present popular arts of music and theater are more than a hobby to the Newtons. Movie and theatrical memorabilia are everywhere, and anyone wanting to research the genre need only settle down with the books on the premises.

If you're lucky, neighbor Maureen Stapleton may pop in for some of Mary's prize-winning sour cream coffee cake or Frank may sit down at the piano and do his own professional rendition of hit songs. He also writes and produces local shows.

"I'm doing all the things I never had time to do when I was a banker," Frank says.

As he took me through the house, we were accompanied by the black and white cat named Cat. "He's usually asleep," Frank observed. Cat gave him a look that said plainly, "Break a leg."

THE GABLES INN, 103 Walker Street, Lenox, MA 01240; 413-637-3416.

A 17-room (private baths) Queen Anne-style bed-and-breakfast inn in the center of Lenox. Queen, double and twin beds. Expanded continental breakfast only meal served, but restaurants nearby. Canopied and high-backed Victorian beds; working fireplace in suite. Open all year. Air conditioned. Swimming pool and tennis courts. Major credit cards. No pets or cigar smoking. One cat in residence. Minimum stay required during Tanglewood season, holiday weekends, and October. CCs: Visa, MC, AE. Mary and Frank Newton, owners/hosts.

DIRECTIONS: From points south, take Rte 7N through Stockbridge, bear left on Rte 7A to Lenox. From east and west, take Mass. Turnpike to Exit 2 (Lee) then west on Rte 20 to 183 west to Lenox. Rte 183 becomes Walker Street and The Gables is on your right.

GARDEN GABLES INN

Lenox, Massachusetts

"The elevator works like a dumb-waiter," Mario Mekenda said, and to prove it, he stepped inside and pulled on the ropes. "If you take the upstairs front room, you can rise under your own power."

This is only one of the surprises in this homey bed and breakfast set well back from Main Street on five flowering acres in Lenox. Another is a 72-foot outdoor swimming pool in the back lawn—the largest in

the county and possibly the first ever installed in this famous Berkshire town. The original house is two hundred years old and was expanded from authentic Colonial to a country house.

Mario was a mechanical engineer in Canada, but now that talent is put to practical hands-on work in updating the guest rooms, putting in new bathrooms, and keeping the inn in top condition. Do-it-your-self-ers will find him happy to share the joys of experience (how many innkeepers can tell you how to build archways?). With Lynn, you can talk poetry.

Although there are two living rooms and a large sunny breakfast room where the walls are decorated with 18th-century Dutch water-colors, the heart of this friendly house is the kitchen. Guests even have refrigerator privileges.

Breakfast is an all-you-can-eat buffet with juices, fresh fruit, yogurt, healthy cereals, croissants, muffins, coffee, tea, and herbal teas. No other meals are served, but port and sherry are complementary and on the sideboard.

Every guest room is different, from the smallest single to the king-bed double with its whirlpool private bath, and each shows the Mek-endas' thoughtful touches. How does it all work so well?

"We spend more time picking a wallpaper than we did buying the inn," Mario says.

GARDEN GABLES INN, 144 Main Street, Lenox, MA 01240; 413-637-0193.

A quiet 14-room (private baths) bed-and-breakfast inn on a garden estate in mid-town Lenox. Twin, double, queen and king beds. Two rooms with fireplaces. Open year-round with very attractive off-season rates. Swimming pool. Air-conditioned. No smoking in guestrooms. No pets. Minimum 3 nights prepaid for holiday, July, and August weekends; 2-night minimum for weekends in June, September, and October. CCs: Visa, MC, AE. Lynn and Mario Mekenda, owners/hosts.

DIRECTIONS: From Exit 2 (Lee) on Mass. Pike, follow Rte. 20 west to Rte. 183. Turn left and continue to statue at town center. Turn right onto Main St. (Rte. 7A) and Gar-den Gables is on your left across from St. Ann's Church.

THE INN AT STOCKBRIDGE
Stockbridge, Massachusetts

When Lee and Don Weitz give driving directions to their inn, they are always very precise about the mileage from Main Street in Stockbridge. The Inn is totally secluded from Route 7, and one can see only a dis-creet hand-carved sign and the driveway entrance from the main road.

It is a pleasant surprise to find that the circular driveway leads up to an imposing Georgian Colonial home, whose four two-story columns

give you the feeling that it would be equally at home in a Southern setting. Two enormous hundred-plus-year-old maples rise majestically above the front of the white clapboard house with dark green shutters. While the outside is inviting, the best is yet to come. Because of the way in which Lee and Don have chosen to run their inn, you might enter and think that you have mistakenly entered a private home where a group of friends were gathered.

One finds no trace of a front office or reception desk, and if you arrive during breakfast you'll see in the dining room sixteen guests talking animatedly at a long candlelit mahogany table set with china, silver, crystal, and linen napkins. Attractive young staff members serve fresh orange juice and fresh fruit, as well as just-baked coffee cakes and main courses which vary from day to day. My favorite was the thickly-sliced French toast, topped with fresh fruit and served with apricot-orange Grand Marnier sauce. Equally poplular are blueberry pancakes with smoked Canadian bacon. Summer breakfasts are served outdoors on the wrap-around porch at tables draped with pink linen. The porch is surrounded with hanging baskets of pink geraniums.

Guests often linger after breakfast to discuss the events of the day. Lee has carefully catalogued all the various schedules—Tanglewood, Jacob's Pillow, Shakespeare and Company, the Berkshire Opera, the Mount, the Berkshire Choral Insitute, the Berkshire Theater Festival, Williamstown Theater, and more.

On warm sunny days you will find guests enjoying the large pool, set back behind a stand of trees. The padded wrought iron chaise lounges are perfect for sunning or napping. Perhaps you would like to visit the nearby fountain and small pond surrounded with flowers in the formal gardens to the rear of the inn. Included on the 12-acre estate is a sweeping front lawn with meadows beyond and views of the distant hills.

I trailed off into the library, a very large room furnished in a most comfortable way, quite reminiscent of an English country house with deep chintz-covered sofas and another big fireplace. Then I crossed over to the other side of the house to see the fourteen-lace Chippendale dinning room table.

The inn was a private house for many years and so most of the eight traditional bedrooms are unusually large. All of them have views of the countryside. Some have a view of a spacious patio where, in warm weather, the tables are set with pink tablecloths and napkins and fresh flowers. Although the property is near the turnpike, the noise which you can hear at times starts to fade as you become entranced with the beauty of the outdoors.

THE INN AT STOCKBRIDGE, Rte. 7, Box 618, Stockbridge, MA 01262; 413-298-3337.

A 7-guestroom (5 private baths) country house about I mi. north of the center of Stockbridge. Full breakfast included. Convenient to all of the Berkshire cultural and recreational attractions. A summer swimming pool on grounds. No pets. CCs: Visa, MC, AE. Lee and Don Weitz, innkeepers.

DIRECTIONS: From NY, take any of the main highways north to Stockbridge, and continue north on Rte. 7 for 1.2 mi. Look for small sign on the right after passing under the Mass. Tpke. Inn cannot be seen from the road. From Mass Tpke.: exit at Lee, take Rte. 102 to Stockbridge and turn right on Rte. 7; go north for 1.2 mi. as above.

INN EVENTS: FEBRUARY 14—Valentine's Day observance: flowers, candlelit champagne breakfast

MAY (FIRST WEEKEND)—daffodils on the grounds and decorations within the inn signal the arrival of spring

JULY 4—special al fresco breakfast, flag cake

NOVEMBER 26—Thanksgiving Dinner

DECEMBER 5–6—tree trimming and open house tour

DECEMBER 31—New Year's celebration with formal black-tie dinner and dancing

MERRELL TAVERN INN

South Lee, Massachusetts

The Merrell Tavern Inn, built in 1794, is an excellent example of a historic building that is being both preserved and granted a new lease on life as a bed-and-breakfast inn.

With the assistance and guidance of the Society for the Preservation of New England Antiquities (SPNEA), the owners of the inn, Charles and Faith Reynolds, have done a remarkable job of preserving the Federalist atmosphere of this former stop on the Boston-Albany stagecoach run. In recognition of their restoration of the 188-year-old inn, the Massachusetts Historical Commission has presented them with a Preservation Award.

The red brick exterior with first- and second-floor porches has remained unmarred by the passing years, and in repainting and installing new plumbing and wiring, the Reynoldses were careful to maintain the house's architectural and visual integrity.

Fabrics and original paint colors have been duplicated wherever possible, and the Reynoldses have supplemented their own collection of antiques with additional circa-1800 pieces. In addition to the four bedrooms created from the third-floor ballroom (quite a customary feature in early inns) there are four guest rooms on the first and second floors with views either of the main road passing through the village of South Lee—located, by the way, not far from Stockbridge—or of the Housatonic River in the rear.

A picture in *Historic Preservation* shows Faith serving breakfast in the original barroom, where perhaps the only remaining circular Colonial bar in America is still intact, even to the little till drawer. The original grain-painted woodwork is protected by an easement.

MERRELL TAVERN INN, Main St., Route 102, South Lee, MA 01260; 413-243-1794.

A 9-guestroom (private baths) beautifully preserved and restored historic tavern in a quiet Berkshire village near Stockbridge. Queen and double beds. Lodgings include a full country breakfast. Open every day except Christmas Eve and Christmas Day. Holiday weekends, 2-night minimum stay; July, Aug., 3-night weekend minimum stay. Within a convenient distance of all of the Berkshire cultural, natural, and recreational activities, including Berkshire Theatre Festival, Tanglewood, and Shakespeare and Company. No pets. CCs: Visa, MC. Charles and Faith Reynolds, owners/hosts.

DIRECTIONS: South Lee is on Rte. 102, midway between Lee and Stockbridge.

THE RED LION INN
Stockbridge, Massachusetts

Sitting in a rocking chair at the Red Lion Inn and watching the town go by is exhilarating.

The old inn has been standing since 1793, not without experiencing any number of modifications and disasters. It was a stagecoach stop on the Springfield-Albany run, and in the years when Stockbridge became a summertime mecca for artists, musicians, and writers— before Tanglewood was started by Serge Koussevitsky, and Ted Shawn made Jacob's Pillow famous—in the era of the splendid Berkshire "summer cottages," Red Lion buggies would collect their guests at the Stanford White-designed railroad station.

The Fitzpatricks set about restoring and refurbishing the Red Lion Inn and turning it into the centerpiece of the village of Stockbridge. The better rooms are not in the main building, but in old homes in back. Although some rooms in the inn are quite adequate, many require you to share a bath with three other rooms, which is far too much for my comfort. If not for the uniqueness of the Inn itself, it would not be listed in this book for that very reason.

As I walked through the lobby and parlors, I was impressed by the beautiful collection of antiques, which includes tables, cabinets, high-boys, clocks, paintings, and prints that seem to be very much at home in the low-ceilinged setting. The collection of teapots was actually started in the middle of the 19th century by a Mrs. Plumb, who owned the inn at the time. All of the rooms and hallways show Jane's attention to detail, and the love and interest she and Jack have devoted to the inn over the years.

Great food is served in either the Widow Bingham's Tavern or the dining room. I listened to a great jazz combo that evening in the Lion's Den downstairs, a pub that features entertainment every night during the summer.

THE RED LION INN, Stockbridge, MA 01262; 413-298-5545.

A 108-guestroom (83 private baths) historic village inn, dating back to 1773, in the Berkshire hills. Queen, double, and twin beds available. European plan. Breakfast, lunch, and dinner. Those sensitive to traffic noises should stay away from the front rooms in the main building. Open year-round. Wheelchair access. Adjacent to Tanglewood, Norman Rockwell's Old Corner House Museum, the Berkshire Playhouse, Jacob's Pillow, Chesterwood Gallery, Mission House, and major ski areas. Outdoor pool. Tennis, golf, boating, fishing, hiking, mountain climbing, and xc skiing nearby. Jack and Jane Fitzpatrick, owners; Betsy Holtzinger, innkeeper/host.

DIRECTIONS: From the Taconic State Pkwy., take Exit 23 (N.Y. Rte. 23) to Mass Rte. 7. Proceed north to Stockbridge. From the Mass. Tpke., Exit 2 at Lee, and follow Rte. 102 to Stockbridge.

THE VILLAGE INN

Lenox, Massachusetts

I was having dinner in the Harvest Restaurant at the Village Inn with innkeepers Cliff Rudisill and Ray Wilson. We were reminiscing about their early days here, when they took over the inn in January of 1982, weathered the winter, and worked on learning the ropes and becoming acclimated.

"After Easter that year," Ray said, "we spent two weeks in England and visited seven country house hotels, sampling marvelous cuisine and learning our way around English teas. As a matter of fact, because of meeting Bronwen Nixon at Rothay Manor, we came back and established an English Afternoon Tea, as well as an authentic High Tea, which we hold, along with a chamber music concert, one Sunday afternoon a month, January through June. Rothay Manor is our 'Twin Inn' in England."

These two men, both from Texas, have established their own unique style at the Village Inn, a two-and-a-half-story yellow clapboard building with a basic Federal design. Built in 1771, and ultimately adapted to meet various needs over many years, it became an inn in 1775, and has been one ever since. Two rear wings, which were once well-constructed barns, form an L-shaped sheltered terrace with a lawn on which there are a number of beautiful maples. Plantings of irises, daffodils, peonies, roses, and tulips brighten the picture during the warmer weather, and the interior of the inn is enhanced by flowers throughout all months of the year.

On the floors above, authentic New England rooms and suites are available for overnight guests or for those with longer stays in mind. All but two of them have their own bathrooms, many have four-poster beds, and some have working fireplaces. All of the rooms have new Colonial wallpaper and new curtains and carpets. They are air conditioned in the summer.

The Tavern in the old cellar is now completely remodeled.

Dinner that evening was delightful and delicious, with a Shaker pie appetizer that had ham and a lovely sauce. The entrée was a perfectly poached salmon steak served with blackberries and a blackberry sauce and a side dish of fresh asparagus. Dessert was a delectable pear and macadamia nut tart. Ray pointed out that they have the area's largest breakfast menu, which includes johnny cakes—a great old New England tradition.

Some special-interest weekends deal with California wines, art and artists, literature, and Shakers, and include workshops and field trips. Write for a brochure describing these interesting weekends.

Cliff points out that "Tanglewood is just a mile down the road, and we continue the tradition of good music all year long. We always have good classical music playing in the background, and our grand piano in the large common room is frequently played by guests who share their talent with us." The inn has also been acquiring some very handsome paintings, including those of William and James Hart and other Hudson River School painters.

THE VILLAGE INN, Church St., Lenox, MA 01240; 413-637-0020. 1-800-253-0917; Fax: 413-637-9756.

A 30-guestroom inn (all with private baths, three in hallway) in a historic Berkshire town, 4 mi. from Stockbridge, 8 mi. from Pittsfield, and 1 mi. from Tanglewood. All sizes of beds available. Breakfast and afternoon tea served daily to travelers. Dinner served Tues. thru Sun. Open every day of the year. Lenox is located in the heart of the Berkshires with many historical, cultural, and recreational features. Swimming in pleasant nearby lakes. All seasonal sports, including xc and downhill skiing, available nearby. No pets. Personal checks accepted. CCs: all major cards. Cliff Rudisill and Ray Wilson, owners-hosts.

DIRECTIONS: After approaching Lenox on Rte. 7, one of the principal north-south routes in New England, exit onto Rte. 7A to reach the village center and Church St. When approaching from the Mass. Tpke. (Exit 2), use Rte. 20W about 4 mi. and turn left onto Rte. 183 to center of town.

INN EVENTS: MAY–JUNE—special weekend packages, including gourmet dinner with wine, that may focus on film, literature (emphasis on Wharton and Melville), museums and galleries, Shaker traditions, and more.

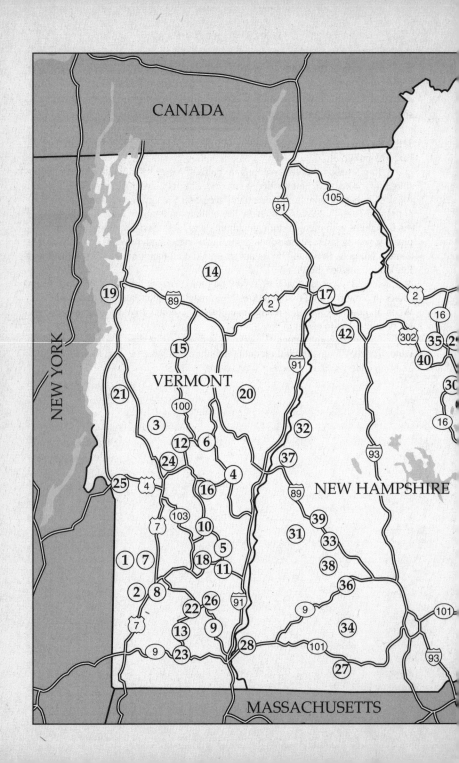

Vermont

1. Dorset, The Barrows House
2. Manchester, Birch Hill Inn
3. Goshen, Blueberry Hill
4. Woodstock, The Charleston House
5. Chester, Chester House
6. Gaysville, Cobble House Inn
7. Dorset, Cornucopia of Dorset
8. Manchester Village, 1811 House
9. Newfane, The Four Columns Inn
10. Ludlow, The Governor's Inn
11. Chester, The Inn at Long Last
12. Pittsfield, The Inn at Pittsfield
13. West Dover, Inn at Sawmill Farm
14. Stowe, The Inn at the Brass Lantern
15. Waitsfield, The Inn at the Round Barn Farm
16. Bridgewater Corners, October Country Inn
17. Lower Waterford, Rabbit Hill Inn
18. Simonsville, Rowell's Inn
19. Shelburne, Shelburne House Farms
20. Chelsea, Shire Inn
21. Middlebury, Swift House Inn
22. Jamaica, Three Mountain Inn
23. Wilmington, Trail's End
24. Chittenden, Tulip Tree Inn
25. Fair Haven, Vermont Marble Inn
26. West Townshend, Windham Hill Inn

New Hampshire

27. Temple, The Birchwood Inn
28. West Chesterfield, Chesterfield Inn
29. Jackson, Christmas Farm Inn
30. Conway, The Darby Farm Inn
31. Sunapee, Dexter's Inn and Tennis Club
32. Lyme, The Dowd's Country Inn
33. North Sutton, Follansbee Inn
34. Francestown, The Inn at Crotched Mountain
35. Jackson, Inn at Thorn Hill
36. Henniker, The Meeting House Inn
37. Etna, Moose Mountain Lodge
38. Bradford, Mountain Lake Inn
39. New London, New London Inn
40. Hart's Location, The Notchland Inn
41. Snowville, Snowvillage Inn
42. Sugar Hill, Sugar Hill Inn

MAINE

Atlantic Ocean

0———10 Miles
0—10 Kilometers

Vermont

Home of fabulous autumn foliage and wonderful winter skiing, Vermont is equally famous for the lovely antiques and country crafts—especially quilts, hand-carved wooden items, and pottery—that can be purchased here. Its picturesque towns and villages, nestled in the Green Mountain valleys, are the quintessence of New England.

EVENTS

JANUARY	Annual Winter Carnival, Stowe: ski races, snow golf, dog sled races, snow sculpture (info: 802-253-7326; 800-24-STOWE)
JANUARY	Winterfest, Newport: contests, dog sled races, ski events, snow sculpture (info: 802-334-7782)
FEBRUARY	Snowflake Festival Winter Carnival, Lyndonville/Burke: crafts, ski events, torchlight parade, snow sculpture (info: 802-626-3317)
FEBRUARY	Winter Carnival, Brattleboro: parade, sugar on ice, ski jumping (info: 802-254-4565)
FEBRUARY	Artisans at the Equinox Hotel, Manchester (info: 802-362-4700)
FEBRUARY	Bromley Torchlight Parade & Fireworks
FEBRUARY	Mogul Challenge, Waitsfield (info: 802-496-3551)
FEBRUARY–MARCH	Woodstock Winter Carnival (info: 802-457-3555)
MARCH	Telemark Festival, Waitsfield (info: 802-496-4387)
APRIL	Festival of Quilts, College of St. Joseph, Rutland
APRIL	Vermont Maple Festival, St. Albans (info: 802-524-5800)
MAY	Champlain Valley Quilt Festival, Shelburne (info: 802-985-3346)
MAY	Noon Music, Stowe
MAY	Great Duck Race, Wilmington
MAY–JUNE	Annual Lake Champlain Balloon & Crafts Festival, Essex (info: 802-899-2993)
JUNE, MIDDLE	Quechee Balloon Festival (info: 802-295-7900)
JUNE	middle Manchester antique & classic car show, Hildene (info: 3621788
JUNE	Burlington Jazz Festival (info: 802-863-7992)
JUNE	Fun Slalom, Killington (info: 802-422-3333)
JUNE	Hildene Classic Car Show, Manchester (info: 802-362-1788
JUNE	Summer Stage, Stowe
JUNE	Ben & Jerry Festival, Stowe

JUNE	Vermont Symphony, Stowe
JUNE–AUGUST	Strattonfest Concerts, Stratton Mountain (info: 800-828-7080)
JUNE–LABOR DAY	Dorset Theater Festival (info: 802-867-5777)
JUNE–JULY	polo matches, Hildene, near Manchester
JULY 4	Londonderry's Old-Fashioned Fourth
JULY 4	Independence Day Celebration, Waitsfield (info: 802-496-3409)
JULY 4	Parade and Picnics, Woodstock (info: 802-457-3555)
JULY 4TH	Chester Craft Sale, Village Green
JULY, 2ND SATURDAY	Chelsea Flea Market (802-685-4460)
JULY, EARLY	West Dover Air Show (info: 802-464-2196)
JULY, MIDDLE	Bluegrass Music Festival, Lower Waterford
JULY–AUGUST	Mountain horse shows and Equestrian Summer Showcase, Killington/Waitsfield/Stowe (info: 802-496-7469)
JULY–AUGUST	Vermont crafters demonstrate stained-glass making, clothes painting, pottery, stenciling, screen making, quilting, basketweaving and more, Waitsfield (info: 802-496-2331)
JULY	Marlboro Music Festival, Marlboro College (info: 802-254-8163)
JULY	Annual Vermont Quilt Festival, Northfield (info: 802-485-7092, 802-773-6563)
JULY	Hand Crafters' Annual Craft Show, Stowe (info: 802-388-0123)
JULY	Hot Air Balloon Festival, Stowe
JULY–AUGUST	Manchester Musical Festival
JULY–SEPTEMBER	Weston Playhouse, Weston
AUGUST	Re-enactment of the Battle of Bennington (info: 802-447-3311)
AUGUST	Stellafare Weekend, Chester: attracts astronomers, star gazers, telescope buffs from across the U.S.
AUGUST	9th Annual Champlain Valley Festival, Ferrisburgh: folk singing and dance (info: 802-849-6968)
AUGUST	Champlain Valley Exposition and Fair, Essex Junction (info: 802-878-5545)
AUGUST, MIDDLE	Castleton, Colonial Day, house tours of 19th century homes
AUGUST	Bread & Puppet Circus, Lower Waterford: political fair
AUGUST	Antique & Classic Car Rally, Stowe
AUGUST	polo matches, Stowe
AUGUST	Mad River Festival, Waitsfield (info: 802-496-7469)
AUGUST	Scottish Festival, Woodstock
AUGUST	Grace Cottage Hospital Days Fair, West Townshend
AUGUST	Horse show
SEPTEMBER, LATE	Peru Fair (info: 802-824-8178)

SEPTEMBER	147th Annual Vermont State Fair, Rutland (info: 802-775-5200)
SEPTEMBER–OCTOBER	Stratton Mountain Arts Festival (info: 802-297-2200 ext. 2555)
SEPTEMBER	Turnbridge World Fair (802-889-5521)
SEPTEMBER	Harvest Week celebration, Waitsfield: herb drying, pumpkin pick-- ing & carving (info: 802-496-7900)
SEPTEMBER	Bach Music Festival, West Townshend (info: 802-257-4523)
OCTOBER	Northeast Kingdom Fall Foliage Festival, Walden/Cabot/Plainfield/ Peacham/Barnet/Groton: church suppers, tours, exhibits. Author's favorite—I spent my honeymoon enjoying this wonderful event. (info: 802-563-2472)
OCTOBER	Antique Show, Stowe
OCTOBER	Craftfair, West Dover (info: 802-464-3333)
OCTOBER	Mount Snow Fall Foliage Craft Fair
NOVEMBER	Burlington Craft Show (info: 802-388-0123)
DECEMBER, EARLY	Victorian Weekend, Chester
DECEMBER	Wassail Christmas Festival, Woodstock (info: 802-457-3555)
DECEMBER	Museum Week, Bennington (info: 802-447-1571)

SIGHTS

Ben & Jerry ice cream factory

Bennington Museum

Billings Farm

Brattleboro Museum

Calvin Coolidge Birthplace

Clark Museum

Crafton, a totally restored but non-commercial village

Fairbanks Museum & Planetarium

Hildene, summer home of Robert Todd Lincoln

Institute of Natural Science

Maple Grove Museum

Marble Exhibit

Merck Forest & Farmland

Morgan Horse Farm

Proctor Marble Factory

Quechee Gorge

Shelburne Museum

Sheldon Museum

Simon Pierce Glassblowing

Southern Vermont Art Center

Stone Village in Chester Depot, stone houses c.1830-50
Vermont Folklore Center
Vermont State Craft Center
Wildflower Farm
Williamstown Museum

THE BARROWS HOUSE
Dorset, Vermont

Sally and Tim Brown have been operating this 18th-century inn since 1986, and love the small Vermont town of Dorset. "We thought that the Barrows House was really a unique property," Sally said. "Its got such a lovely parklike setting, and the multiple buildings offer privacy for guests." The main house was built around 1804, two of the other seven were built in the 19th century, and the remaining five buildings were finished in the mid-20th century. To provide continuity, the Browns have painted all the buildings in the Colonial style: a crisp white with black shutters.

Only a two-minute walk from town, the inn is spread over 11 acres that include two tennis courts and a swimming pool. Neighboring homes are nearby, creating a pleasant rural village atmosphere.

The Barrows House is ideal for family visits. The Browns are only the fourth family to have owned the inn since 1900, and their children often help out during the summer months. Their son Thatcher enjoyed cooking in the inn's kitchen so much during past summers that he has now graduated from Cornell School of Hotel Administration. The only "kid" left at home now are their keeshonds, Katrina, who, according to Sally, "has become a special hostess in the tavern and on our new cocktail terrace," and Beluga.

All of the eight buildings have been completely renovated, and with new rugs, fabrics, curtains, and paint. The common areas are comfortably furnished and, in keeping with the inn's Colonial origins, are decorated with stenciling and many antique period pieces.

The bedrooms are individually furnished in a variety of country styles using combinations of floral and print fabrics interspersed with period and antique furnishings. Television, air-conditioning, and refrigerators are in all the suites, and some of the other rooms. All rooms but two have private baths.

Enhancing the inn's dining reputation was one of the interesting challenges that drew the Browns away from careers in finance. The Barrows House is a full-service inn, where a country breakfast and dinner are served daily. Dinner is a four-course gourmet treat, with six to ten choices of appetizers, a main course, and dessert. A crisp green salad with three dressings comes paired with fresh hot bread.

Breakfast begins with juice, fruit, and cold cereals followed by a pancake special and an egg dish, served with bacon, sausage and great home fries.

Although lunch is not available regularly, a brown-bag picnic can be arranged.

THE BARROWS HOUSE, Rte. 30, Dorset, VT 05251; 802-867-4455.

A 28-guestroom (private baths) 200-year-old colonial country inn on 12 acres in the heart of the picturesque Vermont village. All-size beds. Open year-round. Modified American plan or B&B available. Close to historic Manchester and shopping. Swimming pool and tennis courts on premises. Close to shopping, hiking, and skiing. Well-behaved pets permitted in two of the cottages. Two keeshonds in residence. CCs: Visa, MC. Sally and Tim Brown, owners/hosts.

DIRECTIONS: On Rte. 30 north, 6 mi. northwest of Manchester, VT. Coming from Manchester, the inn is on the right-hand side of the road before the town of Dorset's Green.

INN EVENTS: JUNE–JULY (SUNDAYS)—Littlest Music Festival

BIRCH HILL INN
Manchester, Vermont

The location of this inn sets it apart from other inns in the area. Just a few moments from Manchester and all it has to offer, the inn is situated on a 200-acre property. The farmhouse next door is the only other house that can be seen. From every window and vantage point on the

patio or lawn, there are views of the Green Mountains and Taconic Range. The produce of the extensive vegetable garden is used for the dinners that are served. When I arrived I could see Beefalo grazing in the fields. Jim, the cordial host, explained that they are raised as a low-fat and low-cholestrol beef cattle.

Four generations of Pat's family have lived in this lovely old farm-house, the main part of which is over 190 years old. Pat and Jim decided to turn it into an inn, and have been welcoming guests here since 1981. The original part of the inn dates from 1790; additions were made in 1918 and 1987.

All guest rooms are spacious and individually decorated with antiques, etchings and prints. The country cottage, with a lovely marble terrace, appeals to honeymooners and others with a yen for privacy.

In the large gathering room, an ongoing jigsaw puzzle was challenging some guests. I preferred to curl up with a book in one of the deep couches that flank the fireplace. For more active guests, the inn has its own trout pond and swimming pool.

The plant-filled sunroom provides a sunny spot in winter or a cool one in summer, when huge maples and white birches provide welcome shade. A full breakfast featuring special egg dishes and homemade muffins or pancakes is included.

BIRCH HILL INN, Box 346, West Rd., Manchester, VT 05254; 802-362-2761.
A 5-guestroom (private baths) extremely comfortable country-home inn, with a family cottage, 5 min. from downtown Manchester Center. King, queen and twin beds available. Modified American plan includes dinner and breakfast. B&B plan available. Dinners offered to houseguests Fri. and Sat. nights. Open after Christmas to mid-April, and late May to Nov. Two-night minimum preferred (be sure to make reservations). Swimming pool, xc skiing, trout fishing, and walking trails on grounds. Alpine skiing at major areas nearby as well as tennis and golf facilities; great biking. No pets. Golden retriever in residence. CCs: Visa, MC, AE. Pat and Jim Lee, owners/hosts.

DIRECTIONS: From Manchester Center, where Rtes. 7, 7A, and 30 meet, take Rte. 30 north 2 mi. to Manchester West Rd. Turn left on West Rd. and continue 3/4 mi. to Birch Hill Inn.

BLUEBERRY HILL

Goshen, Vermont

Tony Clark was an innovator in 1972 in what now has become a very popular winter pastime. Today, most inns in New England, or in fact anywhere in the mountains, have some kind of cross-country skiing facilities on the premises or nearby. But despite his devotion to this winter sport, his inn features special outdoor activities in other seasons, too.

"As you know, we are open for skiing from December through March. But, May through October, and especially summertime here in the Green Mountains is just fabulous. We're very popular with summer and fall backpackers and walkers. Many, many of our cross-country trails are used for walking and hiking, and it's possible to use the inn as a central point for such activities or to include it on an itinerary. We use our ski trails as nature and educational paths, providing all kinds of guides to help our guests learn the names of the trees and birds."

Tucked away in the small town of Goshen, you will probably find the inn difficult to locate on your road map. It is in a most idyllic and secluded location, on top of a mountain and on a dirt road, surrounded by the Green Mountain National Forest.

The Dover blue clapboard Inn, built in the early 1800s, was originally an overnight refuge for loggers. Access to most of the rooms is through an exotic greenhouse/solarium with a variety of plants bloom-

ing year round. Bedrooms are plain and simple, with hot water bottles on the backs of the doors and handsome patchwork quilts on the beds. It is truly like visiting a Vermont farm.

Blueberry Hill is very definitely family style. Everyone sits around the big dining room table, and there is one main dish for each meal, cooked in the farmhouse kitchen. This main dish is likely to be something quite unusual, depending upon the cook's gourmet proclivities.

Reservations for winter accommodations should be made as early as possible, as the inn is often booked solid for weeks at a time in winter.

BLUEBERRY HILL, Goshen, VT 05733; 802-247-6735.

A 12-guestroom (private baths) mountain inn passionately devoted to xc skiing, 8 mi. from Brandon. Double and twin beds available. Modified American plan for overnight guests. Open from May thru Oct. and Dec. to March. Public dining by reservation only. Closed Christmas. Wheelchair access. Swimming, fishing, hiking, nature walks, and xc skiing on grounds. Much other recreation nearby. One dog in residence. CCs: Visa, MC. Tony Clark, owner/host.

DIRECTIONS: At Brandon, travel east on Rte. 73 through Forest Dale. Then follow signs to Blueberry Hill.

INN EVENTS: JANUARY—snowshoe race, cross country skiing
FEBRUARY—American ski marathon
MARCH—Pig Race
JULY 26—Goshen Gallop

THE CHARLESTON HOUSE
Woodstock, Vermont

On a frigid January morning in 1934, Farmer Gilbert allowed the first American rope tow to go up his ski hill, and Woodstock hasn't been the same since.

Woodstock is famed not only for its natural beauty but also for its many handsome homesteads: elegant brick Greek Revivals; graceful, white clapboards; some gingerbread Victorians.

One of these, the Charleston House, listed in the National Register of Historic Places, is run by a charming couple, Barbara and Bill Hough. Barbara has left ski-instructing in Colorado to turn breakfast chef here in Vermont.

The furnishings of the Charleston House are those one would expect to find in any elegant home; Oriental rugs, Lawson couches, armloads of books and paintings. The Hepplewhite furniture in the dining room, where breakfast is served, is by Potthast, the last of the great furniture makers of Baltimore. The southern influence continues in the breakfast menu, which includes grits, and also features such continental specialties as strada.

Each of the cozy bedrooms has lots of pillows, comfy comforters, good reading lamps, and a name. Most of the beds are queen-sized four-posters, but one room, named "Good Friends," has four-poster twin beds. And if the inn is filled, the Houghs own a Victorian townhouse one block away, Canterbury House, which is also very nice.

Woodstock's charming Main Street, filled with boutiques, antique shops, and quality restaurants, is only minutes from the handsome black front door. Bicycles are available to the guests who want to explore the byways.

THE CHARLESTON HOUSE, 21 Pleasant St. (Rte. 4), Woodstock, VT 05091; 802-457-3843.

A 7-guestroom (private baths) 1835 Greek Revival homestead, plus a 7-room townhouse, 3 min. from the center of Woodstock. Queen, double and twin beds. Full breakfast. Open all year. TV in common room. An easy drive to 6 major alpine ski areas; xc skiing close by. Golf, tennis, fishing, hiking, biking. Many art galleries and antique shops. Hood Art Museum and Hopkins Center at Dartmouth College in nearby Hanover, NH. No pets. One dog in residence. No smoking in bedrooms. CCs; Visa, MC, AE. Barbara and Bill Hough, owners/hosts.

DIRECTIONS: From I-93 or I-91, take I-89 north to Exit 1, turning left to Rte. 4. Continue approx. 10 mi. to Woodstock Village.

CHESTER HOUSE
Chester, Vermont

Irene and Norm Wright believe in New England hospitality, so they chose its traditional symbol, the golden pineapple, to emblazon on the slate-blue sign welcoming guests to Chester House. The Wrights also believe in providing a beautiful, well-ordered environment, and their immaculate white clapboard inn with its lovely landscaping and perennial flower beds is just that. Originally built in 1780, the inn sits just across from Chester's village green and is listed on the National Register of Historic Places.

As a personnel manager for Mobil Oil Corporation, Norm and Irene spent their lives traveling, meeting new people, and living throughout the U.S. and overseas. When he retired, they decided to open an inn in Norm's hometown of Chester. "I was born and raised on a dairy farm twelve miles from here," he told me. "My family has lived in the area since 1690, so I guess you could say I've returned to my roots."

The inn's interior is just as lovely and ordered as the exterior. All the rooms, including the pleasant guest rooms, have been carefully restored and decorated in the style of 18th-century New England, complete with early American furnishings and Oriental rugs. Guests have full use of the formal living room, spacious family room, and a delightful airy porch that runs the length of the house.

Of the inn's five guest rooms, my favorite was the one with the Jacuzzi. The room was spacious and furnished with a canopied queen-sized bed and American antiques. The other four rooms offer king, full and twin beds. All have private baths with vanities.

Breakfast is a hearty meal that features waffles with real Vermont maple syrup, grapefruit garnished with fresh strawberries, fried apples, and excellent coffee.

To walk off some of those breakfast calories, you might want to stroll around the village and peruse the antique shops. Four major downhill ski centers, plus many cross-country courses, are located

within minutes from the inn. Chester also offers a good home base for day treks to nearby auctions, craft fairs, and cheese factories.

Norm and Irene are a friendly couple who will do everything possible to make your stay at Chester House as relaxing and memorable as mine was.

CHESTER HOUSE, Main St., Chester, VT 05143; 802-875-2205.

An immaculate 5-guestroom (private baths) 18th-century inn across from Chester's village green. King, queen, double and twin beds. Full country breakfast. Open year-round. Central to craft fairs, antiquing, skiing and hiking trails. No pets. Irene and Norm Wright, owners/hosts.

DIRECTIONS: From south or west, take Rte. 11 to Chester. Inn is at center of town next to the Hugging Bear Shop.

COBBLE HOUSE INN

Gaysville, Vermont

If variety is the spice of life, dinner time at Cobble House is a highly flavored affair. The owners don't believe in turning tables so, with a total seating for twenty guests in the dining room, the table was mine for the entire evening. There were ten specials of Italian and French cuisine from which to choose, including rack of lamb, chicken, steak,

and a sumptuous Osso Bucco. I was enjoying a fresh pasta with sundried tomatoes along with maple-glazed salmon and scallops. Preceding this main course had been a hearty Caesar salad. The bread basket was kept full with Beau Benson's favorite homemade herb muffins, and still to come was a mud pie dessert. Beau, co-owner and chef of the family, casually outfitted in shorts and an apron, moved from table to table greeting her guests.

Phil Bensen, or "Farmer Phil" as Beau teasingly calls her husband and business partner, is more the outdoorsman, training Morgan horses, running the Vermont terrain, or swinging his golf clubs. Beau's hand can be seen in the wide variety of plants and flowers in the gardens. Both are avid skiers, and the three acres of Cobble House grounds host cross-country skiing during the winter. They chose Cobble House because of its off-the-beaten-path location along the White River. The old historic house appealed to Beau, while the abundance of outdoor sports seduced Phil. They converted the white-sided 1864 Victorian, complete with barn-red shutters and the traditional widow's walk up top, to a countryside inn in 1984.

Summer days see the hammock swaying lazily on the wide front porch, which offers a peaceful view of the mountains. Inside, wide-planked pine floors, covered in places with colorful latchhook rugs, blend with the country feel of simple furnishings. The common room and parlor display watercolors of the area. Tiring of those, you can settle into the sofa and watch through the tall windows as the horses graze in the meadow. You may enjoy beer, wine or champagne while nibbling on a light afternoon snack of cheese and crackers in the common room. Bedtime took me back to one of the six basic guest rooms, which had a brass bed covered with a calico quilt. Sunrise brought tempting smells of frying ham and Belgian waffles.

Cobble House Inn offers special events throughout the year. One that caught my eye was the Moonlight Cross-Country Skiing, held during the full moons of January and February, which ends with hot cocoa by a roaring bonfire. Historic spots within a hour's drive include Calvin Coolidge's birthplace, Wilson Castle, and the Billings Farm and Museum. I simply could not leave Vermont without visiting the New England Maple Museum.

The simplicity of Cobble House Inn and its surroundings only enhanced the unique dining experience during my stay.

COBBLE HOUSE INN, P.O. Box 49, Gaysville, VT 05246; 802-234-5458.

Victorian restored mansion with 6 guestrooms, includes full breakfast and afternoon hors d'oeuvres. Varied dinner menu, light lunch by arrangement. Queen and double beds. Open year round. Some minimum stays. No smoking. Local or nearby resort skiing, plus a multitude of outdoor sports available. Historic sightseeing within a one-hour drive. Cats, horses and farm animals in residence. No pets. CCs: Visa, MC. Phil and Beau Benson, owners/hosts.

DIRECTIONS: Take I-89 north to Exit 3. Turn right on 107 West at 3 mi. mark. Bear left on 107 approx. 6.5 miles. Turn right at State directional sign saying "Cobble House Inn". Cross the bridge, staying left. Inn on left hand side.

CORNUCOPIA OF DORSET

Dorset, Vermont

We had just settled into our room when Linda Ley, owner of Cornucopia along with her husband, Bill, appeared at our door with two flutes of effervescent champagne.

"Our personal way of welcoming our guests," she explained, as Kitt, the household Vermont mutt, nosed around her to investigate. "There will be tea downstairs later if you want to join us. Come on, Kitt, we have work to do."

We settled into the sitting area of our room, richly decorated in dark blue and rose hues. It held a large four-poster bed draped with a colorful tied quilt. A porcelain washbasin and pitcher sat on an antique table. Rays of light streamed through sheer lace curtains hanging at the windows. Called the Dorset Hill Room, it had a homey presence. Each of the five guest rooms, including the refurbished carriage house, are named after local mountains, and are unique in themes of decor.

Bill and Linda Ley purchased the inn in 1986. Hailing from Greenwich, Bill had attended Cornell (the hotel school) and was president of a wholesale travel company, while Linda ran a marketing company related to travel. They fell in love with the small, cultural village of Dorset and the added advantage of outdoor sports nearby. The previous owners had just completed the renovation of the 1880 Colonial. The location of the white clapboard two-story with dark green shutters was ideal, just a short distance from the village green, excellent dining and the theatre.

When we returned from dinner that evening, we enjoyed a brandy by the fire in the living room, furnished with antiques and heirlooms from both sides of the family. In addition to the living room, the first

floor holds the library, where friendly games of backgammon take place throughout the day. There is a large sunroom, complete with a collection of movies for viewing on the TV and VCR. In the warmer months, patio furniture sits out on the marble patio and side porch. The dining room is large and has that "country kitchen" feel, opening to the kitchen area. Cornucopia breakfasts are served here and bring a whole new meaning to the word "plentiful." Preceded by coffee or tea delivered to your door, breakfast in the dining room begins with a fruit course that might include a melon boat garnished with fresh berries and served with creme fraiche, or, during the cold winter months, warm spiced compote with sour cream and nuts. Chilled cream of melon soup with tempting scents of fresh mint is a summer favorite. Main course selections vary from cinnamon puff pancakes swimming in Vermont maple syrup or cream cheese blitzes topped with warm cranberry and raspberry toppings, to individual souffles slathered in fresh berry sauces or gingerbread waffles.

When we returned to our room each evening, feet aching from touring shops and art galleries, a dimly lit kerosene lamp emitted a warm "welcome back". The bed covers were turned down and soft terrycloth robes hung waiting nearby.

CORNUCOPIA OF DORSET, P.O. Box 307, Route 30, Dorset, VT 05251; 802-867-5751.

Quaint 5-guestroom 1880 Colonial in historic district. King and queen beds. Some fireplaces. Carriage House features full kitchen, loft, and fireplace. Full breakfast included. Afternoon tea. Open year round. Two-night minimum on weekends, three nights during holidays. Short walk to village green, theatre, art galleries and restaurants in Dorset. Hiking, skiing, horseback riding, boating, golf or tennis close by. No pets. Housepets include a mutt named Kitt and Woodstock, the "60s Bunny," who makes his home outside in a hutch or in the garage. CCs: Visa, MC. Bill and Linda Ley, owners/hosts.

DIRECTIONS: Halfway between New York City and Montreal, about 6 mi. northwest of Manchester. Coming from Manchester, the inn is on the right-hand side of the road just past The Barrows House.

1811 HOUSE

Manchester Village, Vermont

Except for the brief period when Mary Lincoln Isham, President Lincoln's granddaughter, used the 1811 House as a residence, it has been used as an inn. Built in the 1770s, the home has been carefully and authentically restored to the Federal period of the 1800s. Twelve-over-twelve windows and clapboard siding are only two of the details that earned the inn its position as a registered National Landmark building.

The inn sits on more than 3 acres of lawn, landscaped with flower and rose gardens, and is directly on the green in Manchester Village. Views through pristine white birches to the Green Mountains and the Equinox Golf Course are exceptional.

All rooms are filled with authentic English and American antiques. I felt as if I had walked into a living museum, yet one where I was encouraged to relax and enjoy the comforts of home. Innkeepers Marnie & Bruce Duff's splendid array of antique furnishings, Oriental rugs, Chinese lamps, and sterling and china artifacts create an ambience that signifies superior taste and sensibilities. The art collection alone, with original oils, prints, and drawings, is of a quality usually seen only in private collectors' homes.

Roaring fires warm each of the public rooms on chilly evenings. You can pull up a chair in the library/game room where a hand-carved chess set waits, or prop your legs over the arm of an easy chair in the restful living room. Whatever your choice, sooner or later you will end up at the hub of the inn, the beam-ceilinged English pub.

In the pub, the hum of conversation and thud of darts goes on long into the evening, enhanced by gleaming brass horns, authentic tavern tables, and a wonderful pewter collection. A well-stocked bar of single malt whiskeys plus other libation are available. Bruce a retired banker, is responsible for the near-regulation dart setup. He has made certain that participants have the best in equipment: a set of balanced brass darts, an illuminated board, and distance markers on the floor, properly placed for anyone who tries to sneak a few feet closer.

The fourteen bedrooms, each with a private bath and shower, exhibit the same tasteful consideration to period decoration as the public rooms. Each room is different. I stayed in Robert Todd Lincoln, with its lovely old four-poster canopied bed and my own fireplace. Plump pillows and cheerful designer fabrics, along with the colorful handmade quilt, made me feel as if I'd been tucked in by someone's loving hands. The modern bathrooms have been expertly designed to blend with the period surroundings.

After a wonderful, restful night, I wandered down to the elegant dining room for a sumptuous breakfast. Amidst Georgian silver and china plates, I enjoyed fresh-squeezed orange juice, a savory English omelet, and rich fresh-brewed coffee with cream. Breakfast can also be taken in the pub, just in case a dart rematch had been planned the night before.

Although the 1811 House sporadically offers dinner, four very fine restaurants are within walking distance from the inn: three serving French cuisine and one serving steaks and seafood. The Duffs are happy to make reservations for you.

The inn is close to many outdoor activities, a perfect way to work off that extra glass of stout. Besides golf and tennis at the Equinox, you might try cross-country skiing or hike one of the trails at the nearby Merck Forest and Farmland Center. Stop at the center on your way back and sample some of the traditional Vermont maple sugar, and give one of the Center's hefty draft horses a pat.

1811 HOUSE, Box 39, Manchester Village, VT 05254; 802-362-1811.

A 14-guestroom (private baths) classic Vermont inn with traditional English pub. King, queen, and double beds. Closed Christmas week. Breakfast included. Restaurants within walking distance. Hiking, skiing, water sports, biking, and antique shops nearby. No pets. Marnie and Bruce Duff, owners/hosts.

DIRECTIONS: In Vermont, take Rte. 7 north to Manchester. Turn left at the blinking light and go back on 7A for 1 mile. The inn is on your left.

THE FOUR COLUMNS INN
Newfane, Vermont

Newfane is a quintessential New England village, and one of the most photographed spots in Vermont. And according to innkeepers Jacques and Pam Allembert, "The Four Columns Inn is one of the reasons why!"

Set back from the main roads on 150 acres of gardens, woodlands, ponds, and streams, the graceful white facade of the main house includes four Greek revival columns. Built by General Pardon Kimball of hand-hewn timbers and beams, the over 150-year-old home has lost none of its stately yet relaxed elegance.

Hiking trails abound, or you can spend a day just lying in the hammock beside the brook—unless you would rather swim in the pool surrounded by lovely gardens personally attended to by Jacques.

Jacques' twenty-plus years as a New York restaurateur have honed his skills as a gracious host to a fine art. "I love the hospitality industry," he told me as he took my bags in the foyer.

The decor of the inn is lovely, with polished antiques, handmade rugs, and attractive accents, like a period spinning wheel tucked into a sunny corner. The living rooms are cozy and invite reading, television watching, or visiting with other guests.

Seventeen unique rooms and suites, all with private baths, are located in the main house, the cottage, and the renovated barn. The clean, airy rooms, some with fireplaces, are decorated with antique and wicker furnishings. Most are papered with quaint prints. The beds range from four-poster to brass. One has a lace-topped canopy. "All our rooms have a living connection with a quiet and relaxing world," Jacques said as we admired the view of the village green from my window.

I accepted his invitation for a glass of wine before dinner and we met at the inn's distinctive pewter-topped bar, which dominates the tavern room. I was impressed with the superb wine list. Victorian and Colonial antiques, along with wide plank flooring and Oriental rugs, provide a warm atmosphere for easy conversation. I could almost imagine General Kimball sitting across from me, tipping a glass of homemade brew to my health.

The excellent reputation of the inn's restaurant had preceded my visit. Over our wine, I asked Jacques to give me a brief overview of the menu. "Well, we offer a blend of fine European and New American cuisine. Our chef, Gregory Parks, uses the finest and freshest Vermont food products. Why don't we go in and you can see for yourself."

As we entered the barn that houses the restaurant, I was impressed by the quality renovation that had been done. The dark beams set off the cream tones of the room, while a large brick fireplace warms one end, and antique copper cook pots, baskets, and country crafts offer interesting accents. Fresh garden flowers and soft candlelight create a romantic mood.

The menu is intriguing. The Chef Parks gives full rein to his creativity, making use of local Vermont gamebird, rabbit, milk-fed veal, and North Atlantic seafood. Unique, inventive sauces are used, such as a blend of rhubarb and radish—yes, radish. The hot-sour-sweet combination is perfect. A full array of desserts, each created in the restaurant's kitchen, can't help but tempt even the most staunch abstainer. I had the creamy chocolate mousse pie, delicately accompanied by blueberries, strawberries, and *real* whipped cream.

After such a splendid dinner, I had doubts about having much more than coffee for breakfast. But the buffet table, set with fresh berries, fruit, homemade granola, and local Grafton cheddar cheese, was too inviting. Besides, what little I did have left on my plate I shared with the inn's two resident white ducks, who seemed genuinely pleased to have my company in the garden.

THE FOUR COLUMNS INN, P.O. Box 278, West St., Newfane, VT 05345; 802-365-7713.

A 15-guestroom (private baths) inn located in one of Vermont's most picturesque rural villages. King, queen, and twin beds. Closed for 2 weeks after Thanksgiving. Breakfast, wonderful gourmet dinner, plus all gratuities included in tariff. Hiking, bicycling, swimming, alpine and xc skiing nearby. Pets by arrangement. One Rottweiler named Jackson in residence. Jacques Allembert, owner/host.

DIRECTIONS: 100 mi. from Boston, and 220 mi. from New York. Take Exit 2 from I-91 at Brattleboro to Rte. 30 north. Inn is 100 yards off Rte. 30 on the left.

THE GOVERNOR'S INN
Ludlow, Vermont

"You've missed our complimentary three o'clock tea," Deedy Marble scolded me, laughingly. "But that's your own fault. It is served on our beautiful Victorian silver service. We actually have second- and third-time guests who try to get here in time for tea. It's a wonderful way to begin a country visit. It gives you a chance to meet the other guests."

Luckily, I had arrived in time for dinner. Each of the gathered guests was individually escorted to our tables in the candlelit dining room by one of the turn-of-the-century-clad waitresses. Deedy, who is

an artist-cum-chef, described the six-course dinner. As each course was served, the dish was again described.

Whether there are five courses or six, dinner always begins with cream cheese and the Governor's sauce (the only recipe, incidentally, not included in the inn's delightfully refreshing cookbook). I don't see how any guest could leave the inn without a jar of this sauce, which is available for purchase.

Here are a few brief hints on the menu: appetizers include mushroom strudel or marinated fish l'orange or steak strips with horseradish cream. Some of the main dishes are Lamb Gourmet, bluefish flambé, and steak Diane. These are augmented by intriguing side dishes. Desserts include chocolate walnut pie and peach ice with raspberry melba sauce.

If all of these seem to be a bit unusual it's because both Deedy and Charlie Marble (he does the wonderful breakfasts) are passionately devoted to cookery. They have attended cooking schools in France, and their skills are evident in the menu.

Another of their innovations is the gourmet picnic hampers, for which the Governor's Inn has now become rather well known.

As Deedy showed me to my guest room on the second floor, she pointed out five generations of family photographs along the staircase. My bedroom had a beautiful brass head and footboard that has been in Deedy's family for over 100 years. The furnishings and decorations are pure Victorian, with the exception of two watercolors by artist Virginia Ann Holt, whose work is also found throughout the inn. Although some of the rooms are on the small side, each is exquisitely decorated with Deedy's personal touches.

Some of the amenities include the option of a morning tray of coffee and sparkling mimosa delivered to your room, some special Governor's Inn chocolates, and in the hallway a "butler's basket" of necessities for guests who have forgotten toothbrushes, toothpaste, and the like. By the way, my bed was turned down at night and my towels had been changed.

The Inn is beautifully furnished with family antiques and all the appointments and decorations are done with impeccable taste. However, those sensitive to traffic should be aware that it is located on a busy road.

THE GOVERNOR'S INN, 86 Main St., Ludlow, VT 05149; 802-228-8830.

An 8-guestroom (private baths) village inn in central Vermont. Modified American plan includes dinner, breakfast, and afternoon tea. Queen, twin and double beds available. Open all year. Downhill skiing at Okemo Mountain and cross-country skiing nearby. Conveniently located to enjoy all of the rich recreational, cultural, and historical attractions in central Vermont. No facilities for pets. Charlie, Deedy and Jennifer Marble, owners/hosts.

DIRECTIONS: Ludlow can be conveniently reached from all of the north-south roads in Vermont. It is located just off the village green, where Rte. 100 crosses Rte. 103.

THE INN AT LONG LAST
Chester, Vermont

Artists are created in many forms: painters, sculptors, writers, composers. Some people, however, are artists of another fashion: artists of life. Jack Coleman is one such artist. Instead of paints or stone mallets, pens or paper, Jack has used his experiences to mold, form, and color a work of art he calls The Inn at Long Last.

Few inns are so representative of their innkeeper's personalities as this three-story Victorian located in the middle of the quiet village of Chester. Author Studs Terkel should have interviewed Jack for his book *Working*, since Jack has had more careers than most of Terkel's subjects: college president, professor, foundation president, blue-collar worker, labor economist, author of seven books, and now an innkeeper. All to satisfy his search for "the dignity of all human beings."

"I've never done anything in which I've used every resource I've got," he told me as we sat in the airy breakfast room drinking coffee. "But every experience I've had I'm drawing on now, and I need everything to make it through the day!" If it sounds as if Jack thinks innkeeping is difficult, he does. But, he also loves what he does: "The work is harder than anybody can possibly describe to you, and the satisfactions are greater than you can ever imagine."

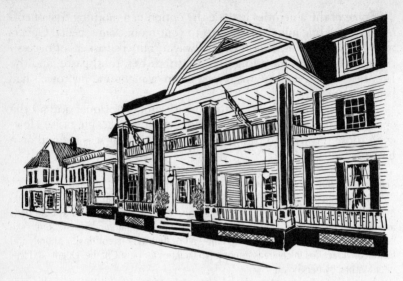

Jack saw the potential of the original old dilapidated inn when he came to see it in 1985. A million dollars later, the once haggard-looking building has been restored to its present grand state. From the moment you enter the lobby, you feel a sense of peace. The inn is spacious, with polished hardwood floors and Oriental rugs. The very large lounge has a huge stone fireplace and comfortable antique furnishings. Jack has a most interesting collection of books in the library, over 3,000, where you will most certainly want to relax by the firelight and share a good-night sherry.

One of the most unique areas of the inn is the upper floors that Jack has turned into a private museum. The thirty guest rooms have been decorated and named for fond memories or passions of his life. Some are named for cities he has called home. Others are named for the experiences he has had, or jobs he has held. His favorite authors, composers, and painters are also represented. For example, one set of adjoining compartments is named for Currier and Ives. "I gave Ives the bigger room because he always comes second," he laughed as we walked to the Grand Opera Room, where programs from some of his favorite operas line the walls.

Breakfast and dinner are eclectic by the chef and Jack helps, of course, and served me a tasty chicken sauté with a spicy peanut sauce. My wife had baked salmon, with dilled Harvarti and Pernod cream, that was absolute heaven. Each entrée includes salad with sourdough rolls. The Shaker lemon pie is luscious.

A Quaker, Jack believes that humility is an essential lesson of life that we all need to learn. Therefore, no task at the inn is beneath him.

You may find him welcoming guests at the front door, taking their bags to their rooms, then scurrying down to the kitchen to whip on his green apron and sprinkle parsley into steaming bowls of split pea soup. Or you may not see him at all as often he is busy doing all the office work required to run some a large operation.

Visit The Inn at Long Last. Visit because it's a comfortable, and gracious inn. But most important, visit for the joy of meeting Jack Coleman and taking part in the art of living.

THE INN AT LONG LAST, Chester, VT 05143; 802-875-2444.

A 30-guestroom (mostly private baths) renovated Victorian country inn. Closed April and mid-Nov. All-size beds. Modified American plan. Historical area, tennis courts, swimming pool, fishing, golf. No pets (except goldfish in their own bowls). No smoking. Jack Coleman, owner/host.

DIRECTIONS: Head north on Rte. 91 in Vermont to Exit 6. Then go 9 mi. on Rte. 103 into Chester. Follow Rte. 11 west one block in Chester to the village green.

THE INN AT PITTSFIELD

Pittsfield, Vermont

"A rose is a rose is a rose," wrote eccentric writer Gertrude Stein. I'm familiar with Ms. Stein's work from a literary standpoint, but my wife is quite the gardener and knows the subtle difference between a Martha Washington and a Tea Rose. Innkeeper Vikki Budasi also knows about these botanical mysteries.

Vikki and her partner, Barbara Morris, came to Vermont from Chicago, bringing with them a sound background in retail management. They chose the area of Pittsfield for its ambiance, and for the inn itself.

Originally built as a stagecoach stop in the 1830s, the inn has housed travelers for almost two hundred years. Remodeling and updating have occurred, including the addition of air conditioning and modern plumbing.

The inn is simply and comfortably furnished with overstuffed sofas and chairs, a glowing pot-bellied stove, and game tables in the living room. The tavern is also welcoming. Any libation you desire can be slid over the genuine Vermont marble-topped bar, and then taken to high-backed chairs around small tables. The bar offers an excellent wine list, and several beers.

Flowers are everywhere, whether in elegant silk and dried arrangements or beautifully displayed in their natural state. Actually, this two-story Colonial has become a gathering place for wildflower enthusiasts. With its three-acre wildflower garden, it has become a spectacular set-

ting for the inn's monthly (June through September) flower-design seminars.

The weekend usually opens with a friendly wine and cheese party on Friday evening. On Saturday morning, while munching on crisp waffles and bacon, participants choose from the list of flowers that had been distributed with the menu. Choices are then obtained from a local florist, fresh and just in time for the flower-arranging session.

While Vikki lectured on a few trade secrets (neither sugar nor asprin help cut flowers—but a bit of bleach does) I left my wife, with gladioli in hand, and ventured out to explore my surroundings.

I wended my way through the inn's backyard of bluebells, clover, violets and Indian paintbrush toward the village of Pittsfield. The general store, post office, library, gas station and church (shared by both Catholic and Universalist denominations) are not re-created tourist attractions but vital, living parts of the town. The circular wooden bandstand just beyond the green looks like a stage prop for "The Music Man."

A small group was relaxing and chatting on the inn's first floor porch as I returned. I caught snippets of the conversation: "I usually use a frog," "peat moss is a must for replanting gardenias."

This made no sense to me, so I decided to retreat to our room for a before-dinner nap. The nine guest rooms are decorated with lovely old quilts, tie-back curtains, antiques and individually designed silk and dried flower arrangements.

The inn's four-course dinner, served in the soft glow of hurricane lamps, may include fish chowder, a tossed salad, Cornish game hens lightly covered with a tomato caper sauce, potatoes speckled with parsely, tender green beans, and a chocolate truffle torte with raspberry sauce. The butternut panelled walls, hand-hewn tables, and many hanging plants make the dining room a warm and inviting environment.

———

THE INN AT PITTSFIELD, Rte. 100, Box 675, Pittsfield, VT 05762; 802-746-8943.

A 9-guestroom (private baths) frame Colonial located in a small Vermont village. Double and twin beds. Near Woodstock and Stockbridge. Open all year. Rates include breakfast and a 4-course dinner. Specializes in weekend seminars highlighting wildflower and floral arranging. No pets. Two dogs in residence. Vikki Budasi and Barbara Morris, owners/hosts.

DIRECTIONS: Take a right on Vermont Hwy. 100 after Killington and go north 10 mi. to Pittsfield.

INN EVENTS: JUNE 26–28—Floral seminar
JULY 24–26—Floral seminar
AUGUST 21–23—Floral seminar
SEPTEMBER 18–20—Floral seminar

INN AT SAWMILL FARM
West Dover, Vermont

With Wilmington behind me, I could now see the buildings of Sawmill Farm on my left. My last turn was over the bridge, which had been reconstructed since a previous visit.

I asked Rod Williams what he would do if all the guests were snowbound. "We would try to amuse them by getting everyone out to cross-country ski," he said. "If you can walk, you can cross-country ski. It's not like downhill. We can even start off with people who have never been on skis. Then we would organize picnics on the trails. We'd keep the fire in the fireplace going bigger and better than ever, and normally we would do tea at four o'clock, but on a snowbound day we start around one."

When Rod and Ione Williams made the "big break" from the pressures of urban life, they brought their own particular talents and sensitivities to this handsome location, and it is indeed a pleasing experience. There was plenty of work to do—a dilapidated barn, a wagon shed, and other outbuildings all had to be converted into lodgings and living rooms. However, over the years, the transition has been exceptional. The textures of the barn siding, the beams, the ceilings, the floors, and the picture windows combine to create a feeling of rural elegance.

Guestrooms have been both added and redecorated, and again I was smitten with the beautiful quilted bedspreads, the bright wallpaper and white ceilings, the profusion of plants in the rooms, and all of the many books and magazines that add to their guests' enjoyment. Lodgings are also found in outbuildings, including the Cider House Studio,

which has a bedroom, dressing room, bath, and living room. The king-sized bed is in an alcove facing a fireplace.

In the living room of the inn there is a superb conversation piece that perhaps symbolizes the entire inn—a handsome brass telescope mounted on a tripod, providing an intimate view of Mount Snow rising majestically to the north.

Brill Williams, Rod and Ione's son, was a teenager when the family moved to West Dover. Now he is officially one of the owners of the inn. The menu changes with the seasons; for example, the fall menu includes grilled marinated duck breasts, backfin crabmeat, fillet of salmon, and a rack of lamb for two. Appetizers include clams Casino, backfin crabmeat cocktail, and cold poached salmon.

INN AT SAWMILL FARM, Box 8, West Dover, VT 05356; 802-464-8131.

A 21-guestroom (private baths) country resort-inn on Rte. 100, 22 mi. from Bennington and Brattleboro. King, queen and double beds available. Within sight of Mt. Snow ski area. Modified American plan omits lunch. Breakfast and dinner served to travelers daily. Closed Nov. 29 to Dec. 18. Swimming, tennis, and trout fishing on grounds. Golf, bicycles, riding, snowshoeing, alpine and xc skiing nearby. No pets. No credit cards. Rodney, Brill, and Ione Williams, owners/hosts.

DIRECTIONS: From I-91, take Brattleboro Exit 2 and travel on VT Rte. 9 west to VT Rte. 100. Proceed north 5 mi. to inn. Or take U.S. 7 north to Bennington, then Rte..9 east to VT Rte. 100 and proceed north 5 mi. to inn.

THE INN AT THE BRASS LANTERN
Stowe, Vermont

Stowe is a typically beautiful New England village. The Brass Lantern is not a typical inn. Mindy and Andy Aldrich have meticulously restored this brick farmhouse and carriage barn to their proper identities as lovely examples of northern New England architecture. Unfortunately, many inns located in this area have modernized, losing the essence of their original design.

The inn's common rooms, including a living room, dining room, and sitting room, are all furnished with antiques and reproductions. Attractive wainscotting links the rooms like a chain. Some modern amenities prevail, like a television in the sitting room and a telephone in the foyer.

Planked floors, handmade quilts, and the traditional colors of mauve and Colonial blue decorate the nine air-conditioned guest rooms. Some have fireplaces and all have clean private baths.

The Aldriches know the importance of food—they not only serve filling country breakfasts, complete with hearty fare, but also bountiful dinners.

The inn is only a half mile from the center of Stowe Village and its quaint shops and fine restaurants.

THE INN AT THE BRASS LANTERN, 717 Maple St., Stowe, VT 05672; 800-729-2980, 802-253-2229.

A 9-guestroom (private baths) New England inn. Queen and double beds. Hearty breakfast. Open all year. Close to Mt. Mansfield, skiing, shops, and restaurants. No smoking. No pets. CCs: Visa, MC, AE. Mindy and Andy Aldrich, owners/hosts.

DIRECTIONS: I-89 Exit 10 to Rte. 100 north. 1/2 mi. from the center of Stowe Village.

THE INN AT THE ROUND BARN FARM
Waitsfield, Vermont

"Our family is in the floral business in New Jersey," Annemarie explained. "My brothers and sisters run it now that my parents and I have moved to Vermont, but, well, it wouldn't be home without flowers."

Not a Simko home anyway. Yet smashing floral arrangements are only one facet of Mad River Valley's extraordinary Inn at Round Barn Farm. First of all, there's the barn itself: a twelve-sided 1910 dairy barn that stood caved-in and unused for twenty years. Then came the Simkos, who decided in 1986 to restore it for the benefit of the community as a theater, classical concerts, weddings, midweek business seminars and community get together (the Vermont Symphony struck

the opening notes). And the 60 foot lap pool now sits where the manure pit was. In the summer, local and visiting artists display their works on the interior walls of the Barn. This informal exhibit changes from week to week and show the diverse talents of Valley artists.

As for the 1810 farmhouse, it was miraculously brought to new life as a B&B and the epitome of *Country Magazine* style in a year and a half—the talk of the valley. There is a fireplaced living room/library where guests sip evening sherry and morning coffee, a less formal game room with a billards table, television and popular boardgames, and six guest rooms, each named for settlers of Waitsfield.

Doreen and Annemarie did the decorating, and the full breakfasts are served in the solarium overlooking the meadow. The large pine Harvest table offers the opportunityu to meet the other guests staying at the Inn and compare travel notes. Expect cinnamon raisin Belgian waffles with maple cream, or cottage cheese pancakes with reasppberry sauce and fresh fruits served in antique cut glass goblets—such stuff as dreams are made of.

Annemarie has been one of the reasons why this Inn is so successful and then she became very self-centered, forgoing the interests of the guests for her own happiness and decided to marry and have a child. Go figure. However the parents are coping with this change of circumstances and since she still comes over to help out all is well.

Among the responsibilities of guests are changing shoes for slippers inside the front door to save the stripped and polished old floors that are hue of maple syrup. Then the Simkos have an outside cat and an inside dog. Naturally the dog wants to go out and the cat wants to come in, so we are implored to pay no attention to the natural order, and keep the door shut.

We can live with that too.

THE INN AT THE ROUND BARN FARM, East Warren Rd., Waitsfield, VT (R.R. Box 247); 802-496-2276 (BARN).

A historic landmark turned elegant bed and breakfast in Mad River Valley, central Vermont. 10 bedrooms (private baths, three with Jacuzzi, 4 with fireplaces). All size beds. Game room with TV and pool table; 60 ft. lap swimming pool & sauna. Snowtime sleigh rides at the door; horseback riding, downhill and xc skiing, biking, canoeing, and fishing available nearby. Full gourmet breakfast. Open all year. No pets or smoking. One cat and dog in residence. CCs: Visa, MC, AE. Jack, Doreen, and Annemarie Simko, owners/hosts; Allison Duckworth, assistant innkeeper.

DIRECTIONS: From Rte. 100 in Waitsfield, drive east on Bridge St. through the covered bridge 1.5 miles up East Warren Road (bear right at joint). Inn is on your left.

INN EVENTS: APRIL–MAY—Vermont Symphony Orchestra
APRIL–MAY—Landscape Painting
JUNE—Theater
JULY—New Voice Theater
JULY—Nature Drawing
JULY—Mozart Festival
AUGUST—Theater
AUGUST—Dinner Dance
AUGUST—Photography Exhibit
SEPTEMBER—Jazz
OCTOBER—Art Show
NOVEMBER—Wreath & Garlands Workshop
DECEMBER—holiday community sing

OCTOBER COUNTRY INN
Bridgewater Corners, Vermont

Richard Sims and Patrick Runkel came to the October Country Inn by a rather circuitous route. As a travel agency manager, Richard became

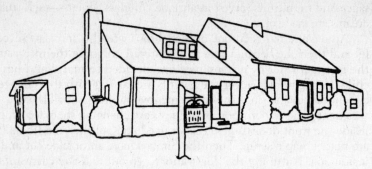

intrigued with the idea of purchasing an inn. Since they both love to scuba dive, why not open an inn in the Caribbean? So, Richard took off to St. Kitts, Antigua, and St. Lucia, and Patrick began working in a restaurant and at a gourmet catering business to prepare himself for the eventual career change.

Unfortunately, what initially sounded quite simple became a bit more complicated, and the two moved their search to the United States, eventually settling in Vermont. After countless hours "pressing our noses against innumerable windows," they finally found the October Country Inn.

Located just 8 miles from the quaint village of Woodstock, the rambling, mid-19th-century New England clapboard farmhouse sits on a hillside on 5 acres. Two airy porches, complete with rocking chairs, and a large flower-framed deck tempt guests to laze away an afternoon. Although civilization is near, the area feels wonderfully rural. There's even a delightful country store only a short walk from the inn.

Indoors, the comfortable living room, with its cozy overstuffed furniture, has a fireplace at one end and a charming pot-bellied stove at the other. It's a great place to relax and peruse the inn's eclectic selection of books. I spent an engrossing evening with E.L. Doctorow, while one of the other guests giggled her way through Gary Larson's humorous view of the world. A variety of interesting games are also available. An unusual art collection, some of it local work, decorates the walls.

Richard and Patrick are gregarious hosts and encourage guests to feel at home. The whole style of the inn conveys a homey feeling. The ten guest rooms are airy and restful, decorated in off-white, pale green, and touches of blue and pink. Two of the rooms have hand stenciling. The beds are comfortable, with new mattresses, and the bathrooms, eight private and two shared, are clean and basic.

In this wonderful family farmhouse atmosphere, I ate one of the most unexpected and memorable meals I have had. The inn specializes in unusual ethnic cuisine, with Patrick conjuring up whatever country's cuisine inspires him. I was served an exotic African menu that began with a flavorful chicken peanut soup. It was followed by tajine of lamb and green beans, traditional couscous, spiced vegetables, vegetarian spiced lentils, a cooling cucumber and yogurt salad, and rich date-nut cakes with orange custard sauce. The pairing of distinctive flavors and textures was a real treat to the palate. The inn has a full liquor license, and just the right wine, beer, or ale is available to accompany the meal. Richard told me that guests often linger after these feasts, laughing and swapping stories until long after the last plate has been washed.

Breakfast starts with a buffet of homemade granola, fresh fruits, juices, and toast. A selection of muffins are then served along with a hot dish, like scrambled eggs with Vermont cheddar cheese.

OCTOBER COUNTRY INN, Box 66, Upper Rd., Bridgewater Corners, VT 05035; 802-672-3412.

A 10-guestroom (8 private baths) 19th-century farmhouse inn on 5 acres, 8 mi. from Woodstock. Closed April and part of Nov. Modified American plan. Double and twin beds. Close to all winter and summer sports. No pets. Two cats in residence. Richard Sims and Patrick Runkel, owners/hosts.

DIRECTIONS: From Woodstock, travel 8 mi. to junction with 100A. Continue for another 100 yards and take first right. At fork in the road, turn right again. Go up the hill. The inn is the second house on the left.

RABBIT HILL INN
Lower Waterford, Vermont

Just above the Connecticut River in the hamlet of Lower Waterford, Vermont, Rabbit Hill Inn rests amid the steepled church, the 150-year-old tiny post office, the honor-system library, and a cluster of restored homes. The village has remained virtually unchanged for more than 150 years. Lower Waterford is one of the most picturesque, and hence photographed, villages in Vermont. The location takes advantage of the spectacular views of the White Mountains and accompanying outdoor sports, including fishing, sailing, canoeing, nature walking, mountain climbing, and downhill and cross-country skiing.

The inn boasts two wonderfully restored buildings, originally built in 1795 and 1825. Wide pine floor boards, five spacious porches, and eight fireplaces accompany antique and reproduction furnishings. As you arrive, you are welcomed into the Federal-period parlor for a full high tea, which includes freshly baked pastries such as scones slathered with fresh whipped cream and preserves.

Each of the eighteen guest rooms has a special theme to the decor: hat boxes and bonnets, reproduction wooden toys, or antique letters.

My room was based on the life of an early-20th-century woman named Clara. For the suite at the top of the tavern, owners John and Maureen Magee have re-created a Victorian Dressing Room, right down to items in the wardrobe and letters of the period. The Tavern Secret Room does hold a real secret for its guests, but you'll have to stay there to find out. You can choose from king, queen, double, and twin beds, most with canopies. All rooms have private baths.

Guests may congregate for conversation and relaxation in the Federal-period parlor, the After-Sports Lounge, or the Library Nook. A television, VCR, and small video library are available, and chamber music concerts take place almost every evening. A large selection of musical tapes has been recorded for guests to use with their in-room radio-cassette players. Lawn games inspire healthy competition, and guests may choose to venture out on snowshoes or toboggans in the winter, or canoes in the summer.

Breakfast, dinner, and high tea are all included in the room rate. Dinner is outstanding, offering five courses superbly prepared by chef Bob Reney, who was trained in the European tradition. Maureen seated me in the lovely candlelit setting, then quietly disappeared. As I enjoyed my appetizer of chicken and smoked cheddar cheese in puff pastry, salad of garden lettuce, and entrée of steak Elizabeth—a filet mignon wrapped in bacon and topped with shrimp—I was pleasantly surprised to hear Maureen in another role, that of flutist, as she unobtrusively entertained from the next room!

Breakfast offers juice, homemade granola, rice pudding, cobblers, homemade doughnuts, an egg dish, or pancakes and French toast. "We often concoct our special breakfast treat, the Rabbit Hill banana split. It's made with yogurt or whipped cream cheese, granola, and fresh fruit," John told me as we sipped our first cup of fresh roast coffee. "You know, people who have stayed here have given us wonderful memories. One of the best was the couple who fell asleep on the second-floor porch, and remained there all night!"

After two years of work, the Magees have created a one-of-a-kind audio experience for their guests. They have researched those persons who were part of the inn's history and then represented their voices on cassette with an individualized script. Each person has their own theme representing a different year. For example, Victoria Cummins, who lived in 1825, tells the story of her uncle's "Big House" (the main inn building) and of the Green Mountain Boys and Vermont's achievement of statehood. Samuel Hodby, who was quite a visionary and established the Inn as the Hodby Tavern in 1795, explains the politics of the late 1800s. On another tape, an 1850s guest who couldn't square his bill tells how he made the eagle that graces the inn's facade today. Taken together, the tapes tell the entire Rabbit Hill Inn story, the high points of Vermont's history, and what it means to be a Yankee in the Northeast Kingdom.

————

RABBIT HILL INN, Rte. 18, Lower Waterford, VT 05848; 800-76-BUNNY, 802-748-5168.

An 18-guestroom (private baths) restored country inn in one of the most photographed villages in Vermont. All size beds available. Closed April and the first 2 weeks in Nov. Modified American plan; includes high tea. Evening chamber music concerts. Hiking, swimming, boating, summer hayrides, xc skiing, golfing. Warmly hospitable. No pets. CCs: Visa, MC. One collie-shepherd in residence. John and Maureen Magee, owners/hosts.

DIRECTIONS: From I-91, take Exit 19, then Exit 1 onto Rte. 18 south. From I-93, take Exit 44, Rte. 18 junction; turn north (left) on Rte. 18.

INN EVENTS: FEBRUARY—week-long Valentine's Celebration
MARCH—Mystery Weekend
JULY 4—Party
OCTOBER 30–31—Mystery Weekend, Pumpkin Carving Contest
NOVEMBER 25–26—Old-Fashioned Thanksgiving
DECEMBER 23–25—Old-Fashioned Christmas

ROWELL'S INN
Simonsville, Vermont

————

Established in 1820 as a stagecoach stop, the venerable Rowell's Inn presides over a bend in Route 11 between Manchester and Chester beside bubbling Lyman Brook. Lovingly restored by Innkeepers Lee and Beth Davis, the Inn's five guest rooms and five common rooms, are brimming with antiques and oddities that make it a constant discovery even for its many loyal repeat visitors.

The Inn, admitted to the National Register of Historic Places, boasts broad-shouldered re-brick walls and expansive porches lined with welcoming rockers which invite the traveller to watch the traffic go by with a morning cup of coffee or while away a lazy afternoon awaiting one of Beth's New England feasts.

The library features a cozy fireplace, built-in bookcases, enveloping wing chairs, Stagecoach prints and a plush, custom-woven English carpet. The library offers a tranquil moment with a good book, or a late-afternoon catnap as a retiring sun yawns over neighboring Green Mountains.

Through a dining room complete with stamped tin ceilings, antique hutches, floor of alternating cherry and maple planks and portraits of stern-faced Edwardian ancestors, is the Tavern Room. A 1790 farmhouse in its earlier life, the Tavern Room was painstakingly rolled from a nearby hill to expand the Inn's food and drink services near the turn of the century. A hand crafted pub-style bench and table (fashioned by Lee and a local artisan friend) at one corner furnish the perfect spot to sip a glass of wine or sample one of the many English ales, porters and stouts available at a bar complete with old-fashioned soda fountain, pretzels, and peanuts in the shell. Overstuffed chairs, beside a toasty woodstove are surveyed by a curious moosehead and a pot-bellied bass that didn't get away many Vermont summers' past.

Adjoining the Tavern Room is a toasty sun room which brings the outside in. At one end a crackling fireplace is guarded by a colonialist's long-silent musket, while at the other an ancient cheeseboard, hors d'oeuvres, Beth's cookie jar and a dizzying variety of teas make an afternoon snack irresistible. The sun rooms's French doors open to a patio of jigsaw slate with Adirondack chairs from which to watch the open-air ballet of flitting wild birds dancing to the Brook's music on a bird-feeder stage.

Upstairs guest rooms feature brass beds, pedestal basins, claw foot tubs and heated towel racks.

Beth's five course dinners offer hearty Yankee fare like her old-fashioned Sunday chicken dinner or weekly boiled New England dinner, with an ample measure of gourmet innovation and flare. Traditional here, never means tired, and specialities like Fiddlehead soup are spiced with fresh herbs from an extensive herb garden steps from Beth's kitchen. Tempting desserts include Old Vermont Chocolate Cake, Bread Pudding and Oatmeal or Apple pie.

Christmas at the Inn is Beth's domain and labor of love. It begins early with a tree-trimming weekend for guests and ends late, as handcrafted decorations fill every corner until around Valentine's Day. Beth's priceless collection of Santas, many gifts from Inn guests are everywhere, and nowhere could the jolly old elves feel more at home.

ROWELL'S INN, RR 1 Box 269, Simonsville, VT, 05143; 802-875-3658.

A 5-guestroom (private baths) inn in the mountains of central Vermont. King, double and twin beds available. Modified American plan with 2-day minimum on weekends. Bed and breakfast also available midweek. Dinner is served by request to houseguests only. Closed 3 wks. in April and 1 wk. in Nov. Convenient to all the cultural, recreational, and historic attractions in the area, including, hiking, biking, trail riding, golf, tennis, fishing, theaters, downhill and xc skiing. Children over 12 welcome. No pets. No credit cards. Beth and Lee Davis, owners/hosts.

DIRECTIONS: Rowell's Inn is between Chester and Londonderry on Rte. 11.

SHELBURNE HOUSE,
INN AT SHELBURNE FARMS
Shelburne, Vermont

The remaining 1,000 acres of the farm and its wonderful old mansion were on the verge of collapse. It was the year 1969 and a gathering of the Webb descendents had been called to announce the intention to sell the property off for real estate development. Murmurs rose to cries of disapproval from the ranks. Spearheaded by two of the brothers, and supported by their siblings, an idea to save the farm was being born. Even more approriate was the timing. The idea of environmental consciousness was on the rise. Rejuvenation of the farm to a non-profit conservation education organization took place in the following years. The last part of the farm to be rejuvenated was the old house, which finally opened its doors in 1986.

Looking like a castle, the country manor house of red brick rests on

the cliffs of Lake Champlain. Most of the furnishings and decor are original, and a combination of Renaissance Revival, Empire and Colonial Revival, reflective of its late 1800s origin. Another reflection of the era is the lack of heating in the guest rooms, which the owners have tried to offset by being open during the warmer seasons (somewhat of a challenge for the cold-blooded).

Stepping into the foyer, my eyes caught the ornate design on the carved mantel of the marble fireplace. Heavy wooden beams supported the ceiling and needlepoint pillows rested in the arm chairs near the warmth of the fire. The library has bold green walls, brightly designed Oriental rugs, and even a purple sofa, establishing an atmosphere for animated conversation to all within the room. The Tea Room, tipping the scales in the opposite direction, has soft, pink walls trimmed with scrolled, white wanscoating. Late afternoon found me on the edge of the gilded sofa, elegantly sipping tea and nibbling finger sandwiches. The dining area in the Marble Room offers a spectacular view of Lake Champlain through tall windows. As the sun goes down, flickering candlelight from the tables casts odd shadows along the deep red walls. The gold framed portraits appear to come alive. My grilled-to-perfection Beef Tenderloin Filet smothered with oyster-mushroom sauce was preceeded by a red pepper fettuccine appetizer with goat cheese, pinenuts, and greens all enjoyed with a glass of excellent Cabernet wine, selected from the full house bar. The Grand Marnier parfait with Almond Tuile cookies led me to believe I was not only living like a king within these walls, but I was eating like one, too.

Compared to the elaborate design and decor of the rest of the house, my room appeared quite simple at first glance. The brass bed, surely one of the originals to the house, was covered with a white, cot-

ton duvet. Wallpaper with pale, yellow and white stripes p
sunny, yet peaceful look to the room. A winged-back chair sit
to the window looked over the lush, green pastures. There w
the old-fashioned wash basin and pitcher. I chose to use th̶e̶ ̶.̶ore
modern bath adjacent to my room. I decided I liked the simplistic contrast, and the comfortable, cozy feeling of the room, despite the lack of
heat. I even had a restful night's sleep on the old bed that had wit-
nessed many dreams.

Warm crepes, stuffed with orange, ginger and cinnamon ricotta
along with a fresh berry compote and several slices of crisp bacon were
served to me the following morning before I began my tour of the farm,
and explored some of the hiking trails around the lake. Why, I might
even do some canoeing! I spent a whole day browzing through the
Shelburne Museum down the road. One of first American Folk Art
Museums, it displayed intricate quilts, hand-painted duck decoys, and
antique fire-fighting equipment, plus many more examples of our heritage.

SHELBURNE HOUSE, INN AT SHELBURNE FARMS, Shelburne, VT 05842; 802-985-
8498.

24 guestroom country manor house with some shared baths on the bluffs above
Lake Champlain and surrounded by 1,000 acres of farmland. Built in 1889, it has 4
common rooms. Tea is served each afternoon, and a full house bar available each
evening. Breakfast and dinner served in the dining room. Open mid-May through mid-
Oct. with some minimum stay requirements. Smoking is allowed only in one common
room. Abundant in activity for the outdoors type. Canoeing, bicycling, winter skiing,
tennis, croquet, hiking, fishing, or touring Shelbourne Farms. Two miles from the
quaint town of Shelbourne. Reservations recommended. CCs: MC,V,AMEX. Marnie
Davis, manager.

DIRECTIONS: Located off Rte.7, also known as Shelburne Rd., at the junction of Bay
Rd. and Harbor Rd. in Shelburne.

SHIRE INN
Chelsea, Vermont

If the word "idyllic" had not already been created, I would have
invented it myself just to describe this bucolic scene.

Standing on a sturdy wooden bridge immediately behind the Shire
Inn, gazing down on a branch of the White River below, I caught the
flash of a trout slipping through the cool, rushing waters. Some early
owner of the house so appreciated this scene, he placed a bench long
enough to hold eight people here on the bridge.

I had just driven through some exceptionally beautiful Vermont
country, following Route 14 north from Lebanon, alongside the White

River, to Chelsea. The village is listed on the National Register of Historic Places, and has two commons and several early-18th-century homes and buildings.

Built of Vermont brick in 1832 and surrounded on all sides by gardens and lawns, the Shire Inn, with its fanlight doorway and black shutters, is certainly one of the most attractive of these historic homes.

The entrance hallway is dominated by a handsome circular staircase. On one side of this hallway is a most comfortable living room with deep chairs and sofas, as well as lots and lots of books. "This is the gathering room for our guests," remarked Mary Lee Papa, who with her husband, James, is the innkeeper.

"We're open year around," James told me, "and it's a good base from which guests can explore the variety of recreational and cultural opportunities that abound up here in this area. We've got good cross-country skiing here in Chelsea—actually, right from our own backyard."

The six guest rooms are most attractively furnished and four of them have working fireplaces. The beautiful "pumpkin pine" floorboards have been brought back to their lovely natural finish. All the guest rooms, named after Vermont counties, have a bountiful supply of books and magazines, but each has its own distinctive quality.

Breakfasts are really almost beyond description. There are three courses, and the emphasis is on fruits of all kinds, including baked fruits, as well as all kinds of pancakes and homemade breads. There is also a cream cheese omelet, now and then served with mint.

Dinner could include scallops in a caraway sauce, veal
sauce, chicken in a spice or curry sauce, pork chops with ca
ing, or fillet of sole in wine. For dessert there might be fres
pie or an amaretto mousse, chocolate-brandy cake, a g
mousse, or chocolate cheese cake.

SHIRE INN, Chelsea, VT 05038; 802-685-3031.

A 6-guestroom (private baths) village inn in a beautiful central Vermont setting.
King, queen and double beds available. Open all year with a vacation break in Nov.
and Apr. Breakfast included in room rate. Evening meal available by advance reservation. Bicycles available. The Justin Morgan horse farm, the Joseph Smith memorial, xc
and downhill skiing, fishing, swimming, boating, and walking nearby. No pets. One
Scottish Deerhound in residence. No smoking. James and Mary Lee Papa,
owners/hosts.

DIRECTIONS: From I-89 use Exit 2, proceed west on Rte. 14, then northward on Rte.
110 to Chelsea. From 1-91, take Exit 14 and turn left on Rte. 113 proceeding northwest to Chelsea. Both of these roads are extremely picturesque.

SWIFT HOUSE INN

Middlebury, Vermont

"Every day is special at Swift House," said Andrea (Andy) Nelson, in
response to my question about special events available. She heard no
argument from me.

Andrea and John Nelson have been owners of Swift House Inn for
the past six years. John, having spent thirty years as a manager for
IBM, retired into innkeeping. Andy brought along the public relations
skills she had gleaned from real estate sales. According to Andy,
innkeeping is "always changing and always challenging."

Swift House has seen many changes in its lifetime. Over the years
the estate increased to three houses. The main house was built by
Samuel Swift in 1815, later becoming home to Vermont Governor
John W. Stewart and his daughter, Jessica Stewart Swift. The Carriage
House was added in the late 1800s, and the Gatehouse, of Victorian
design, was completed at the turn of the century.

The buildings are set upon three acres of expansive lawns and formal gardens, terraced by low stone walls. A tree swing hangs from the
branches of a tall shade tree that has undoubtedly seen much history in
its years of growth.

The Main House has five antique-filled common rooms, including
the dining room with a marble fireplace warming the cherrywood paneling. My favorite candlelight dinner began with an appetizer of escar-
got, followed by a main dish of mouth-watering sautéed soft-shell crab.

I passed up the tempting chocolate terrine and had strawberry short-cake for dessert. I ended this elegant dining experience sipping a brandy in the full service bar. Throughout the Main House and Gate-house the theme of Queen Anne's era continues with winged-back chairs, floral print sofas, and large area rugs, brilliantly colored, over hardwood floors. The many fireplaces have ornate carvings. Strategi-cally-placed window seats invited me to curl up with a book. Inn guests can enjoy the sauna or steamroom, complete with waiting fluffy terry robes. Winding staircases accessed the upper floor guest rooms, which have private baths holding old-fashioned, claw-foot tubs.

My room was in the nearby Carriage House, which has been recently modernized with whirlpool bathtubs and air conditioning for sultry summer nights. The bedroom would not have been complete, however, without the traditional four-poster bed, rose-printed wallcov-ering, and the added touch of my own fireplace accompanied by a hefty supply of wood.

The next morning found me sitting on the veranda munching sticky buns and fresh popovers for the continental breakfast, which was included with my room. Full breakfasts are available in the dining room, but I chose to eat lightly before I headed off to view the local sights.

SWIFT HOUSE INN, 25 Stewart Lane, Middlebury, VT 05753; 802-388-9925.
Main House, Gatehouse, and Carriage House have a total of 21 elegantly-designed guestrooms. Three acres in historic Middlebury. King, queen, and twin beds. Continental breakfast included. Full breakfast available and dinner served Thurs.-Mon. Sauna and steamroom. Restricted smoking. Open all year. Concerts, theater, shopping, and historic points of interest within walking distance. No pets. CCs: Visa, MV, AE, DC. John and Andrea Nelson, owners/hosts.
DIRECTIONS: Stewart Lane is just off Rte. 7 in the middle of Vermont, halfway between Rutland and Burlington. Inn can be seen from the road.

THREE MOUNTAIN INN
Jamaica, Vermont

When I dropped in on Charles and Elaine Murray, innkeepers of the Three Mountain Inn, they were poring over their "Backroads" maps, helping guests to plan excursions. Elaine particularly enjoys getting to know each guest's special interest, whether it be a particular Vermont antique or crafts store, a quaint village to tour, or spectacular photo sites for avid shutterbugs.

Charles excused himself to escort a just-arriving couple to their country-decorated room in the converted stable wing of the inn. This room has a unique original post-and-beam ceiling. All the bedrooms are lovely with four-poster beds (some with canopies), comforters, cheerful flowered wallpaper, and private baths. Additional guest rooms are located next door in Robinson House, which dates back to 1820.

Here guests can lounge on the spacious lawn and enjoy spectacular views of Shatterack, Ball and Turkey mountains. The small farm house across the street, Sage Hill House, has kitchen facilities and is particularly suited to families and couples.

The Three Mountain Inn dates back to the early 1790s and features three marvelous fireplaces on the main floor. In the main sitting room a bee-hive fireplace provides cozy warmth during those icy Vermont winters. Each of the dining areas also offers a fireplace, adding a romantic touch to breakfast or dinner. The original wide plank pine walls and floors, called "Kings Wood," were highly valued during the eighteenth century; much of it was exported to England.

Elaine abruptly leaped up from the table as the kitchen timer buzzed. "Oh my gosh!" she said, "I almost forgot my bread." Elaine is the inn's chef and bakes all the breads and desserts. She also whips up savory sauces and salad dressings. The inn serves dinners, which may offer favorite recipes such as trout almandine, scallops maison, chicken paprikash, or carrot vichy soup, followed by butter pecan ice cream pie

with hot caramel pecan topping. Guests have a choice of appetizers and entrées, as well as three or four great desserts.

I wandered around behind the inn one morning and strolled past the landscaped pool where a few guests were soaking up the end-of-summer sun to find Charles stacking yet another cord of wood to keep the wood furnace, fireplaces, and three wood stoves glowing when the chill hit. "It gets cold here," he laughed. "But there's just something about wood heat I love. You know the old saying, 'Wood heats you twice: once when you split it, and again when you burn it.'" I knew just what he meant.

THREE MOUNTAIN INN, Rte. 30, Jamaica, VT 05343; 802-874-4140.

An 18-guestroom (14 private baths) inn—some rooms adjacent to main house—located in a pleasant village in southern Vermont. All-size beds. Modified American plan (rates include breakfast and dinner). Dinners also served to travelers nightly except Wed. Closed Apr. 15 to May 15; Labor Day to Sept. 10. Swimming pool on grounds. Tennis, golf, fishing, horseback riding, nature walks and hiking trails in Jamaica State Park, downhill and xc skiing. Marlboro Music Festival, Weston Playhouse within a short drive. No pets. No credit cards. Charles and Elaine Murray, owners/hosts.

DIRECTIONS: Jamaica is located on Rte. 30, which runs across Vermont from Manchester (U.S. 7) to Brattleboro (I-91).

TRAIL'S END
Wilmington, Vermont

Many inns close, or certainly lose their charm, when winter puts a frost on the countryside and activity. But the rustic quality of Trail's

End lends itself to all seasons. Nestled among pines, the inn was opened to guests about the same time that nearby Mount Snow started operation as a ski resort—1956. Ever since then it has been providing travelers with traditional New England hospitality.

Bill and Mary Kilburn are the owners of Trail's End. The two have a large inn to manage. With a living room, library/game room, plant-filled loft, and 18 guest rooms to look after, they are busy folks.

The common rooms are comfortably furnished with family pieces and antiques. A large fieldstone fireplace radiates enough heat to warm the room right up to its cathedral ceiling. In the winter, hot cider and cookies magically appear; in summer, the beverage changes to chilled lemonade. And for those with a constant appetite, candy, apples, and nuts are available all the time!

Ranging in size from family suites to more intimate rooms with one double bed, the guest rooms blend well with the simple country atmo-

sphere. But elegant touches, like brass headboards, oak dressers, and fluffy comforters, add a luxurious touch. Some rooms have fireplaces and all have private baths.

The morning fare consists of juice, a choice of eggs, blueberry pancakes, thick-sliced French toast, bacon or sausage, coffee or tea, and some of the best homemade granola I've ever crunched. Dinner is often available, and on Thursday nights during the summer, there's a steak fry by the pool.

TRAIL'S END, Smith Rd., Wilmington, VT 05363; 802-464-2727.
An 14-guestroom (private baths) rustic New England inn in Vermont's Green Mountains. Four rooms with fireplaces. Queen, double, and twin beds. Full breakfast; dinner occasionally. Open Thanksgiving to April, and Memorial Day to October 31. Close to cross-country skiing, hiking, horseback riding, canoeing, tennis, and golf. No pets. CCs: Visa, MC. Mary and Bill Kilburn, owners/hosts.
DIRECTIONS: At traffic light in Wilmington, take Rte. 100 north for 4 mi., then turn right and follow inn's signs.

TULIP TREE INN
Chittenden, Vermont

Like the town crier, innkeeper Ed McDowell announces breakfast and dinner at the Tulip Tree Inn by ringing a bell and, in a resonate baritone, descriptively recites the menu. Does this sound a bit dramatic? Well, that's only one of the dramatic roles Ed plays as owner-host. "I never get sick of being the host because that's the fun of the job. If you want to hide out, what's the sense of being an innkeeper?" He and his wife, Rosemary, left New York City, where Ed owned a taxi and limousine service and Rosemary worked for the Carnegie Foundation, to open a country inn in Vermont.

Ed's wonderful sense of humor is infectious. With a theater background, he is no stranger to storytelling, and willingly spins yarns while guests lounge on comfortable couches around the huge stone fireplace in the spacious sitting room. Windowed on three sides, you feel as if you are sitting outdoors. A comfortable living room and a small library/pub are also available for guests. The pub has a wide selection of imported beers including stout, spirits, and wines.

Nestled in the Green Mountain National Forest, the Tulip Tree is an ideal example of what you should expect from a country inn. Built as a farmhouse in 1842 and purchased by Thomas Barstow, a wealthy collaborator of Thomas Edison in the early 1900s, the serene forest-green house, with its crisp white shutters and trim and airy porch, could be a model for a picture postcard.

This inn is one of my favorites. Although its location inspires solitude, Ed and Rosemary make certain you're never bored or lonely. In

fact, from the moment Ed greets you and personally shows you to your room, you will be entertained, by the McDowells, their playful shag of a sheep dog, Guinness, or the other charming guests.

The eight guest rooms vary in size, but are all warm and cozy. Tucked under the fluffy French print comforter of my oak four-poster, I fell asleep listening to the sound of the river drifting through my open bay window. The McDowells have made every effort to decorate the rooms authentically, and have purchased New England-made braided rugs and furniture. All guest rooms have private baths, some with Jacuzzis.

Both breakfast and dinner are served in the pleasant dining room, where everyone sits communally at two or three large tables set with tasteful china and silverware, and glasses for water, wine, and an after-dinner sherry or liqueur.

Our dinner began with a lovely hot curried carrot soup, swirled with tangy plain yogurt. The color alone was heavenly. The soup was followed by a crisp green salad with juicy sections of ripe tomato, Vermont cider sorbet, strips of succulent veal in white wine and cream, tender egg noodles, steamed broccoli, and a luscious dessert of pumpkin cheesecake with warm Vermont maple syrup. Breakfast is just as appetizing.

After dinner, I took my glass of sherry and joined some of the other guests in the living room, only to be met by a reproachful-looking Andrew Carnegie staring down from his portrait on the wall. Had he seen how much I'd eaten? I didn't care. I was happy, contented, and ready for an evening of Ed's storytelling.

TULIP TREE INN, Chittenden Dam Rd., Chittenden, VT 05737; 802-483-6213.

An 8-guestroom (private baths), lovely, small country inn nestled in the Green Mt. National Forest. Open Memorial Day weekend thru end of March. Queen beds. Modified American plan. Hiking, fishing, and xc skiing at the doorstep. Guinness an old English sheep dog and Hoover a black cat in residence. CCs: Visa, MC. Ed and Rosemary McDowell, owners/hosts.

DIRECTIONS: From Rutland, VT, go north on Rte. 7. Just past the red brick power station on the left, watch for a red country store. Keep right of the store, and go approximately 6 mi. Just past the fire station, go straight 1/2 mi. The inn is on your left.

VERMONT MARBLE INN
Fair Haven, Vermont

What do three people who had careers in the fields of insurance, cab driving, and machine tools have in common? For one thing, a desire to provide excellent service to the public by doing whatever it takes to

make the customer happy. Another thing they have in common is the Vermont Marble Inn.

Innkeepers Shirley Stein and Bea and Richard Taube used to live and work in New York City. In 1986, the three decided to open a country inn and leave the big city life behind. Why did they make this decision? "That's a very good question!" laughed Bea. "Sometimes I think we were out of out minds."

Looking for an appropriate inn proved time-consuming, but ultimately worth the trouble. "We were looking for a mansion," Shirley remarked, "but we were never looking for anything this grand." Bea and Richard agreed. "There are mansions, and then there are *mansions*."

This splendid, delicately veined, golden Vermont marble-block mansion was built in 1867 by Ira C. Allen, reportedly a member of the renowned Ethan Allen family. The main mass is almost square, with two and one-half stories and a mansard roof surmounted by an elaborate cupola. A wonderful example of Second Empire Italianate Victorian styling, the home has seven chandeliers suspended from imposingly high ceilings, elaborate plasterwork decoration, carved marble fireplaces, and an Art Deco suite that was added in the 1930s.

Immediately upon entering the heavy walnut doors, one is enfolded in luxury. Comfortable furnishings in the double parlors are grouped around the fireplaces for easy conversation. Wing-back chairs in the cozy library encourage evening reading.

The twelve beautifully decorated guest rooms, named after the owners' favorite poets, are romantic and luxurious. Some of the rooms are complemented with high, four-poster queen-size beds, draped with antique hand-crocheted lace curtains, while others have wood-burning fireplaces. All have lush linens and private baths.

A late afternoon English tea with homemade cookies, cakes and tarts is served in the library for guests who need refreshment after a hard day of Vermont sightseeing. Before dinner, cocktails in the parlor precede a sumptuous feast in the dining room.

Past the towering staircase and down the long hallway are the inn's two dining rooms. Although the main dining room is small, barely ten tables, it is charming and gracious. The goblets sparkle, as does the elaborate crystal chandelier overhead, and the entire ambience reflects Victorian elegance. It overlooks the five acres of tastefully landscaped grounds with its delightful herb garden. The other, more formal, room displays an elaborate ceiling of papier-m[aca]aché and plaster, cast in a design of fruit bordered with grape leaves.

Within these two dining rooms you will be served with what chef Donald Goodman calls gourmet American, which according to Don means "that I can take different styles from Italy or France, everywhere, and apply them to regional American concepts using ingredients indigenous to New England." I had the chilled shrimp marinated with garlic, capers and olives, and a main course of chicken breast stuffed with zucchini, roasted red pepper and chevre. Each entrée on the menu is handled in an innovative way.

After dinner, you can retire to the drawing room for an after-dinner drink, or to the library for a board game or a movie on the VCR, or just nestle into a cozy chair with a favorite book.

VERMONT MARBLE INN, 12 West Park Pl., Fair Haven, VT 05743; 802-265-8383.

A 12-guestroom (private baths) mansion with 8 fireplaces and 3 in public areas, located on the town green in Fair Haven. Queen, double and twin beds available. Open all year. Continental breakfast. Gourmet dinner available. A short drive from one of the largest ski areas in the East, golf, tennis, fishing, hiking, and horseback riding. Bea and Richard Taube, and Shirley Stein, owners/hosts.

DIRECTIONS: From New York, take State Thruway to Exit 24 to Northway, to Exit 20. Then take Rte. 149 east to Rte. 4; then go north to Exit 2. Follow sign to Fair Haven. From Boston, take Rte. 93 north to Rte. 89; then go north to Rte. 4 west (sign reads to Rutland), to Exit 3. Follow signs to Fair Haven.

INN EVENTS: JANUARY—Chocolate Lovers' Weekend
    FEBRUARY—Lovers' Weekend
    MARCH—Wine Lovers' Weekend
    JUNE—Hikers' Weekend
    SEPTEMBER 11–12—Wine Lovers' Weekend
    NOVEMBER 26–29—Thanksgiving Weekend
    DECEMBER 24–26—Christmas Holiday Weekend
    YEAR-ROUND—Murder Mystery Weekends by special arrangement

WINDHAM HILL INN

West Townshend, Vermont

"Aren't you lucky!" I exclaimed. Linda and Ken Busteed were showing me some of the wonderful treasures they had found in the attic—trunkloads of memorabilia and all kinds of furnishings that belonged to the Lawrence family, the original 1825 homesteaders and owners of the house. "We found that quilt in the attic," Linda said, pointing to a beautiful antique quilt hanging on the wall in the Wicker Room.

"William and Matilda Lawrence had twelve children," Ken took up the story, "and Miss Kate was the last of the Lawrences. She farmed the land until she died in her mid-eighties in the late 1950s."

This rambling old farmhouse, perched on a remote hillside with spectacular views of the West River Valley and the eastern edge of the Green Mountains, was turned into an inn a few years before Ken and Linda bought it in 1982. They have since created a most delightful, truly country inn, simply but fetchingly furnished and decorated with country fabrics, many antique pieces, and all sorts of interesting touches, such as Linda's collection of antique high-button shoes (the handmade white calf wedding shoes are captivating). Three sitting rooms allow you to join other guests or be alone.

While we were chatting in the cheerful, floral Wicker Room, a guest came to tell us there was a deer in the yard, and we all rushed to the parlor window to look. Sure enough, there was the big, beautiful creature grazing on the lawn and not at all concerned about the two wood sculptures of black and white Herefords standing nearby.

Ken and Linda are very relaxed with their guests. They have two dining rooms, one with an oval mahogany table for up to twelve, and the other with several smaller tables. "Sometimes," Linda observed, "guests who originally preferred a separate table, decide they want to sit at the group table. We've had some lively conversations there."

The dinner was exquisite. We had asparagus en cro[acu]te, sherry-peach soup, an endive salad with mustard-vinaigrette dressing, a homemade strawberry-rhubarb sorbet with mint, scallops provençale with herbs, onions, garlic, and swiss cheese served with snow peas, homemade poppy seed rolls, and a wedge of scrumptious frozen chocolate cheesecake.

For guests who are inclined toward activities beyond sitting on their balconies, drinking in the spectacular scenery, dreaming in the natural gardens, listening to the birds and the bees, and watching the butterflies, there are walking and hiking trails in the summer, which become cross-country ski trails in the winter. Ken told me they are right next to a preserved area of 1200 acres that will never be developed. Forget about traffic noise—there isn't any.

When we were standing on the deck of one of the guest rooms in the barn, Linda pointed out a couple of the trails that led out through openings in the old stone walls. "The trail that goes over the third mowing is a little steeper than the others," she said. Linda then explained that they created a cross-country learning center with a private trail system for the use of inn guests only.

Standing on the balcony outside my room before climbing into bed, I felt as if I could reach out and touch the brilliant moon and the millions of stars. This is indeed one of my favorite special country experiences.

WINDHAM HILL INN, West Townshend, VT 05359; 802-874-4080.

A 15-room (private baths) 1825 country farm inn on 160 acres of secluded hillside in the scenic West River Valley of southern Vermont, 23 mi. northwest of Brattleboro. All size beds available. Modified American plan includes breakfast and dinner. Open mid-May to Nov. 1; Thanksgiving; mid-Dec. to April 1; 2-night minimum stay on weekends. Nature walks, biking, xc skiing and lessons, swimming, summer chamber music concerts, and horse-drawn carriage picnics on grounds. Backroading, Marlboro and Bach Music Festivals, state parks, and antiquing nearby. No pets. One cat and two dogs in residence. No smoking. Handicapped access. CCs: Visa, MC. Ken and Linda Busteed, owners/hosts.

DIRECTIONS: From I-91, take Exit 2, following signs to Rte. 30. Take Rte. 30 north 21-1/2 mi. In West Townshend, turn right at red country store and drive 1-1/2 mi. up hill to inn.

INN EVENTS: JULY 4—Evening of Chamber Music
                    JULY 11—Mainstream Jazz
                    JULY 18—Traditional Jazz
                    AUGUST 1—New Orleans Jazz
                    AUGUST 15—Mainstream Jazz
                    AUGUST 21–22—3rd Annual Mushroom Hunt
                    NOVEMBER 25–29—Taditional Thanksgiving
                    DECEMBER 25—Old-Fashioned Christmas
                    WINTER—XC skiing and instruction as soon as snow falls

New Hampshire

The granite-faced White Mountains, tallest in the Northeast, make New Hampshire a center for rock and ice climbing, hiking, skiing, and fantastic natural sightseeing. Visitors have flocked to see the Old Man in the Mountain rock formation, ride the cog railway up Mount Washington, and travel through Franconia Notch for well over a century.

EVENTS

JANUARY	WinterFest, Conway: ice sculptures
MAY	New Hampshire Sheep & Wool Festival, New Boston (info: 603-428-7830)
MAY	Lilac Time Festival, Lisbon (info: 603-838-6777)
JUNE MIDDLE	season opening of Mt. Division Railway scenic train ride
JUNE	Market Square Days Celebration, Portsmouth (info: 603-431-5388)
JUNE	Turn of the Century Weekend, Sunapee region: explore nine historic inns. (info: 800-258-3530, 603-526-6271)
JUNE	Old-time Fiddlers' Contests, Lincoln/Stark (info: 603-636-1325)
JUNE	Portsmouth Jazz Festival (info: 603-436-7678)
JUNE, LATE	climb to the clouds auto race up Mt. Washington
JULY 4	Pollyanna Day, Franconia
JULY 4	Lincoln-Woodstock's Old-Fashioned 4th
JULY 4	Family Day Celebration, Jackson
JULY	Antique & Classic Boat Show, Laconia (info: 603-524-0348)
JULY–AUGUST	North Country Chamber Players, Franconia (info: 603-869-3154)
AUGUST, EARLY	Craftsmen Guild Fair, Newbury (info: 603-224-1471)
AUGUST, MIDDLE	Mt. Washington Valley Equine Classic
AUGUST	Milton, Old Time Farm Day, Milton: festival of farming as practiced from 1780 to 1930 (info: 603-652-7840)
AUGUST, MIDDLE	world championship rodeo at Attitash
AUGUST, LATE	Lakes Region Fine Arts & Crafts Festival, Meredith (info: 603-279-6121)
SEPTEMBER, MIDDLE	Iron Man Triathalon, Sunapee
SEPTEMBER, EARLY	Francestown Festival (info: 603-547-2174)
SEPTEMBER	Manchester Riverfest (info: 603-669-7377)
SEPTEMBER, MIDDLE	Highland Games, Lincoln (info: 603-745-6621)
SEPTEMBER, MIDDLE	world mud football championship

SEPTEMBER, LATE	Fryeburg fair
OCTOBER, MIDDLE	Canterbury Shaker Village: special Columbus Day Weekend events (info: 603-783-9511)
OCTOBER	Fall Foliage Festival, Warner (info: 603-456-3098)
OCTOBER	Sandwich Fair (info: 603-284-7062)

SIGHTS

Canterbury Shaker Village

Currier Gallery of Art

Franconia Notch State Park

Franklin Pierce Homestead

Mount Monadnock

Mount Washington

New England Ski Museum

Pisgah Park

Robert Frost Home

Ruggles Mine

St. Gauden's National Historic Site

Spofford Lake

White Mountain National Forest

Winnesquam Pond (of *On Golden Pond* fame)

THE BIRCHWOOD INN

Temple, New Hampshire

Judy and Bill Wolfe and I were enjoying a quiet moment in the back parlor of the Birchwood Inn, and I could see by the light in his eye that Bill was most enthusiastic about being an innkeeper.

The Birchwood Inn, sitting on one corner of the village green, is listed on the National Register of Historic Places and is believed to have been in operation since 1775. The present Federal-style brick building, along with the adjacent barn, was probably built about 1800, and the records document a history of changing uses that mirror the evolution of the small town tavern in New England.

The small, tucked-away village of Temple has no telegraph wires in the center of the town, and it's pretty much the same as it's been for two hundred years, with the Grange Hall, Congregational Church, village store, Revolutionary cemetery, and old blacksmith shop.

In 1965, probably the most interesting and prized feature of the inn was discovered when some early wall murals were uncovered under

layers of old wallpaper. The paintings proved to be the work of the well-known muralist Rufus Porter, painted between 1825 and 1833. Fortunately, they were restored and are now being carefully preserved by Bill and Judy.

Today, the inn is characterized by comfortable furniture, a Steinway square grand piano, wide floorboards, checked tablecloths of yellow, red, brown, and blue, music in the background, and many tiny little areas where guests can enjoy a tête-à-tête. On the other hand, there is much opportunity for sociability. Judy said, "We have developed countless friendships with lovely people from all over the world without ever leaving the comforts of our little inn. The opportunity to reach out to people of all interests is a rare privilege afforded to both innkeepers and their children alike." The Wolfes find that their three children enjoy being involved with inn activities.

The guest rooms are decorated according to different themes—there is the Music Room, the Seashore Room, and the Train Room, among others. Homemade quilts add a real country touch. Five rooms have private baths, while two rooms share two hall baths.

The kitchen is handled in an interesting way because Bill does the cooking. Judy bakes breads and desserts, including blueberry-lemon bread, blueberry cobbler, chocolate cake, and various pies and tortes. The evening menu is on a slate blackboard, and on the night of my visit included crab soup, baked stuffed lobster, and chicken piccata. They have a new cookbook, titled *The Birchwood Sampler*, with 255 of their most requested recipes.

THE BIRCHWOOD INN, Rte. 45, Temple, NH 03084; 603-87?
A 7-guestroom (5 private baths) village inn in southern N
and twin beds available. Open year-round. Breakfast includ
not served on Sun. or Mon. Wheelchair access. Hiking,
hayrides, summer theater, ice skating, superb backroading
houses nearby; also the Cathedral in the Pines. One cat in residence. No credit
Judy and Bill Wolfe, owners/hosts.

DIRECTIONS: Take Rte. 3 north to Nashua. At Exit 7W follow Rte. 101 west through
Milford to Rte. 45. Turn left 1-1/2 mi. to Temple. From I-91 at Brattleboro take Rte. 9
east to Keene to Rte. 101 through Peterborough, over Temple Mtn. to Rte. 45. Turn
right, 1-1/2 mi. to the inn.

CHESTERFIELD INN

West Chesterfield, New Hampshire

I've always had a soft spot in my heart for country inns that have histo-
ries as farmhouses. The Chesterfield Inn is one of these. The traditional New England center-hall Colonial, with its two attached barns,
is more than 200 years old. Built in the 1780s, the building first func-
tioned as a tavern and then as a private farmhouse. The clapboard
structure was renovated in 1984. Sitting on a hill above the Connecticut River, the panoramic views are to the lovely Vermont Green
Mountains to the west.

After looking at more than eighty country inns, Phil and Judy Hueber hiked the Chesterfield Inn's 10 acres and knew it was "the one."

...ad been a marketing director for Dun & Bradstreet and Judy a ...ager for Mutual of New York prior to the move to their "dream ...n" and a much less stressful way of life.

One of the most attractive aspects of the inn comes from its unusual construction. In order to reach the three intimate dining rooms, one must walk through the kitchen. The candlelit dining room tables are set with crisp white linens, Dudson floral china, and crystal water glasses. The rooms are softened by Oriental carpets.

Dinner is leisurely. My first course was a colorful salad of roasted red peppers with fresh basil. An exotic main course of Brazilian fish and shrimp, stewed in a sauce of coconut, tomatoes, peanuts, and ginger, was exceptional. A crisp garden salad, using tender bibb lettuce from the inn's garden, was tossed with a tangy, homemade house dressing. Along with my after-dinner espresso, I ordered pumpkin cheesecake, one of Carl's specialties. I made a mental note to ask him how he makes it so creamy.

Cathedral ceilings, weathered barn boards, and exposed beams highlight the nine spacious guest rooms. Many of the walls are hand-stenciled, and period antiques and handmade quilts—a hobby of Judy's—decorate the comfortable rooms. As an avid reader, I particularly appreciated the rooms' cozy sitting areas and three-way reading lamps. All rooms have full baths, two with Jacuzzis, and thick, large towels. Some have fireplaces and two have balconies. My room had a lovely view onto the inn's pond.

The Huebers have stocked the rooms' small refrigerators with chardonnay, champagne, mineral water, and imported beers. Air-conditioning is quiet, and telephones and television are available.

A beehive fireplace dominates the sitting room. Colonial furnishings, a brass chandelier, a 20-foot-high ceiling, and lots of windows make this room a wonderful place for relaxing.

Judy whips up a super breakfast that might include fruit-filled crepes or summer vegetable custard and is served on the cheery remodeled sun porch or outside on the terrace.

CHESTERFIELD INN, Rte. 9, West Chesterfield, NH 03466; 603-256-3211.

A 13-guestroom (private baths) country inn with a guest cottage of four garden, patio fireplace rooms on a hill above the Connecticut River Valley. Open all year. King and double beds. Breakfast included. Gourmet dinners Wed. to Sun. Close to outdoor activities and cultural offerings. Two cats in residence. Judy and Phil Hueber, owners/hosts.

DIRECTIONS: Traveling north on Rte. 9, take Exit 3 and follow to lights. Go straight, across river, 2 mi. Inn is on the left. From Keene, NH, travel west on Rte. 9 for 20 min. Inn is on the right.

CHRISTMAS FARM INN

Jackson, New Hampshire

Christmas Farm was given its name many years ago, and Sydna and Bill found it inspirational. Using subtle variations of red and green in the decor, naming their guest rooms after Santa's reindeer and elves, sending out semiannual newsletters from the North Pole, and having a big Christmas celebration in the middle of July, they keep the feeling and spirit of Christmas alive all year.

As I drove up the country road my first view of the inn, with its white clapboards and green shutters, was very inviting. The main house, built in the 1770s, is set back on a little knoll, across a green lawn with huge maple trees and masses of flowers. The green rocking chairs on the long front porch with its overhanging roof, hanging plants, and flowers seemed to beckon me to "come and set a spell." The screen door is the kind I expected to slam when it closed.

Bill obligingly took me on a tour up the little road that wound around the hill and through the woods. There are several cottages with names like the Sugar House, the Smoke House, and the Livery Stable, in a lovely, woodsy setting, with little yards and porches where you can sit out and enjoy the birds and the flowers. They are all different, with attractive and comfortable furnishings. Some have fireplaces, and all have beautiful mountain views. The 1777 Saltbox and the Barn are closer to the main house and have several guest rooms and suites. The ground floor of the huge Barn is also a leisure center with table tennis, a piano, and a TV.

Guest rooms in the main house are decorated in Laura Ashley fabrics and antique reproductions. Two rooms have Jacuzzis. Cheerful plaids cover the settees and chairs in the two cozy sitting rooms; one room has a corner fireplace with a raised hearth, and the other has a TV and VCR. There's an old-fashioned phone booth in the entry.

My dinner in the pleasant dining room with its many windows overlooking the flower gardens was delightful. Everything was excellent, from my appetizer of ravioli of crab with saffron and chives, to the entrée of grilled tuna with spinach, garlic, herbs, and diced tomatoes, to the ambrosial finale of an amaretto-soaked sponge cake served in a raspberry sauce and topped with chocolate. All of the breads and rolls are freshly baked. I gently awakened the next morning to that wonderful aroma wafting in my bedroom window.

CHRISTMAS FARM INN, Jackson, NH 03846; 603-383-4313.

A 37-guestroom (36 private baths) comfortable farmhouse inn with cottages and suites on 14 acres on a country road in the rolling farmlands and forests of the White Mountains. Modified American plan. Breakfast and dinner served to travelers by reservation. Open year-round; various packages available. Swimming pool, sauna, putting green, horseshoes, shuffleboard, volleyball, table tennis on grounds. Golf, tennis, fishing, hiking, all summer/winter sports, and cultural and sports events nearby. No pets. No smoking in dining room. Sydna and Bill Zeliff, owners/hosts.

DIRECTIONS: From Rte. 16, go through village. Follow Rte. 6B up the hill 1/2 mi. to the inn.

THE DARBY FIELD INN

Conway, New Hampshire

There's a real sense of adventure involved in just making the last stage of the journey to reach Darby Field Inn. I turned off Route 16 and followed the Darby Field sign, plunging into the forest on a wonderful dirt road that seemed to climb ever upward. Following this road through the forest, again I had the great feeling of expectation that something would emerge at the top of the mountain that was going to be grand, and grand it is.

The Darby Field Inn has a most impressive panoramic view from its terrace dining room and many of the bedrooms. On this particular day Marc and Maria Donaldson, the innkeepers, took turns making sure that I saw all of the redecorating that had been accomplished in the inn, and we also had a chance to talk about the great view of the mountains.

"Over there is South Moat Mountain," Marc explained, "and that's Mount Washington just to the right. We can also see Adams and Madison and White Horse Ledge in the center."

The Darby Field Inn sits on the edge of the White Mountain National Forest, where guests can cross-country ski, snowshoe, and hike to nearby rivers, waterfalls, lakes, and open peaks. Fortunately, there's a very pleasant swimming pool on the terrace, providing guests with not only a cooling dip in the hot days of summer, but still another view of the mountains.

Maria and I did a short tour of the rooms. "Each room has its own country personality," she observed. "Some have four-poster beds, patchwork quilts, and braided rugs. Most of them have private baths and, as I'm sure you've noticed, many face our special view of the valley."

There is a cozy little pub where both guests and Marc and Maria's friends can come together. This is adjacent to the living room, which has as impressive a stone fireplace as I have ever seen.

I was curious about the origins of Darby Field Inn. "Samuel and Polly Chase Littlefield first came up here in 1826, when it was hard work farming through all those generations of hard winters and long distances," Maria recounted. "Later on, the home took in summer guests, and it was then that the innkeeping tradition began. In the 1940s, a man from Boston and his family came here, and the original farmhouse became the living room section of what was to be known as the Bald Hill Lodge. The barn and blacksmith shop came down and in its place the dining room and kitchen section was built. The swimming pool was added and even a small ski lift for guests."

As one might expect, the menu is a bit on the hearty side with lamb chops, filet mignon, veal piccata, and roast duckling satisfying outdoor-oriented appetites.

Marc and Maria met in Venezuela, Maria's homeland, and came to Darby Field in 1979. They saw it as a country home for their children and an opportunity to meet guests from all parts of the world.

As Marc and Maria walked me out to the car, she said, "We can't let you go without pointing out our garden where we get so many of the good things we serve at the inn, including snow peas, peppers, cabbage, corn, lettuce, and brussels sprouts."

THE DARBY FIELD INN, Bald Hill, Conway, NH 03818; 800-426-4147 (NH: 603-447-2181).

A 16-guestroom (14 private baths) White Mountain country inn, 3 mi. from Conway. All size beds available. Modified American plan. Closed Apr. Bed and breakfast offered at various times, so I would suggest checking with the inn in advance. Within convenient driving distance of all of the Mt. Washington Valley cultural, natural, and historic attractions, as well as several internationally known ski areas. Swimming pool and carefully groomed xc skiing trails on grounds. Tennis and other sports nearby. One dog in residence. CCs: Visa, MC, AE. Marc and Maria Donaldson, owners/hosts.

DIRECTIONS: From Rte. 16: Traveling north turn left at sign for the inn (1 mi. before the town of Conway) onto Bald Hill Rd., and proceed up the hill 1 mi. to the next sign for the inn and turn right. The inn is 1 mi. down the dirt road on the left.

DEXTER'S INN AND TENNIS CLUB

Sunapee, New Hampshire

What a day! The sky was the bluest of skies, the sun was the sunniest of suns, and New Hampshire during the last week in June was really showing off for the rest of the world. I crested the hill and found Dexter's Inn basking in all of this glory, its bright yellow paint and black shutters blending well with the black-eyed Susans, Queen Anne's lace, and other summertime flowers and the green trees in the background.

As I looked east from the summit of the hill a magnificent scene of green foliage and Sunapee Lake came into view. I strolled up the granite steps of the inn, and stepped into the entrance, over which was the date 1804. Here again was the comfortable library-living room with some appropriate paintings of New Hampshire mountains and countryside. The furniture had been brightly slipcovered, and the room was wonderfully cool after the midday heat. I took a moment and stepped out to a screened-in porch with white wicker furniture and a ceiling painted to look like a canopy. It looked like a wonderful place to spend an evening.

Now I opened the door to the side terrace with its round tables and bright yellow umbrellas, remembering that I first sat here perhaps ten

years earlier. There were tennis courts on both sides of the broad lawn and some tennis players were having a lively game. I could hear guests splashing in the swimming pool.

I went to see some of the guest rooms in the main house, which are reached by funny little hallways that zigzag around various wings, and also the guest rooms in the barn across the street. Everything looked tiptop. Extra towels awaited me in my room—someone knew I planned to play tennis. The Holly House cottage is a real plus. Because it is fully equipped with a kitchen, washer/dryer, living room with fire-place and two bedrooms with king and twin size beds along with their own private baths, it is well suited for families, two couples traveling together or small seminars.

In the fall you will find apples in your room. You can eat one and take the others to the field to feed Alvin, Annie and Carolyn, the Scottish Highland cattle who roam the pastures. They are fascinating to watch.

At mealtime expect to find homemade soups and breads, fresh poached salmon, thick lamb chops, brandied chicken, rosemary had-dock, or exceptional filet mignon. A sampling of desserts includes lemon mouse, chocolate walnut torte, and butterscotch pecan pie.

———

DEXTER'S INN AND TENNIS CLUB, Box 703R, Stagecoach Rd., Sunapee, NH 03782; 603-763-5571, 800-232-5571.

A 19-guestroom (private baths) resort-inn in the western New Hampshire moun-tain and lake district. All-size beds. Modified American plan; European plan available in late June and Sept. Breakfast, lunch, and dinner served to travelers by advance reservation; closed for lunch and dinner on Tues. during July and Aug. Lunches served only in July and Aug. Open from early May to mid-Nov. Three tennis courts and teaching pro, pool, croquet, and shuffleboard on grounds. Lakes, hiking, backroading, and championship golf courses nearby. Pets allowed in Annex only. CCs: Visa, MC. Michael and Holly Simpson-Durfor, owners/hosts.

DIRECTIONS: From north and east: use Exit 12 or 12A, I-89. Continue west on Rte. 11 for 6 mi.—just 1/2 mi. past Sunapee to a sign at Winn Hill Rd. Turn left up hill and after 1 mi., bear right on Stagecoach Rd. From west: use Exit 8, I-91, follow Rte. 103 east into NH—through Newport /2 mi. past junction with Rte. 11. Look for sign at Young Hill Rd. and go 1-1/2 mi. to Stagecoach Rd.

INN EVENTS: JUNE—Nostalgia Weekend
JUNE—Super Senior Tennis Tournament
JULY 5–10—Rug Hooking Classes
JULY 17–19—Senior 60s Tournament
JULY 20–24—Landscape Painting
SEPT 13–18—Rug Hooking Classes
OCTOBER 9–11—Columbus Day Weekend

THE DOWD'S COUNTRY INN
Lyme, New Hampshire

The Dowd's Country Inn, on the scenic Lyme Common, is a picture-perfect white Colonial built in the 1780s. An old country store and a historical hardware establishment are the Inn's neighbors. A brick walkway leads past the quaint picket fence to a stone patio, and up to the sunny porch furnished with white wicker.

The Inn is set on six acres complete with a tranquil pond frequented by ducks and resident turtles. I had arrived just in time for complimentary afternoon tea, so over flaky scones, innkeepers Mickey and Tami Dowd told me how they happened to end up in Lyme.

"Mickey was the executive steward at the Waldorf-Astoria before we made the move. Then prior to opening the inn, he had a restaurant at Dartmouth College," she continued. "Right," Mickey added. It's

named "Everything but Anchovies"! Later, they purchased the inn and immediately began renovation work.

Two comfortable common rooms offer restful settings for reading or visiting with fellow guests. The sunken living room, with its cozy wood stove, piano and television, was designed from an old carriage house and still has the basketweave brick floor and old beams.

Country touches like handmade quilts and shams, stenciled walls, cheerful wallpaper, and wide-board floors create a homey atmosphere. Some of the rooms have fireplaces, and all have private baths and queen-sized beds. Tucked behind the gardens, a separate cottage with its own small kitchen is a perfect accommodation for honeymooners or families.

A homemade country breakfast is served in the sun porch or dining room, and at Sunday brunch, eggs Florentine are a special treat. During the summer, chicken and lobster barbecues take place on Lyme Common and, of course, the fall colors are always spectacular. The inn also has a short nature walk that meanders around the water-iris-filled pond, then beyond to New England's oldest smoke house.

THE DOWD'S COUNTRY INN, #5 on the Common, Lyme, NH; 603-795-4712.

A 22-guestroom (private baths) Colonial inn on Lyme Common. Queen beds. Full country breakfast and afternoon tea. Open year-round. Near Dartmouth College and biking, hiking and snowmobile trails. Children welcome. No pets. Smoking permitted. Tami and Mickey Dowd, owner/hosts.

DIRECTIONS: The Inn is located on Main St. in Lyme, approximately 8 mi. north of Hanover on Rte. 10, or 7 mi. south of Orford on Rte. 10.

FOLLANSBEE INN

North Sutton, New Hampshire

When the Reileins purchased Follansbee Inn in 1985, they were already in love with the area surrounding the small country village of North Sutton. Dick left a career in computer sales and Sandy gave up her position as a hospice worker to realize their dream of having an inn. "We wanted an inn since staying in many in England on our honeymoon," Sandy told me. "And since we've had one, we have no regrets!"

The Follansbee Inn is nestled near lovely, peaceful Kezar Lake, four miles from, as Sandy says, "the nifty New England town of New London." The Follansbee family built the rambling, distinctive farmhouse in 1840, and it was expanded in the 1920s. Crisp and clean, the white clapboard and green-trimmed house has a traditional old fashioned front porch for evening "dawdling."

"We don't have any television here," Dick told me as he ushered me into the cozy sitting room, "just great conversation." I was pleased to practice this rather rare art as we sat in overstuffed chairs next to the wood-burning stove. The room is paneled with weathered barn wood, which lends an air of timelessness. Another meeting room has comfortable sofas, a fireplace, and a small service bar.

In the winter months, hot kir and cider are served around the fire: a welcome treat after an afternoon of cross-country skiing. Summers bring Follansbee slush, served as guests relax on the front porch. The inn also has a nice selection of wines and beer. Several local brews are offered. By the way, Follansbee is a nonsmoking inn. "We want our guests to enjoy this clean New Hampshire air, inside and outside," Dick said.

The twenty-three guest rooms are each decorated differently. Carpeting, new mattresses, and lovely antiques create a comfortable atmosphere. Shared baths are large, with claw tubs and showers, and private baths have either tub showers or shower stalls. The bayberry soap waiting in my soap dish was an aromatic surprise.

One of the most wonderful things about Follansbee Inn is Kezar Lake. First of all, the view to the lake is spectacular. There's something about the sight of a peaceful lake the first thing in the morning that just starts the day off on the right note. Dick and Sandy invited me to the inn's private lakefront and pier to show me their new handmade wooden rowboat one afternoon. "Isn't she great!" Sandy proudly said. "We have quite an armada now: a sail board, rowboat, canoe, and paddleboat." For an afternoon of lazing, take one of the boats to the small island in the middle of the lake and enjoy one of Sandy's picnic lunches as you soak up some sun.

Breakfast begins in the dining room, with homemade granola, juices, coffee, and tea. Guests are then invited into the cozy kitchen to feast on lots of fresh fruit, muffins, and either an egg casserole, pancakes, or French toast. Evening dining is leisurely. Dick can suggest just the perfect wine to accompany your meal.

FOLLANSBEE INN, P.O. Box 92, North Sutton, NH 03260; 603-927-4221.

A 23-guestroom (11 private baths) authentic New England country inn on Lake Kezar. King, double, and twin beds. Closed portions of Nov. and April. Hearty breakfast included; picnic lunch and dinner available. Boating, fishing, hiking, biking, picnicking, golf, tennis, xc skiing from doorstep, summer playhouse, and musical concerts. Downhill skiing 4 miles away. No pets. One dog in residence. No smoking. Dick and Sandy Reilein, owners/hosts.

DIRECTIONS: Take I-89 to Exit 10. Follow signs to North Sutton, about 2 miles. The inn is behind the big white church.

THE INN AT CROTCHED MOUNTAIN

Francestown, New Hampshire

Once again I turned off Route 202 at Bennington, New Hampshire, and followed Route 47 toward Francestown. I noticed that an unusual number of beaver dams had been built by our industrious friends. Admiring the farms on both sides of the road, I wound my way ever upward through the grove of trees, coming once again to the Crotched Mountain Inn, just a few paces from the base of a ski area.

The inn was originally built as a farmhouse in 1822. The first

owner constructed a secret tunnel from his cellar to the Boston Post Road, incorporating his home as a way station to shelter runaway slaves on the Underground Railroad. During the late 1920s, it was to become one of the most spectacular farms in New England, boasting an internationally recognized breed of sheep, champion horses, and Angora goats.

Unfortunately, the house was destroyed by fire in the mid-30s, rebuilt, and John and Rose came on the scene in 1976.

Rose is an attractive Indonesian woman. She is in complete charge of the kitchen, doing a great deal of the cooking. The menu includes roast duck with plum sauce, sautéed bay scallops, and Indonesian-style scallops with sautéed tomatoes, onions, pepper, and ginger. There is a low ceiling pub with a roaring fire for after dinner guests to enjoy their night cap.

As I was leaving, Rose walked out to the car and said, "Do tell your readers that we love children to come here, and we have many things for them to do and see, and they always seem to have a good time."

THE INN AT CROTCHED MOUNTAIN, Mountain Rd., Francestown, NH 03043; 603-588-6840.

A 13-guestroom (8 baths) mountain inn in southern New Hampshire, 15 mi. from Peterborough. Double and twin beds. European plan. Open from mid-May to the end of Oct., and from Thanksgiving thru the ski season. During winter and holiday periods, dinner is served on Fri. and Sat. Dinner is served from Tues. thru Sat. during the remainder of the year. Within a short distance of the Sharon Arts Center, American Stage Festival, Peterborough Players, Crotched Mt. ski areas. Swimming pool, tennis courts, xc skiing, volleyball on grounds. Golf, skiing, hill walking, and backroading in the gorgeous Monadnock region nearby. No credit cards. Two dogs in residence. Rose and John Perry, owners/hosts.

DIRECTIONS: From Boston, follow Rte. 3 north to 101A to Milford. Then Rte. 13 to New Boston and Rte. 136 to Francestown. Follow Rte. 47 for 2-1/2 and turn left on Mountain Road. Inn is 1 mi. on right. From New York/Hartford, take I-91 north to Rte. 10 at Northfield to Keene, NH. Follow 101 east to Peterborough, Rte. 202 north to Bennington, Rte. 47 to Mountain Rd. (approx. 4-1/2 mi.); turn right on Mountain Rd. Inn is 1 mi. on right.

INN AT THORN HILL

Jackson, New Hampshire

What a transformation! When I last saw Mount Washington from my guest room, it had been at sundown the previous day. The mountain's eminence had caught and reflected the last rays of the sun, until it finally disappeared in the ever-deepening hues of blue that marked a mid-September evening in northern New Hampshire. This morning

the top of the mountain was completely white. A 6-inch snowfall had powdered several peaks of the Presidential Range, and Jack Frost had brushed some streaks of red, orange, yellow, and russet through the greenery. When I went down for breakfast there was an electricity in the air that comes with the arrival of a change in season.

Innkeepers Jim & Ibby Cooper moved to village of Jackson in 1992. During their lifetime, they had been accustomed to a much more cosmopolitan environment than the village of Jackson (population 650) provided. But the Coopers had no trouble adapting, and quickly left any attachment to their previous careers in hotel management and teaching, where Ibby taught in a one school house for the homeless. The Inn at Thorn Hill Inn was designed by noted architect Stanford White, who also designed the Washington Square Arch in New York City. Gossip holds that White was shot to death by a jealous husband. Built originally as a private mansion for Katherine Prescott Wormeley, a distinguished translator of the works of Balzac, the property with its gambrel-roofed main house on 7.5 quiet country acres became her winter abode. The quintessential grand country residence was completed in 1891. Three different types of accommodations are available at the inn: the main inn, the carriage house, and the cottages. Each room has a private bath and is individually decorated with Victorian antiques. The inn is by no means rustic, catering to a clientele who appreciate a genteel atmosphere. The first floor, with its forty-two-seat dining room, has a Victorian flavor. The parlor offers the inn's only television and a baby grand piano, and the spacious drawing room with its soapstone wood stove, lace curtains, and antique furnishings provides a comfortable ambience that is hospitable and welcoming.

The inn's long living room has been divided into three separate areas where guests can gather for conversation or for games at the gaming tables. Views to the surrounding mountains, and unique Victorian accents, highlight the guest rooms. The Carriage House next door offers a 20- by 40-foot great room with a fireplace, seven comfortable guest rooms and a jacuzzi. Decor is country-inspired and the environment perfect for group get-togethers. The other three cottages offer the ultimate in privacy with the option to participate in the group environment. All rooms and cottages have modern baths with either showers or shower/tub combos. The inn's dining room is reserved for the public by reservations. In addition to individual tables for those who desire romantic privacy, there is a common table that seats eight, for the adventurous who love to swap travel stories and good conversation. Besides the scrumptious, full breakfast, a varied dinner menu is prepared to order, offering appetizers like a country pâté of veal, pork, and chicken livers flavored with brandy, and entrées of lobster pie and roast breast of duck with montmorency sauce. All entrées are served with fresh vegetables. The inn's built-in pool and winter sports, including the Jackson Ski Touring cross-country trail network, provide enjoyable exercise for any season. Plays, dance troupes, and concerts take place at various times during the year. Art and quilt workshops are conducted various weeks thoughout Spring and Fall.

INN AT THORN HILL, Thorn Hill Rd., Box A, Jackson, NH 03846; 603-383-4242.

A 20-guestroom (private baths) inn within sight of Mount Washington. Various packages available, including European, Modified American, and B&B plans. Breakfast and dinner served daily. All-size beds. Closed April. Many cultural and recreational activities nearby. No Smoking. Kennel nearby. Jim and Ibby Cooper, owners/hosts.

DIRECTIONS: Take I-95 to the Spaulding Turnpike and follow Rte. 16 north to Jackson. Once in the village, take Rte. 16A through the covered bridge to Thorn Hill Rd. and turn right; go up the hill.

THE MEETING HOUSE INN
Henniker, New Hampshire

Located in the beautiful Contoocook Valley, nestled at the base of Pat's Peak Ski Area, The Meeting House waits for those who love and appreciate a small rural environment. Henniker is home to New England College and takes its name from the original meeting house, built more than 200 years ago, at the base of Craney Hill.

Located on a quiet, secondary country road, the refurbished farmstead is bordered by two meandering mountain-fed streams. Its 5 acres

of wooded land provide wonderfully peaceful hiking trails. As innkeeper Cheryl Bakke stated, "The inn is a quiet jewel awaiting your discovery."

And a jewel it is. Bill and June Davis, and Cheryl Davis Bakke and her husband, Peter, have owned and operated The Meeting House Inn and Restaurant for many years. They were charmed by the quaint town of Henniker, and chose it as an ideal location to begin "hands-on" innkeeping. For them, the "hands-on" part started immediately. They purchased the buildings, which previously had not been used as an inn, and began renovating. "We literally started from scratch," Bill, the former owner of an executive search firm, told me. "We wanted the inn to have our own signature."

That unique family signature is apparent throughout The Meeting House. The style is eclectic, with personal family antiques and treasures in all the rooms. Even the intricate needlepoint pieces have been stitched by family members.

Each guest room has its own personality. "Rooms are *chosen* by our guests rather than *assigned*," Cheryl told me as she showed me to my romantic suite. "We want people to relax in the comforts of their own personalities and thoughts."

Wide pine floors, canopy brass beds, comfortable furnishings, designer sheets, and fluffy extra pillows are just part of what encourage total relaxation. All rooms have private baths. I really luxuriated as I soaked in a deep, hot bath, made fragrant by a few drops of complimentary homemade Henniker wild rosewater cologne.

The common room has a phone, television, VCR, and some interesting mystery puzzles that can be taken back to your room for an evening of *who-dunit*. A solar recreation area, comprised of a hot tub and sauna, is also available for guest use. Tiny twinkling Christmas tree lights peep from the plants surrounding the tub, creating a magical atmosphere.

Breakfast is always a surprise. Delivered in a charming country basket, each morning's unwrapping brings a delightful selection, including a home-baked goody. The menu is changed seasonally. Accompanied by Grensil, the inn's affectionate Maine coon cat, I took my treasure basket to breakfast on the sunny deck where I could appreciate the rock gardens and flowers that surround the inn.

In the evening, hearty New England cookery can be enjoyed in The Meeting House restaurant, housed in the inn's authentic, carefully preserved barn. Open to the public, dinner is available Wednesday through Sunday. The recently added solar greenhouse bar is just the spot to have one of Bill's famous fourteen-ingredient Bloody Marys. The bar is full-service, and includes nonalcoholic selections. An extensive wine list is also available.

A unique display of small plastic bags, filled with sand from around the world, hang from the restaurant walls: "The Sands of Time." What began as one guest's way of sharing a vacation experience has grown into a nostalgic collection that former guests send from such exotic locations as Mt. Everest and the floor of the Atlantic Ocean. Such "sharing" is an indication of just how much warmth and friendliness is found, and remembered, at the Meeting House. As the inn's brochure states, it is "A place in time to return to again and again."

THE MEETING HOUSE INN, 35 Flanders Rd., Henniker, NH 03242; 603-428-3228.

A 6-guestroom (private baths) country inn located in the Contoocook Valley. All-size beds. Open all year. Breakfast included, dinners available Wed. through Sun., Sunday brunch. Gift and antique shops, downhill and xc skiing, water sports, theaters nearby. No smoking or pets. Maine coon cat in residence. June and Bill Davis, and Cheryl and Peter Bakke, Owners-hosts.

DIRECTIONS: From Henniker, take Rte. 114 south about 2 mi. to Pat's Peak Sign. Turn right (Flanders Rd.); the inn is about 1/2 mi. on the right.

MOOSE MOUNTAIN LODGE
Etna, New Hampshire

Up the hill I drove to the lodge and its fabulous view.

Moose Mountain Lodge is a rustic building high on the western side of Moose Mountain, built in 1938, mostly of logs and stones gathered from the surrounding forests and fields. The broad porch extends across the entire rear of the lodge, and has foreground views of the rolling New Hampshire countryside and, in the distance, of famed Ver-

mont peaks as far away as Rutland. Peter Shumway the owner is fond of saying there is a 99-mile view.

I passed through the new entryway and walked into the kitchen, as almost everyone does, joining Peter and Kay Shumway around the big table for a wonderful breakfast visit.

The kitchen is one of the centers of activity at Moose Mountain Lodge. "We run an open kitchen here," Kay said. "I like it when guests wander in and ask 'What's for lunch?' Incidentally, most of the time it's soup and salad." This is Kay's domain and it reveals her many interests besides cuisine, including flowers and plants. In the middle of the big butcher-block table was a copy of *Webster's New Collegiate Dictionary*. How can you go wrong in a kitchen that is also a haven for the intellectually curious!

There are twelve lodge-type, rustic bedrooms with colorful quilts, lots of books and magazines, bunk beds and conventional single and double beds, and a rustic air that I seldom find these days.

"Many things are different here in the summer, including the menus," Kay remarked. "Summer meals have lots of fish and some meats with light sauces; all of the vegetables from the garden and all the fresh fruits that I can pick (right next to the front door); sometimes cold soups. We have salads and homemade breads and generally fruit desserts.

"However, in the wintertime we serve stuffed squash, lots of potatoes and big roasts, and always a huge salad and all kinds of desserts. Everything is put out on the buffet table so guests can have whatever they want and they can sit wherever they wish."

In winter there are extensive cross-country ski trails everywhere, and the winter scenery is spectacular. It's great to come in after skiing and grab a cookie from the seemingly bottomless cookie jar.

Hanover and Dartmouth College are seven miles down the road. It's easy to attend a concert or sporting event or browse through the Dartmouth bookstore, the largest and most complete in New England. The Shumways are involved in several Biking, Canoeing and Hiking Inn to Inn programs.

MOOSE MOUNTAIN LODGE, Etna, NH 03750; 603-643-3529.

A 12-guestroom (5 shared baths) rustic lodge a few miles from Hanover, NH. Queen, double, and twin beds available. Open from Dec. 26th-March 20th and late May until Oct. 20th. Breakfast, lunch, and dinner served to houseguests only. Xc skiing for all abilities on grounds or nearby. Ski equipment available. Hiking, biking, walking, canoeing, backroading, and many recreational and cultural attractions nearby, including Dartmouth College. No pets. One dog in residence. Peter and Kay Shumway, owners/hosts.

DIRECTIONS: If arriving for the first time, stop in Etna at Landers Restaurant or the Etna Store and telephone the lodge for directions. The last mile up the mountain is steep, and when the road is icy, guests are met at the bottom parking lot with a 4-wheel-drive vehicle. Etna is on the map, a few miles east of Hanover.

MOUNTAIN LAKE INN

Bradford, New Hampshire

I took one look at the wide expanse of manicured lawn that stretched from the screened-in front porch of the Mountain Lake Inn and my hands began to itch for a croquet mallet. Located in the foothills of the White Mountains on 167 acres of woods and streams, the inn has served guests since it was built in 1760. White with black shutters, the immaculately maintained inn overlooks a spectacular view to its own private sandy beach just across the highway on Lake Massasecum.

Carol and Phil Fullerton spent almost six years searching for just the right inn when they decided to leave the Boston area, where Bill was a stock and commodity broker and Carol ran a successful catering business. Neither have regrets about the change of careers. "We find this life-style rejuvenating," Carol said. Their search was over when they stayed one night at the Mountain Lake Inn. "We fell in love with it driving up the driveway," she continued. Well, you've heard of love at first sight; the next day the inn became theirs.

The Fullertons are hard-working partners. They immediately used their skills of refinishing and restoring "just about everything in our various urban and suburban houses during the last thirty years" to upgrade the inn's nine homey guest rooms and private baths. Ameri-

can and English antiques combine fluidly with contemporary furnishings. Soft earth tones, quilts, crisp eyelet curtains, stenciling and wallpapers, along with unique touches like Phil's Scottish grandfather's 1820s clock, create a relaxed atmosphere. Handmade New England crafts are tucked here and there.

Currier and Ives prints decorate the charming front parlor with its large fireplace. Another pine-paneled sitting room, where you will enjoy your country breakfast of fresh fruit, homemade muffins, cereals, and either a hot egg dish or French toast, has a cozy wood stove and a beautiful view of the front lawn.

Carol gives full vent to her creativity preparing dinner. After years of catering for a variety of epicures, she has developed a repertoire of recipes to please even the most discriminating. My mouth still waters at the thought of the tender beef burgundy, in a sauce with a hint of sweet paprika and thick with mushrooms, that was served my first evening a the inn. I also sampled the beef fondue, accompanied by Carol's three diverse sauces for dipping: zippy horseradish, sweet-hot mustard, and a rich wine sauce.

Dinner is served in the antique-decorated dining room where unique mismatched chairs surround polished wood tables spread with woven mats. An eighty-five-year-old pool table dominates one corner. The dining room is open to guests only, so dinner is usually an intimate affair.

Carol and Phil enjoy the company of their guests. After raising five sons, their in-house family is now limited to a pair of cats, Pepper and Casey, and Parker, their "extremely friendly" English springer spaniel. Having been parents, they understand the need for time away from the kids, so are happy to arrange for babysitting.

Besides swimming and sunbathing, fishing, canoeing, skiing, and snowshoeing are available. A horseshoe pit and badminton net also lie in wait.

MOUNTAIN LAKE INN, Rte. 114, P.O. Box 443, Bradford, NH 03221; 603-938-2136.

A 9-guestroom (private baths) charming country inn in the foothills of the White Mountains. Near 3 major ski areas. Closed 2 weeks in November. All size beds. Modified American plan. Restaurant for guests only. Private sandy beach on lake. No pets. Two cats and one dog in residence. Children welcome. Smoking restricted. Carol and Phil Fullerton, owners/hosts.

DIRECTIONS: From Boston, take I-93 north to Exit 5, then west to Rte. 114. Go north 5 mi. From New York, take I-84 to I-91, north to Exit 3 in VT. Go east on Rte. 9 to Henniker, then 5 mi. north to Rte. 114.

NEW LONDON INN
New London, New Hampshire

On three lovely landscaped acres, the New London Inn overlooks the town green of the village of New London. Located on the main street of what will soon be a designated historic area, the three-story white clapboard, green-shuttered, Federal-style building has been operated as an inn for more than 150 years. Innkeepers Maureen and John Follansbee informed me that they would soon be applying for inclusion in the National Historic Register.

Extensive renovation of the inn began three years ago. The thirty guest rooms, decorated in subtle shades of green, yellow, lavender, blue, and pink, are furnished with antiques and wicker. The result is a fresh, airy atmosphere. Telephones were recently installed in each room. The private baths were modernized, but some still offer the old-fashioned charm of claw-foot tubs.

After busy careers in New York, Maureen and John made the decision to pool their talents and open an inn. Maureen had spent seventeen years in human resources, and John had worked for twenty-five years in international insurance, prior to their search for an inn. When they finally found what they wanted, the cart rather came before the horse. "First, we fell in love with the town and the area," Maureen told me. "Then we decided we really wanted the challenge of restoring this beautiful inn."

Maureen is an avid gardener, and eager to give you a guided tour of her prize-winning horticultural masterpieces. John can direct you to the nearby cross-country ski areas. A golf course and the Mount Sunapee lake region are less than two miles away. And, for those who

love the thrill of uncovering that long-sought-after, one-of-a-kind hat pin, antique shops are in the immediate area.

A cozy mixture of antique and contemporary furnishings assure comfort in the common rooms. Television is available in the living room and bar. The inn has a full liquor license, and serves beer, wine, and spirits.

Breakfast is included with the room tariff and is served in the lovely dining room. Surrounded by Federal-period wallpaper, raised paneling, and new Windsor chairs, you will be treated to fresh fruit, juice, and a choice of entrée and side dish. On chilly mornings, the 200-year-old fireplace warms the room.

Dinners offer wonderful appetizers, such as pepper pasta with Italian bacon and fresh vegetables. Soup usually follows, and could be something like chilled tomato lime and scallop. I had an entrée of spiced beef medallions with lime-cilantro butter and avocado sauce. What a combination of flavors!

NEW LONDON INN Main St., P.O. Box 8, New London, NH 03257; 603-526-2791.

A 30-guestroom (private baths) Federal-style inn on 3 acres overlooking the New London village green. Open all year. All-size beds. Breakfast included, dinner available. Skiing, golf, public beaches, antique shops, and theater nearby. No pets. Maureen and John Follansbee, owners/hosts.

DIRECTIONS: From I-89, inn is approximately 3 mi. off Exit 11 from the south, or Exit 12, from the north. Follow signs to New London.

THE NOTCHLAND INN

Hart's Location, New Hampshire

New Hampshire has the highest mountains in the Northeast, including the majestic Mount Washington. The air is almost crystalline, and

the granite, evergreen forests, and icy snow-fed streams offer an invigorating atmosphere for body and soul.

Only 10 miles from Mount Washington, at the entrance to Crawford Notch, The Notchland Inn sits on a picturesque knoll with a commanding view of the Saco River valley. The Inn's 400 acres spread to touch the bases of four different mountains.

Off a major highway, the inn has served travelers for more than a century, and played an active role in the history of New Hampshire's White Mountains. Dr. Samuel Bemis, a successful dentist and inventor, completed the English-style manor house in 1862. Using native granite and timber, the handsome mansion was constructed by methods Dr. Bemis had studied in Europe. To achieve the clean cuts so obvious in the stone even today, the granite was drilled by hand at intervals. The holes were plugged with wooden dowels, which, when wet, split the granite with amazing precision.

John and Pat Bernardin purchased Notchland in 1983. The inn had been abandoned for some time, so the Bernardins began the work-intensive process of restoring the inn to its former Victorian grandeur. The huge brick chimneys, embossed metal ceilings, tiled fireplaces, and hardwood interior have been carefully and lovingly refurbished. Modern updating, like private tiled baths, has been done to complement the Victorian design. The atmosphere is delightfully casual and comfortable.

All eleven guest rooms have their own fireplaces and private baths. The rooms are bright and airy and are furnished with local and English antiques and decorated with designer wall coverings and fabrics. The placement of beds and chairs takes advantage of the incredible views to the mountains beyond.

Pat and John are a couple with varied interests and an unending flow of energy. Believing in the tradition of the country inn, where the family runs the business, they have no staff, choosing rather to do everything themselves. And they do *everything*. When I asked John, a former nuclear engineer, what he did for fun, he laughed and said, "I like bicycling, skiing, and fixing up the place, and fixing up the place, and ..."

One of the Bernardins' hobbies is their sanctuary for endangered species of domestic animals. I had never heard of endangered domestics, but Pat immediately educated me. "They're rare, almost extinct, breeds of goats and sheep." You can visit their collection of llamas, minauture horses, and their famous golden retriever, Ruggs, who has rescued many a misdirected hiker. Wild critters also wander in now and then: deer, moose, and that masked bandit, the raccoon. Recently a large barn complex was completed to house the animals. A team of Belgian draft horses has been added to the menagerie to take the guests for hay/sleigh rides through the woods.

It's difficult to imagine Pat having much time to spend whipping up gourmet breakfasts and dinners, but she does. A former chief chef, she focuses her culinary expertise on preparation of fabulous five-course dinners that include hearty homemade soups, crisp salads, a choice of three of four entrées, like beef Wellington, and luscious desserts. Breakfast is equally wonderful. Both meals are served in the inn's intimate dining room by the fire.

Notchland has a wealth of outdoor sports. John just recently cleared five miles of cross-country ski trails to add to the 12 already in use. After a nippy day in the snow, you can return for a soak in the hot tub by the pond, and then relax in the library with a video. Or read in one of the other three sitting rooms, where you'll find comfortable chairs and warming fires.

THE NOTCHLAND INN Hart's Location, NH 03812; 603-374-6131, 800-866-6131.
An 11-guestroom (private baths) Victorian manor house nestled in the mountains near Crawford Notch. King, queen and double size beds. Modified American plan. Open all year. Excellent winter sports, hiking, and boating. Antique shops, outlet centers, and theaters nearby. No pets. Ruggs, a golden retriever, in residence. CCs: Visa, MC, AE. Pat and John Bernardin, owners/hosts.

DIRECTIONS: From North Conway, follow Rte. 302 north for 20 min. into the White Mt. National Forest. The inn is very noticeable on a knoll above the highway.

INN EVENTS: MAY—White Mountain Waterfalls Tour
JUNE—Presidential Tranverse, biking with downhill-only option
JULY 25—Guided Canoe Tour of Upper Androoscogin River
SEPTEMBER 12–13—Early Foliage Hiking Tour

SNOWVILLAGE INN

Snowville, New Hampshire

Frank, Trudy, and Peter Cutrone are a family after my own heart, and Snowvillage Inn is one of my favorite inns. Not only is it unusual to have a father-mother-son team pool their diverse skills to operate an inn, but Trudy also shares my interest in writing. The trio purchased the 1900s inn in May 1986. "When we do 'business', I call my parents partners," Peter informed me, smiling. "When we talk 'family', it's Mom and Dad."

Originally a retreat for historical writer Frank Simonds, the country inn is located 1,000 feet up Foss Mountain in the New Hampshire rural village of Snowville. Mr. Simonds valued the peace and solitude, the absolutely spectacular view of the White Mountains, and the property's 10 acres of forest and lawns that keep neighbors and traffic at bay. The Cutrones chose Snowvillage Inn after first deciding to adopt a new life-style, then agreed on their approach to innkeeping: "country casual." Snowvillage was to be a place where guests could relax and put up their feet. And it is.

Coming up the graceful, flower-edged drive, three attractive buildings meet your gaze: the many-gabled main house with attached chalet, the converted 150-year-old red barn, and the quaint chimney house. Though separated by a lush center lawn and old stone walls, the three buildings are closely connected by driveways. The New England architecture is enhanced with colorful window boxes of flowers.

The living room and lounge are elegant, adorned with Oriental rugs, a huge brick fireplace, and well-stacked bookcases. Games like chess and Tak-a-Radi are available in a beautiful, hand-carved Swiss cupboard. Peter's expertise as a wood craftsman is apparent in his handsome oak grandmother clock in the comfortable living room. Paintings of Trudy's Austrian ancestors smile down from the walls, and sprays of fresh flowers appear everywhere.

In keeping with the inn's literary heritage, each of the eighteen guest rooms is dedicated to a writer and displays a selection of the author's work. The rooms are romantic and cozy with a blend of New England and Alpine Provincial furnishings ranging from period antiques to quality reproductions. Colors of dusty rose, blue, mint, and fiery poppy red accent country cottons and natural muslin linens. I found the welcome basket in my room a particularly friendly gesture, especially when I uncovered the buttery chocolate chip cookies. A new room has been recently added by combining two rooms; its twelve windows offer a breathtaking view from your pillow of Mt. Washington and the White Mountains.

Dining at Snowvillage Inn is exquisite. My dinner began with a warm loaf of walnut beer bread, accompanied by a salad course of greens topped with an unusual bourbon dressing. This was followed by creamy tomato soup and an entrée of Viennese beef tenderloin in a delicious sauce, rice pilaf, and a colorful sauté of squash with yellow and red peppers. Trudy's luscious French silk pie, slathered in whipped cream and shaved chocolate curls, completed the meal. Breakfast is also included with the room fee.

I was treated to an exceptional final evening at Snowvillage Inn when I attended Trudy's Americanized version of her native Austria's traditional Solstice Festival, a celebration of the return of light to the land. Tiki torches stood in for more traditional ones, but the spirit brought on by song, wine, and good food created an evening truly worthy of this ancient ritual.

SNOWVILLAGE INN, Snowville, NH 03849; 603-447-2818.

A 18-guestroom (private baths) mountain inn retreat. Closed April. All-size beds available. Modified American plan; breakfast with B&B rates. Clay tennis courts, sauna, fitness course in woods, volleyball, horseshoes, and a wide, restful screened porch on premises. Llama hikes with gourmet lunch during summer. No pets. Two dogs and three cats in residence. CCs: Visa, MC, AE. Frank, Trudy, and Peter Cutrone, owners/hosts.

DIRECTIONS: 120 miles from Boston and 55 miles from Portland, ME. From Boston take I-95 N to Spaulding Turnpike North in Portsmouth, NH (Exit 4). When the turnpike ends after Exit 18 it becomes Rte. 16 North. (Do not get off turnpike prematurely.) Follow Rte. 16 North to Rte. 25; take a right and go east for 5 miles. Take a left on Rte. 153 North. (Do not take Rte. 153 before this point.) Go 10 miles on 153 North; pick up Inn sign and turn right at Crystal Lake Beach to Snowville (1 mile). Turn right at Inn sign and come up the mountain 3/4 mile. Congratulate yourself.

INN EVENTS: FEBRUARY—Cook & Ski health-oriented cooking school

    MAY 2, JUNE 13, JULY 11, AUGUST 22, SEPTEMBER 19 AND OCTOBER 24—
        Llama Hikes with gourmet lunch

    MAY—Queen Victoria Weekend: shop until you drop treasure hunt

    MAY—Memorial Day Antiquing

    JUNE—Wildflower Walk and Barbeque

    JULY 4—Lobster Weekend

    AUGUST 9–13—One Grand Week: special activities for grandparents
        with grandchildren

    SEPTEMBER 12—Artist Weekend: lecture and wine tasting

    NOVEMBER 14—Veterans Remembrance Day, Big Band Dance

SUGAR HILL INN

Sugar Hill, New Hampshire

Stepping onto the wide veranda of Sugar Hill Inn, with its flowers and white wicker furnishings, I was reminded of the gracious old homes I've visited in the South. The 17th-century farmhouse is set on a natural rock foundation, and is stretched along a spacious lawn dominated by an old horse-drawn surrey. A powerful telescope on the veranda invites night-time star searching.

Sugar Hill Inn was built as a home for one of the hardy early-American families who came to the White Mountain area in search of a better way of life. The home was built in the traditional way, using post and beam construction, and relied on handsome rock fireplaces in the principal rooms for heat. Wide pumpkin pine boards were used for woodwork and flooring. Over the years, three cottages were added in a cluster to the west of the original inn. In 1972, improvements were made to the total facility and the inn was renamed Sugar Hill Inn.

Jim and Barbara Quinn, Rhode Island residents who had been in the grocery business, purchased the inn in 1986 and made substantial efforts to infuse the inn with their own personal warmth and, in Jim's

words, "their desire to develop first-time guests into longtime friends."

The two charming common rooms have original fireplaces, mantels, and stone hearths. Decorated in a Colonial style, with beautiful sugar-maple flooring accented by Oriental rugs, the rooms are quite lovely and comfortable. The living room has an antique 1906 player piano with a large assortment of piano rolls. I had particular fun with the rousing rendition of "Alexander's Ragtime Band" that we played during an after-dinner sing-along. A television is available, and board games and a variety of reading materials and puzzles are set out for entertainment.

I stayed in one of the country cottages adjacent to the main inn and found it spacious and homey. Each cottage has its own covered front porch for enjoying the evening twilight. All the guest rooms are individually decorated with handmade quilts on antique beds and hand-braided rugs on the floors. Barb has used her artistic flair to design and paint wall stencils modeled after original patterns found during renovation. As an inveterate late-night reader, I was happy to find good lighting for reading in bed. All rooms have immaculate private baths with mostly tub/shower combinations.

The inn's light, airy dining room is a perfect spot for enjoying a breakfast of such specialties as walnut pancakes, along with fresh fruits and home-baked muffins served on country crockery. In the evening, the ambience is changed with candlelight for a dinner that features two entrées and the finest of fresh and locally grown fruits, vegetables, poultry, and meats. Jim prepares all of the meals and has some wonderful specialties like his chicken Washington, a tender chicken breast stuffed with rich crabmeat and sauce. I recommend the excellent pecan bourbon pie for dessert. The inn has a fine selection of wines, beer, and full spirits to accompany your dinner.

SUGAR HILL INN, Rte. 117, Sugar Hill NH 03580; 603-823-5621.
A 16-guestroom (private baths) traditional New England inn and cottages 5 mi. from Franconia. Open May thru mid-Nov., and Dec. 26 thru March. All-size beds. Full breakfast included; dinner available on premises. B&B rates not available during fall seasons or holidays. All seasonal sports. Antique and outlet shopping, museums, theater, and chamber concerts nearby. No pets. No smoking. CCs: Visa, MC. Jim and Barbara Quinn, owners/hosts.
DIRECTIONS: From Boston, take Exit 38 from I-93. Turn right on Rte. 18 through Franconia. Turn left on Rte. 117. The inn is 1/2 mile up the hill on the right. From New York, take Exit 17 from I-91. Go east on Rte. 302 and turn right onto Rte. 117. The inn is on the left 1/2 mile before Rte. 18.
INN EVENTS: FEBRUARY–MARCH—cross-country touring gourmet getaway
MAY–JUNE—spring break guided tours with hikes and lunches
JULY 4—guests help with inn's parade float; hot air ballooning
OCTOBER—Great Pumpkin Contest

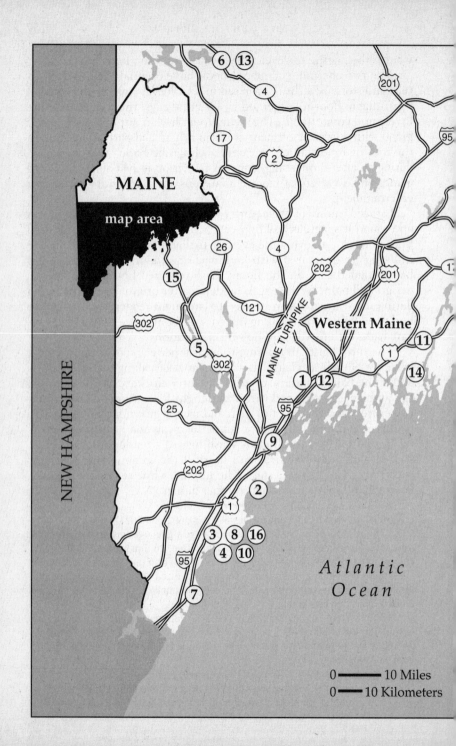

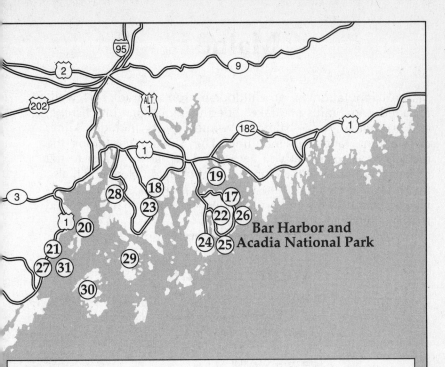

Bar Harbor and
Acadia National Park

Maine

Maine

Maine's reputation as an outdoorsperson's paradise is well-founded. Mountains and lakes offer hiking, swimming, fishing, and canoeing in the summer; winter sports include skiing, dogsledding, and snowmobiling. The 5,000 inlets along the famous rocky coast let you get right down to the water to dig clams or just observe the dramatic tidal changes. Here you'll also find historical tributes to the state's seafaring past, charming villages, antique shops and art galleries, and the amazingly varied terrain of Acadia National Park.

Western Maine

EVENTS

JANUARY	weekend sled dog races and Snodeo (snowmobile festival), Rangeley (info: 207-864-5571)
JANUARY	White White World Week, Carrabassett Valley (info 207-237-2000)
FEBRUARY	Winter Wonderland Week, Bethel (info: 207-824-2187)
MARCH (LAST SUNDAY)	maple sugarhouses statewide open doors to public (info: 207-289-3491)
MARCH	Bronco Buster Weekend, Saddleback Mountain
APRIL	Fishermen's Festival, Boothbay Harbor (info: 207-633-4008)
MAY MIDDLE	A Victorian Affair, Kennebunkport (info: 207-967-0857)
MAY	Maine State Parade, Lewiston/Auburn (info: 207-784-0599)
MAY, AUGUST–OCTOBER	Good Company theater
JUNE LATE	Taste of the Port Food Festival, Kennebunkport (info: 207-967-2000)
JUNE	Garden Tours, Bath (info: 207-443-3471)
JUNE	La Kermesse Parade, Biddeford (info: 207-282-1567)
JUNE	Windjammer Days, Boothbay Harbor (info: 207-633-2353)
JUNE	Garden Tours, Freeport (info: 207-865-3471)
JUNE	Old Port Festival, Portland (info: 772-6828)
JUNE	Pittston Agricultural Fair (info: 207-737-2797)
JUNE–AUGUST (TUESDAY EVENINGS)	Sebago Chamber Music Festival
JULY, EARLY	Schooner Fare Concert, Rangeley

JULY 3–5	Heritage Days, Bath (info: 207-443-9751)
JULY 4	Freeport Celebration (info: 207-865-6171)
JULY, MIDDLE	River Oyster Festival, Damariscotta (info: 207-563-8340)
JULY, MIDDLE	Clam Festival, Yarmouth (info: 207-846-3984)
JULY, LATE	Logging Museum Festival & Parade, Rangeley
JULY, LATE	Oxford Bean Hole Festival
JULY	Antique Auto Exhibit & Parade, Bath (info: 207-443-1316)
JULY	Sidewalk Festival, Lewiston (info: 207-784-3611)
JULY	Deering Oaks Family Festival, Portland
JULY, MIDDLE	fiddlers contest, Rangeley
JULY–AUGUST	Friends of the Arts Weekly Concert Series, Rangeley
AUGUST, EARLY	Norway Sidewalk Art Sale
AUGUST, EARLY	Sidewalk Art Show, Rangeley
AUGUST, MIDDLE	Blueberry Festival, Rangeley
AUGUST, LATE	Gun Show, Rangeley
AUGUST	Thomas Point Clearing House Picnic, Brunswick (info: 207-725-6009)
AUGUST	Maine Festival, Brunswick (info: 207-772-9012)
AUGUST	Downeast Wildlife Art Festival, Freeport (info: 207-397-4742)
AUGUST	Topsham Fair (info: 207-729-3443)
AUGUST	Wiscasset Antiques Show (info: 207-882-6817)
AUGUST–SEPTEMBER	Cumberland Fair (info: 207-443-2787)
SEPTEMBER	Thomas Point Bluegrass Festival, Brunswick (info: 207-725-6009)
SEPTEMBER	Sidewalk Art Show, Lewiston (info: 207-783-8956)
SEPTEMBER	Common Ground Country Fair, Windsor (info: 207-623-5115)
OCTOBER, MIDDLE	Fall Foliage Festival, Boothbay (info: 207-633-4727)
OCTOBER	Fryeburg Agricultural Fair (info: 207-935-3268)
NOVEMBER, MIDDLE	Chili & Chowder Challenge, Portland (info: 207-722-6828)
DECEMBER, EARLY	Chester Greenwood Day, Farmington: honoring the inventor of the earmuff (info: 207-778-4215)
DECEMBER, EARLY	Christmas Prelude Season, Kennebunkport (info: 207-967-0857)
DECEMBER 31	Portland Celebration (info: 207-772-9012)
DECEMBER	Giving Tree Program, Rangeley

SIGHTS

Angel Falls

Appalachian Trail

Dodge Point

Jones Glass and Art Gallery

Knott House

L.L. Bean, Freeport

Laudholm Farm Wildlife Preserve

Longfellow House

Maine Maritime Museum

Marginal Way Cliff Walk

Mingo Springs

Music Box Museum

Old Port District, Portland

Pemaquid Colonial Restoration

Portland Head Light

Portland Museum of Art

Rachel Carson Wildlife Refuge

Reid State Park

Sabbathday Lake Shaker Community

Sugarloaf Mountain

Two Lights State Park

Washburn-Norlands Living History Center

White Mountains

Wiscasset antique shops

THE BAGLEY HOUSE
Freeport, Maine

"Always welcome strangers into your home, even if you have not much to give, because one day you will be a stranger and will need the same kindness," advised the old Eskimo woman to Sigurd Knudsen, Jr. during the ten years he worked in Social Services in Alaska. This piece of advice Sig eventually brought back home to Maine.

Sig grew up in Freeport. In 1987, bringing a twenty-four year career in social work to an end, he purchased The Bagley House.

He is only the fourth owner of the old Greek Revival Colonial house, with its attached ell, built in the early 1770s. The Bagley family lived in the ell and rented rooms out in the main portion of the house. Israel Bagley, quite a participant in the growing community, used the house as a store, a church meeting place, and even a schoolroom for the children.

I learned of this history while sitting in the country kitchen one morning visiting with Sig. This was a feature I loved—being able to enjoy breakfast the old fashioned way, right at the kitchen table. The nearby brick fireplace, lit early that morning, warmed my back as I sat with other guests at the large baker's table. The aroma of fresh-baked muffins hung in the air.

"Don't overdo," warned Sig. "There's more to come."

Right he was as heaping platters of Decadent French Toast appeared, a tasty recipe made with croissants, orange rind, eggs, cream, cinnamon, and Triple Sec. Crisp fried bacon arived on its heels. A guest told me she had enjoyed Belgian waffles topped with local wild blueberries and yogurt the preceding morning. I could see that daily walks on the surrounding six acres would be in order or I would leave ten pounds heavier. So right after breakfast, I changed into my hiking shoes.

Fall had arrived in full glory, and the maples surrounding the two-story white house were alive with color. Heading towards the woods, I was treated to the sight of some deer feeding near an old apple orchard. Wild blueberries, raspberries, and blackberries, abundant in the warm months, were dying off in the face of the coming cold. A stay during the winter means strapping on your skis right at the back door and pushing off for cross-country skiing.

Upon my return, I strolled into the library. Sig's collection of

Eskimo artifacts and Alaska photos are on display here. Helping myself to a bottle of sparkling water from the small refrigerator, I sat down at the antique oak library table to look over brochures of local information. Connected to the library is the living room, with large windows that allow sunlight to warm up the atmosphere, while Oriental rugs brighten the dark wood of the antique furniture. Sig's wooden and soapstone bird collection, which I found to be quite interesting, makes its home here.

Floors in all the guest rooms are of wide pine planks. Hand-stencilled rugs, crafted by Sig's sister, Karen, adorn most rooms. She was also responsible for some of the stencilling seen along the walls. My room held a four-poster bed painted a soft yellow, a small antique sewing stand, a student desk, and an oak dresser. A cushioned rocker sat in the corner. The spacious bath had a pedestal sink dating back to yesteryear. All rooms have private baths; however, two are not connected to their rooms, but are found right down the hall.

Freeport, only a ten-minute drive from Bagley House, offers shopping and restaurants. A coastal town, it also has boat tours and sailboat rentals.

THE BAGLEY HOUSE, RR3, Box 269C, Freeport, ME 04032; 207-865-6566.
A 5-guestroom (private baths) 17th century Greek Revival B&B. Queen and double beds. Hearty breakfast included. Open year-round. Minimum 2 nights on holidays & college weekends. No smoking. Local attractions include shopping, dining, and boat excursions in nearby Freeport. City of Portland and several state parks within 30 minutes. No pets. CCs: Visa, MC, AE, DC, ENR. Sigurd A. Knudsen, Jr., owner/host.

DIRECTIONS: From I-95 take Exit 20. Follow Rte. 136 north six miles. Look for Inn on the right.

BUFFLEHEAD COVE
Kennebunkport, Maine

When I received a letter of invitation from Harriet and Jim Gott, Bufflehead Cove's innkeepers, I was excited to learn that the inn's namesake, the small, glossy black, bufflehead duck, winters in the cove right next to the inn.

"Oh yes, they fly in each fall," Harriet told me when I called for reservations.

I grabbed my binoculars, threw in National Geographic's Field Guide to the Birds of North America, and was off.

The warmth and friendliness I felt from Harriet on the phone was immediately apparent as I arrived at the turn-of-the-century, gray shingled inn. Long strides carried her across the wrap-around porch, hand

outstretched in welcome. White wicker chairs with plump chintz cushions were placed here and there.

"You're just in time for afternoon cheese and wine in the dining room," she said, a hint of New England accent coating her words.

I turned for a moment to take in the view. The languid Kennebunk River lay in front of me, a small boat rocking tethered to the dock. Feathery trees, awash with fall color, lined the river banks. Then I noticed it...the quiet. You'd never believe that tourist traffic, both car and boat, is only a half-mile down river, and the town of Kennebunkport only a mile away.

Harriet and Jim have lovingly remodeled their grand old home. I call it a home, because that's just what it was.

"We raised our family here," Harriet told me as we climbed the pine staircase to my room. "And we've tried to keep that comfortable, homey family feel in the guests' portion of the inn."

I didn't argue, I truly felt at home here. I joined the other guest in the expansive dining room where Jim was pouring wine. Hand stencilling skirted the walls and decorated the shiny plank flooring.

"Look out the window, up river," Jim suggested. "You might be able to see some buffleheads in the cove." Dusk blurred in the landscape, so I could only imagine them, with white buffle heads tucked under wings, readying for the falling darkness.

With wine in hand, I wandered into the living room where firelight played on the beamed ceiling and illuminated the rich colors of Oriental rugs. Bookshelves lined the walls over cushioned window seats and large picture windows offered water views. I was tempted to settle into a good mystery, but dawn makes for the best bird (or duck) spotting.

Decorated in soft, restful colors, all the inn's rooms are attractive and comfortable with private baths. Harriet settled me into the Balcony Room. A large brass bed and French doors opening onto a charming window-enclosed balcony awaited me.

The Teal Room, with its brass bed, and the River Room, with its collection of folk art and handcrafted double bed, provided a cozy, romantic atmosphere for two of my fellow guests, who allowed me a quick peek into their rooms. Before I left, Harriet let me tour the two largest rooms: The Suite, two rooms with double beds and views to the cove and river; and the Garden Suite, with its queen-sized bed, sitting area, kitchen, private entrance and patio, perfect for a family.

Although breakfast is normally served at 8:30, Harriet kindly accommodated my request for an earlier start. Over a warm, walnut-stuffed, baked apple resting in English custard, spicy ginger pancakes, and hot coffee, she suggested that after my bird-watching I might want to stroll into town and visit St. Anthony's Franciscan Monastery. "And for a real treat," she said, "buy a fresh-cooked packed lobster for an alfresco lunch."

As I walked into the crisp fall morning, binoculars around my neck, I rather felt like James J. Audubon. However, I doubt he had the comforts of Bufflehead Cove to come home to.

BUFFLEHEAD COVE, P.O. Box 499, Kennebunkport, ME, 04046; 207-967-3879.

A 5-guest room, turn-of-the-century shingled inn on the Kennebunk River. Queen, double, and twin beds. Open April-December; 2-night minimum stay on weekends. Full gourmet breakfast included; complimentary afternoon wine and cheese. Two miles to beach; 1 mile to town; golfing; antiquing; whale watching; duck watching; and hiking. James and Harriet Gott, owners/hosts.

DIRECTIONS: Take Exit 3 from Maine Turnpike. Turn left on route 35 south. At intersection of routes 35 and 1 continue on 35 for 3.1 miles. Watch for Goldberg Realty sign and turn left just beyond it. Follow lane to inn.

BLACK POINT INN

Prouts Neck, Maine

The Black Point Inn was recently described as one of the "last bastions of clean air, pure water, peace—and finger bowls." It is one of the few remaining American-plan resort hotels that were so numerous along the New England coast at the turn of the century. The atmosphere is genteel, friendly, and understated, with gentlemen in coats and ladies in summer dresses for dinner and later dancing to a small orchestra, which also plays during luncheon at poolside.

It's always exhilarating to stand on the flagstone terrace, looking out across the gaily colored umbrellas around the pool to the vast blue sweep of ocean. There are fine sandy beaches, tennis courts, and an 18-hole golf course a few steps away. Normand Dugas joined me, and we stood for a moment watching the American and Canadian flags snapping in the breeze and the white sails of a boat on the horizon.

"Our new 28-foot fishing boat, called *The Blue Lady*, departs with a surprising number of guests at 5 A.M., in order to catch the rascals before they wake up!" Norm said. "Our guests are able to do some fishing and still get back in time for breakfast by 9 A.M. We have mackerel, bluefish, stripers, a few small sharks, and an occasional sea bass."

Norm and I walked into the indoor swimming pool room, which he tells me has been extremely well received by all of the inn guests. Those staying slightly off season have particularly appreciated this pool, since the ocean is too cold before mid-June and after mid-September. The walls of the room are lined in beautiful California red cedar, and the pool overlooks the rose garden and the putting green.

Another interesting addition to the Black Point is the "Atlantic House Library." The Atlantic House Hotel, also on Prouts Neck, is now closed after 146 years of continuous operation, and the BPI acquired most of its library books and some other memorabilia. A lovely two-tier outside deck just off the library has been constructed for nice sunny-day reading.

The Prouts Neck path, or Cliff Walk, starts from a point next to the sea just a few steps from the main entrance of the inn and continues along the cliffs and rocks, cutting back through nooks and crannies between stately summer homes. At one point it passes in front of the studio of Winslow Homer, many of whose finest oil paintings were inspired by this coastline.

The evening menu emphasizes freshly caught Maine fish, and there is always lobster in some form; if you're lucky, you might even find lobster salad at the poolside luncheon buffet. Meals are essentially New England fare.

The dining room is cheerful, with windows looking out on the colorful rose garden, and the lounges are gracious and comfortable. Rooms are more readily available during the months of May, June, September, and October, when the modified American plan is optional.

BLACK POINT INN, Prouts Neck, ME 04070; 207-883-4126.

An 80-guestroom (private baths) luxury resort-inn on Rte. 207, 10 mi. south of Portland. All size beds available. Open May to late Oct. American plan during July and Aug. Optional MAP May, June, Sept., Oct. During high season, 3-night minimum stay. Indoor pool, Jacuzzi, and sauna, fresh-water whirlpool, heated salt-water pool, bicycles, sailing, dancing, golf, tennis, and ocean bathing all within a few steps. L.L. Beane is 16 miles away. In June, 8 miles away, is the Old Port Festival and Yarmouth Clam Festival is 15 miles away. No children under 8 during July and Aug. No pets. Normand H. Dugas, manager.

DIRECTIONS: From Maine Tpke., take Exit 7. Turn right at sign marked Scarborough and Old Orchard Beach. At second set of lights turn left on Rte. 207. Follow 4.3 mi. to Prouts Neck.

INN EVENTS: MAY—Memorial Day Weekend Package
MAY—Mother's Day Brunch
OCTOBER—Columbus Day Weekend Package

THE CAPTAIN LORD MANSION
Kennebunkport, Maine

I remember it very well: in fact, it was only last summer. It was a Wednesday morning in mid-July and I joined the Captain Lord breakfast group at nine-thirty. (There had been an earlier breakfast group at eight-thirty.) Many of the guests were seated in a large but somewhat formal dining room enjoying coffee and planning the day's activities. A large jigsaw puzzle was on the dining room table and a couple of guests were playing Chinese checkers in one corner. The Chippendale chairs, beautiful cabinets, and crystal chandelier were indications that this was indeed an important room during the many years of the mansion's existence.

Meanwhile, the morning breakfast chimes were rung, and almost as one, the waiting guests rose, crossed the hallway, and walked into the ample Captain Lord kitchen, where breakfast is served.

I took advantage of the moment to walk around and admire the handsome woodwork and lovely period wallpapers of this mansion, built during the War of 1812.

I walked to the front of the house where a beautiful curving banister led up a rather formal staircase to the third floor. Throughout the mansion, Rick and Bev have displayed antiques, Oriental rugs, and other tasteful *objets d'art*. One parlor has been set aside as a gift shop offering attractive mementos of the area, as well as smaller items such as cups, saucers, plates and the like.

Ample use has been made of the generously-sized hallways on the second and third floors, which contain handsome cabinets, antique children's sleighs, duck decoys, quilts, prints of sailing ships, a spinning wheel, and even a basket of washed wool.

I peeked into a few of the spotless guest rooms whose doors were open, and there fluffy comforters, handmade quilts or 100% wool blankets, and Posturepedic mattresses reigned supreme. There are additional rooms in Phoebe's Fantasy, a beautiful Federal house next door, named for Captain Lord's wife. Furnished in much the same manner, it has king- and queen-sized four-posters and canopied beds, antiques, and working fireplaces.

I returned to the kitchen where the guests were all seated around the lovely harvest table, listening to Rick tell his tales and wonderful jokes. There was lots of laughter and appreciative comments about the breakfast of orange juice, fresh homemade breads, muffins, toast, and coffee, and, if desired, a soft-boiled egg.

Being in the hospitality business as long as I have, I begin to appreciate those innkeepers that not only are successful, but give something back to the industry without always looking for a handout. Rick and Bev are always ready and willing to give advice on the telephone to fledgling newcomers or packing a bag to speak at seminars or conferences throughout the U.S. I'm also grateful to them for their advice in my task of updating this book.

THE CAPTAIN LORD MANSION, Box 800, Kennebunkport, ME 04046; 207-967-3141.

A 16-guestroom (private baths) mansion-inn in a seacoast village. All size beds available. Lodgings include breakfast. No other meals served. Open year-round. Near the Rachel Carson Wildlife Refuge, the Seashore Trolley Museum, the Brick Store Museum, and lobster boat tours. Bicycles, hiking, xc skiing, deep-sea fishing, golf, indoor swimming, and tennis nearby. No pets. One house cat in residence. Bev Davis and Rick Litchfield, owners/hosts.

DIRECTIONS: Take Exit 3 (Kennebunk) from the Maine Tpke. Take left on Rte. 35 and follow signs through Kennebunk to Kennebunkport. Take left at traffic light at Sunoco station. Go over drawbridge and take first right onto Ocean Ave., then take fifth left off Ocean Ave. (3/10 mi.). The mansion is in the second block on left. Park behind building and take brick walk to office.

CHARMWOODS
Naples, Maine

Charmwoods is a unique type of inn. Once a private lakefront estate, the inn radiates all the flavor and ambience of the Maine woods but is a mere 2-1/2 hour drive from downtown Boston.

As hosts, Marilyn and Bill Lewis are a perfect combination. Bill, a former editor at the *Boston Globe* and *Boston Herald*, has unusual interests that Charmwoods's guests find to be a pleasant diversion. For example, he often entertains with his 1890 Thomas A. Edison phono-

graph, drawing from a collection of about 500 cylindrical recordings.

Marilyn is vivacious and delights in giving her guests personal attention. Her penchant for decorating is particularly evident in the spacious bedrooms, with their selection of handsome coordinated sheets, blankets, towels, and other accessories in distinctive colors.

The focus of activity at Charmwoods is frequently the commodious and gracious living room, with its massive fieldstone fireplace and panoramic view of lake and mountains. Striking undersea photographs by the Lewises' son, Jonathan, are on display.

Adjoining the living room is a broad deck ideal for a sunny breakfast or for chatting under the stars. A path leads down a few steps to the shoreline of this delightfully clear lake, where a rowboat and canoe are docked in the boathouse. Swimming from the white sandy beach or private sundeck is perfect, and a trim cabana provides numerous amenities, including telephone service.

During my last visit at Charmwoods, nearly all the guests clutched tennis rackets, and the all-weather court saw plenty of play. There is a lakeside golf course and riding stables just a few minutes away.

CHARMWOODS, P.O. Box 217, Naples, ME 04055; 207-693-6798.

A 5-guestroom (private baths) lakefront bed-and-breakfast inn, plus a guest cottage, on the west shore of Long Lake, approx.3/4 hr. from Maine Tpke. Open late June to mid-October. Breakfast included. Variety of outdoor sports on grounds and nearby. Summer playhouse just down the road. No pets. No CCs. Marilyn and Bill Lewis, owners/hosts.

DIRECTIONS: From Boston, follow Rte. 1 north to I-95 and take Exit 8 (Portland-Westbrook). Turn right and follow Riverside St. 1 mi. to Rte. 302. Turn left (west) to Naples, about 30 mi. ahead. Charmwoods is just beyond on the right. From North Conway, NH, follow Rte. 302 through Bridgton. Charmwoods sign and driveway off Rte. 302 just before Naples.

THE COUNTRY CLUB INN
Rangeley, Maine

Rangeley, Maine, is one of those places in the world that has a special kind of charisma. There are few locations that offer such beauty and grandeur in all seasons. The combination of wide skies, vast stretches of mountain woodland, and the placid aspect of Rangeley Lake have been drawing people to this part of western Maine since long before the roads were as passable and numerous as they are today.

Innkeeper Sue Crory of the Country Club Inn says, "The dramatic lake and mountain scenery surrounding us will tranquilize even the most jangled nerves." At an elevation of nearly 2,000 feet, the Country Club Inn offers a magnificent view. Each of the guest rooms has a

picture window, and the dining room and lounge both offer a scenic view of the lake, which reminds me of similar stretches of lake and mountains in certain sections of Scotland—Loch Ness being one. The cathedral-ceilinged living room has heavy beams, wood paneling, and many, many different comfortable sofas, armchairs, and rocking chairs. There are jigsaw puzzles in various states of completion, huge shelves of books, and a great moosehead over one of the fieldstone fireplaces.

Sue elaborated on how they are enjoying being a year-round operation and mentioned the many activities during the summer season—excellent fishing (landlocked salmon and square-tailed trout), hiking the many trails (including the Appalachian Trail, which goes through this area), boating, canoe trips, a swimming pool, and a variety of lawn games. For those who love golf there's a challenging 18-hole public golf course adjacent to the inn. Tennis courts are nearby.

The inn is located in the heart of the northwestern mountains of Maine's ski country, surrounded by Saddleback and Sugarloaf mountains, which offer downhill and cross-country skiing.

THE COUNTRY CLUB INN, P.O. Box 680C, Rangeley, ME 04970; 207-864-3831.

A 19-guestroom (private baths) resort-inn overlooking Rangeley Lake in western Maine, 45 mi. from Farmington. All size beds. Modified American plan. Breakfast and dinner served to travelers by reservation. Open mid-May to mid-Oct. and late Dec. to late March. Near many cultural, historic, scenic, and recreational attractions. Swimming pool, horseshoes, bocci, volleyball, and croquet. A public 18-hole golf course adjacent to the inn. Tennis and lake swimming nearby. Fishing, hiking, and canoeing. Snowmobiling and xc skiing at doorstep. Downhill and xc skiing at Saddleback and Sugarloaf Mts. Two dogs in residence. CCs: Visa, MC, AE. Sue Crory and family, owners/hosts.

DIRECTIONS: From Maine Tpke., take Auburn Exit 12 and follow Rte. 4 to Rangeley. From VT and NH, take I-91 to St. Johnsbury; east on Rte. 2 to Gorham and Rte. 16 north to Rangeley. From Bar Harbor, Rte. 1A to Rte. 2 to Rte. 4. From Montreal, Rte. 10 to Rte. 112 to Rte. 147 to Rte. 114; then Rte. 26 to Rte. 16 to Rte. 4.

DOCKSIDE GUEST QUARTERS
York, Maine

Harriette Lusty and I were having a light luncheon on the porch of the restaurant at Dockside Guest Quarters. It was a day such as I have experienced here many times in the past, watching the wonderful harbor traffic as all kinds of craft make their way through the harbor to the ocean. Even though it had been a very hot day out on I-95, here on this lovely porch there was a wonderful breeze that made even sitting in the sun a joy.

"Oh, we do some very wonderful things here on the Fourth of July," Harriette exclaimed. "We have a thirty-five-foot-long flag with only thirty-seven stars that is brought out, and placed on the lawn, because it is much too large for any flagpole. At noontime we set off our cannon, and all of our staff and their families and friends, as well as our neighbors, come over and stand by. It's really quite a ceremony and we leave one of our postcards at each door, inviting all the guests to come up to the shoot. It takes place right over there by the flagpole. We use that brass one-pounder saluting cannon usually kept in the hallway near the front door. Everybody gets into a wonderful Independence Day mood."

The Dockside Guest Quarters is composed of the original New England homestead of the 1880s, called the Maine House, and four multi-unit cottage buildings of contemporary design, with guest rooms that have their own porches and water views. The three-level restaurant is also separate and overlooks the harbor and marina docks.

The innkeepers are the David Lusty family. David is a real "State of Maine" man, complete with a wonderful Down East accent. The Lustys have raised four sons at Dockside, and now their second son, Eric, and his wife Carol have returned to take a hand in the running of the inn. Third son Philip and his wife Anne have also joined the family business. Philip is the new manager of The Restaurant.

There's always a great deal of Colonial history to share in the York area; the center of town is a National Historic District. This is within a pleasant walking distance of Dockside. Tours are conducted by the York Historical Society. "Our statue of a Civil War Confederate soldier instead of a 'Yankee in Blue' is always an object of curiosity," David told me. "Our Union soldier statue has been located in a small town in South Carolina."

DOCKSIDE GUEST QUARTERS, P.O. Box 205, Harris Island Rd., York, ME 03909; 207-363-2868.

A 21-guestroom (19 private baths; some studio suites with kitchenettes) waterside country inn 10 mi. from Portsmouth, N.H. American plan available. All size beds available. Continental-plus breakfast served to houseguests only. Restaurant serves lunch and dinner to travelers daily except Mon. In May, open Fri. and Sat. only; daily from Memorial Day weekend thru end of Oct. York Village is a National Historic District. Wheelchair access. Lawn games, shuffleboard, badminton, fishing, and whale-watching from premises. Golf, tennis, and ocean swimming nearby; safe and picturesque paths and roadways for walks, bicycling, and jogging. Clipper is their cat in residence. CCs: Visa, MC. Eric, Carol, David, and Harriette Lusty, owners/hosts.

DIRECTIONS: From I-95 (northbound) take exit 4 (last exit before the northbound toll gate at York) to U.S. 1, then south on Rte. 1 to first light. Left at light onto Rte. 1A. Follow 1A thru center of Old York Village, take Rte. 103 (a side street off Rte. 1A leading to the harbor) across York River bridge. First left after crossing bridge and watch for signs to the inn.

THE INN AT HARBOR HEAD

Kennebunkport, Maine

"... surrounded by sea roses, an ocean view and the tang of salt air," said the brochure describing the Inn at Harbor Head. When this sensual description materialized before my mind's eye, I leaned back in my office chair and knew it was time to head for the seaside.

The inn sits on a knoll overlooking Kennebunkport's Cape Porpoise Harbor. The weathered gray of the shingled, rambling old farm house mirrors the soft hues of the rocky, sheltered shoreline. If I were a painter, I would find unlimited material here.

Interestingly enough, I discovered that innkeeper Joan Sutter is an artist who has gone from sculpture to what she calls "wall painting." Her artistic touch can be seen throughout the inn: in the spectacular guest rooms' highly expressive murals; in her refined choice of furnishings; in the subtlety of color.

The inn's seaside cottage ambience encourages a sandals-and-soft-cotton freedom outdoors, yet the interior is sophisticated and elegant. The formal sitting room is appointed with lovely Oriental rugs, a Chinese screen, and a twinkling crystal chandelier. But don't feel restrained by this elegance; just snuggle into a wingback chair and relax.

The five romantic guest rooms have luxurious tiled baths; two have whirlpools. Each is tastefully decorated in a highly individual fashion. I was given the Garden Room, a study in Zen tranquillity. Here Joan has created a serene environment, from the "little river of rocks" that crosses the path to the canopy bed, to her drawings of plum and peach blossoms that seem to float on the wall. Even the spare lines of a twisted pine outside the French doors that open onto a private sun-deck enhance the mood.

Guests have full use of the grounds, the waterfront dock, and the sun-warmed floats. Just ask for a beach permit, grab a fluffy towel and beach chair—and off you go! But before heading out with your suntan lotion and a romance novel under your arm, linger over breakfast. Mine began with with tender poached pears and continued with eggs baked in puff pastry with a perfect, lemony hollandaise sauce.

THE INN AT HARBOR HEAD, Pier Rd., Cape Porpoise, RR2 Box 1180, Kennebunkport, ME 04046; 207-967-5564.

A beautifully decorated 5-guestroom (private baths) home overlooking Cape Porpoise Harbor. King and queen beds. Full breakfast. Closed Thanksgiving and Christmas weeks. No smoking or pets. CCs: Visa, MC, AE. Joan and David Sutter, owner/hosts.

DIRECTIONS: Take Rte. 9 thru Kennebunkport for 2-1/2 mi. to the village of Cape Porpoise. At Wayfarer Restaurant, leave Rte. 9E. Proceed on Pier Rd. 3/10 mi. to inn.

INN EVENTS: JANUARY—Mystery Weekend Treasure Hunt

FEBRUARY—Valentine's Day special

INN ON CARLETON
Portland, Maine

Innkeeper Susan Holland and her competent staff of two sons, Jamin and Will, basset hound Max, and cat Merlin, operate the Inn on Carleton with warmth and enthusiasm. Located in Portland, home of poet Henry Wadsworth Longfellow, the inn is set in the city's historic district. The brick Victorian was built as a "spec" house in 1869.

Susan's avocation as a restoration bookbinder created a need for a location in downtown Portland where she could establish a bindery, and she bought the Inn on Carleton in 1988. Plans for a B&B were

scheduled for some time in the future. "But when I saw the property," she told me, "I decided to just do it now!" Although the inn takes up the majority of her time, Susan is happy to show guests her downstairs bindery, where she restores old books and designs new bindings.

The common rooms and guest rooms are simple, yet comfortable, mostly furnished with Victorian antiques. The front parlor has a lovely bay window, and the steady tick-tock of the grandfather clock is calming. The guest rooms are large. While only three rooms have private baths, all rooms have access to full baths, complete with claw-foot tubs. Breakfast is served family style in the dining room.

After Jamin and Will were securely ensconced at the kitchen sink doing the breakfast dishes, Susan invited, "Come and join me in the bindery. You can watch me 'round and back' a book." My curiosity got the best of me, and I decided that Longfellow could wait a few more hours.

INN ON CARLETON, 46 Carleton St., Portland, ME 04102; 207-775-1910.

A 7-guestroom (3 private baths) brick Victorian townhouse in the seaside town of Portland. Queen, double and twin beds. Open all year; 2-night minimum stay on weekends July–Oct. Full breakfast. Close to seasonal sports and shopping. No smoking or pets. One dog and cat in residence. CCs: Visa, MC, Dis. Susan Holland, owner/host.

DIRECTIONS: Take Rte. 295 toward Portland. Take Exit 5A for Congress St. Follow Congress approx. 1 mi. Go right on Neal St. for 2 blks., then left on West St. Go 1 blk., then left on Carleton.

THE MAINE STAY INN & COTTAGES
Kennebunkport, Maine

"Just what is a flying staircase?" I asked Carol Copeland, owner of the Maine Stay. She offered a visual explanation and led me to an ornately carved, suspended spiral staircase. It's just one of this inn's unusual features. Others include a fainting couch, sunburst crystal glass windows, carved fireplace mantels, and a sizable cupola, the third story watchtower over the inn's two stories of block Italianate design.

In 1983, when the floors were lifted to install insulation, old newspapers, artifacts, and other historical remnants were found tucked in the attic eaves. All this evidence supportd what was known of the building's history: that The Maine Stay was built around 1860 by Melville Walker as a family dwelling, was sold in 1891, and underwent major renovations in the early 1900s under the direction of George Little, its owner at that time. It was not until 1941 that the house was dubbed "The Maine Stay," and the owners, the Eldridges, began to

rent rooms. Title to the old house passed several more times, and the
house was placed in the National Register of Historic Places in 1976.
Current owners Carol and Lindsay Copeland purchased The Maine
Stay in April 1989.

Carol showed me the living room, which is graced with sparkling
crystal chandeliers and a deeply colored carpet. The wingback chairs
invited me to settle in with a good book and warm myself by the fire.

"I think you'll be happy with your choice of this two-room suite,"
Carol said, leading the way. It had a comfortable sitting area framed by
a large picture window. A four-poster bed, draped overhead by a white
ruffled canopy, furnished the bedroom. Tiny pink roses were lined up
symmetrically on the off-white wallpaper.

From the open window, I heard the tapping of a croquet mallet hit-
ting the wooden ball and saw two guests engaged in a friendly game on
the lush carpeting of lawn. Beyond were several of the eleven cottages
which are part of the inn. All have full kitchens, and some have fireplaces and knotty pine wood panelling.

Guests are treated to a full breakfast on the weekends, formally
served at the two tables in the dining room. A more casual continen-
tal-style morning meal is set out during the week. If you are staying in
a cottage, front-door delivery of a breakfast basket can be arranged.

Carol and her husband Lindsay both spent their childhoods in
nearby Massachusetts; as adults, they relocated to the west coast to
pursue careers in the banking industry. With the arrival of two daughters and increasing weariness of their high-stress careers, they longed

to be closer to family. Owning a bed and breakfast inn gave them a way to support their return to the east coast and also to achieve the simplified lifestyle they desired.

THE MAINE STAY INN & COTTAGES, 34 Maine St., P.O. Box 500A, Kennebunkport, ME 04046; 207-967-2117.

A 6-guestroom (private baths) main house and 11 cottages with full kitchens located in heart of the Historic District. Queen, double, and twin beds. Open year round. Minimum weekend stays. Restricted smoking. Easy hike to beach, shopping, or restaurants. No pets. CCs: Visa, MC, AE. Carol and Lindsay Copeland, owners/hosts.

DIRECTIONS: Exit #3 off I-95 and left onto Rte. 35. Turn left on Rte. 9, cross over a bridge, then right onto Main St.

THE NEWCASTLE INN

Newcastle, Maine

A bright green awning accents the entrance to this beautiful white clapboard Federal-style Colonial. Built in the 1800s as a Cape carriage house, the structure began its life as an inn during the 1930s. It is a classic New England country inn, just what Ted and Chris Sprague were looking for when they began their search in 1985.

"I'd become a bit disenchanted with teaching," Ted confided to me, "yet I still wanted a career where I could have a positive influence on others. Innkeeping offers that opportunity." After two years and many hours spent in research, on seminars, consultants, and visits to over one hundred inns, they ended up on Newcastle's stoop.

Ted and I were relaxing in lawn chairs under a towering backyard shade tree. The yard edges up to the banks of the Damariscotta River, a tidal river met by the sea, and the pristine sands of Pemaquid Beach.

"Chris is a natural at this (innkeeping)," he continued, with obvious pride. "She grew up working in her father's gourmet grocery and knows good food."

Chris' award winning recipes may be sampled at breakfast and dinner, both of which are included in your room rate. In the morning, the sunlight illuminates the tones of the dining room's quarter-sawn yellow pine floors and the room just seems to glow. Breakfast includes a special homebaked bread, juice, fresh fruit and entrée. Just imagine the heady aroma of spicy gingerbread still warm from the oven! Entrees may include an egg dish, Grand Marnier French toast, fluffy lemon zest pancakes, or bread and butter pudding. Ham or country sausage accompanies your entrée.

Complimentary hors d'oeuvres are served prior to dinner. The inn has a full liquor license and offers beers, imported ales, and a variety of wines. The five-course dinner is elegant yet simple, and a real delight. Served on lovely botanical-patterned china, the menu changes with Chris' whim, and the seasons. When I visited, George's Greek lamb with kaseri cheese was the evening's special.

After dinner I took my hefty slice of apple almond-cream pie into the common room. This room's unique stenciled floor is a sample of Chris' artistry, as are the pieces of intricate crewelwork and needlepoint displayed throughout the inn.

There are two other comfortable areas for relaxation: the more formal fireplace-warmed living room, and the wicker furnished glassed and screened-in porch, a popular gathering spot during the spring and summer.

The inn's spacious hallways and staircases give way to the fifteen intimate second and third floor guest rooms. Traditional Colonial colors appear in wallpapers, borders, and bed coverings. Some rooms have canopied beds and all have private, modern bathrooms. My room, as do many of the others, had windows facing the river.

The Newcastle Inn offers seclusion, an unhurried schedule, excellent food, and charming innkeepers in Ted and Chris. They certainly made the right career change.

THE NEWCASTLE INN, River Road, Newcastle, ME 04553; 207-563-5685.

A 16-guestroom (private baths) traditional New England country inn on the Damariscotta River. Open year-round. All sized beds. Modified American plan. Swimming, fishing, boating, bird watching, antiquing nearby. No smoking. No pets. CCs: Visa, MC. Chris and Ted Sprague, owners/hosts.

DIRECTIONS: In Maine take Rte. 95 north to Rte. 1 Exit (Bath/Brunswick). Go 7 mi. north of Wiscasset. Watch for Inn sign on right; go right on River Rd.

INN EVENTS: FEBRUARY 14–15—Valentine Weekend
MARCH, MIDDLE—Cooking with Chris
MAY—birding

JUNE—Monhegan Adventure
JUNE—hiking
JULY—Symphony Weekend
NOVEMBER—Thanksgiving Celebration
DECEMBER 25–27—Christmas Weekend

181 MAIN STREET BED & BREAKFAST
Freeport, Maine

"We got the old roof ripped off just in time to enjoy the first snowfall
of the season...from inside the house!" said Ed Hassett, co-owner of
181 Main Street with his longtime friend, David Cates. After two
years of searching through seven eastern states, Ed and David finally
settled on the rundown 1840 Greek Revival cape house in Freeport for
three reasons: it was the right vintage; even in its decayed condition, it
had obvious potential and lots of room; and, most important, it was situated along Route 1, Maine's major tourist highway. Ed left behind a
New York career of working with the mentally handicapped, and
David his combined careers of college professor and air flight atten-
dant, and they moved into the house one chilly day in 1986 to under-
take renovation from the inside out. Ed oversaw most of the manual
labor, while David picked out wallcoverings, color schemes, and decor
from stacks of samples at his bedside. Then, combining their personal
collections of antique furniture, paintings, and rugs to furnish the
seven-guest room inn, they opened for business in July 1987.

The cape house is connected to an ell and a barn, typical of homes
of the era. The gray wood siding is trimmed in white and black, sur-

rounded by shrubs and flower gardens. There's a backyard swimming pool for the warm season, and an outdoor grill available for guest use. David displays his culinary talents with an endless breakfast variety of homemade breads and muffins, poached pears with yogurt and strawberry sauce, or Belgian waffles.

The kitchen, located in the ell that connects the house and barn, definitely had a country look with pine cabinets, a beamed ceiling, and beige print wallpaper that matches the tile floor. Nearby are two dining rooms, where hand-hooked rugs provide spots of color on the refinished wide-plank floor. There are seven tables, allowing private dining space to accommodate each room's guests. Oil paintings grace the walls.

Both parlors have comfortable wing-backed chairs and camel-back sofas accented in reds, greens, and blues. Lots of books and magazines are stacked about.

A white-bannistered staircase leads to the second floor landing. When I admired the quilt on the antique bed in my room, David told me his mother had made quilts for each of the guest rooms. Mine appeared to have been made from a collection of fabric scraps which blend together into a collage of color. A massive dresser with an ornately carved mirror covers one wall of this room. A wing-backed chair with a reading lamp is tucked in the corner. Sunlight, filtering through sheer window coverings, cast shadows on the flower-printed wallpaper.

The inn is only a five-minute walk to the famous L.L. Bean outlet in downtown Freeport.

---

181 MAIN STREET BED & BREAKFAST, 181 Main St., Freeport, ME 04032; 207-865-1226.

Intimate 7-guestroom bed & breakfast on one acre with swimming pool. Open all year. Breakfast included. Queen and double beds. No smoking. Walking distance to Freeport. Drive to ocean, parks, and historic sights. No pets. CCs: Visa, MC. Ed Hassett and David Cates, owners/hosts.

DIRECTIONS: Exit 20 off I-95 to Main Street (US Rte. 1).

RANGELEY INN

Rangeley, Maine

Coming into the town of Rangeley, perched on scenic Rangeley Lake, I thought the big blue clapboard building with the long veranda across the front had the look of one of those grand old summer hotels.

Meeting Fay and Ed Carpenter in the roomy lobby with its country-print wallpaper and comfortable wing chairs and sofas, I had an immediate feeling of warmth and friendliness. I was not surprised to discover they had earned an Innkeeper of the Year award. "We've found innkeeping to be a very rewarding career," Ed told me. "We really enjoy getting to know our guests with all their varied backgrounds and interests."

Looking through some of the comments and letters from their guests, I realized that their cuisine played an important part in the overall picture. "Our daughter Sue is responsible for making our kitchen one of the finest in Maine," Fay said. "She's self-taught, and there just isn't anything she can't do." "That's absolutely true," Ed broke in, "I never cease to be amazed by how creative she is with her seasonings, garnishes, textures, and taste."

I had the opportunity to sample Sue's cooking, and it was indeed a pleasure. I tried the sole Victoria, which was stuffed with crabmeat, shrimp, cream cheese, finely chopped vegetables, and wrapped in phyllo dough. Some other interesting entrées with blueberry chicken, sautéed in fresh blueberries, blueberry schnapps, and spices, and lemon grass shrimp, prepared with garlic, ginger, sliced carrots, scallions, snow peas, peppers, water chestnuts, and lemon grass.

The dining room, with its high ceiling and many windows, has an elegant but informal atmosphere. The dining tables were carefully laid with china and stem-ware on double rose tablecloths. The fresh flowers and candlelight added a note of romance.

"That's a beautiful antique ceiling," I exclaimed, looking up at the peach-colored, ornate pressed tin admiringly.

"I'll tell you a secret, I put that ceiling up myself," Ed replied, with refreshing candor.

I think refreshing candor may be the keynote of this inn. Ed and Fay and their two daughters, Sue, who is the chef, and Janet, who served me breakfast with a most infectious smile, have a straightforward, friendly manner that puts everyone at ease.

The guest rooms are simply furnished with country-print wallpapers and various-sized beds. Fay told me that some of the rooms still have the old clawfooted, cast-iron "soakers." "We've started to add the old-fashioned shower heads and duck curtains." There are additional motel-style rooms in a separate building, which looked very clean and comfortable.

Ed showed me around the several acres of lawn and garden bordering on Haley Pond, a bird sanctuary. Not only are there ducks, Canada geese, and herons, but at the moment, Ed tells me, they have two pairs of loons.

RANGELEY INN, P.O. Box 398, Main St., Rangeley, ME 04970; 207-864-3341 or 5641.

A 51-guestroom (private baths) village inn and motor lodge on the eastern shore of Rangeley Lake in western Maine. Breakfast and dinner served daily; limited dining in early Dec. and late spring. Wheelchair access. Summer events such as Blueberry Festival and Fiddlers' Contest and evening entertainment, also pool table and board games on premises. Guided canoe trips, dogsled races, and all the summer and winter activities of lake and mountain areas. No pets. One cat in residence. Limited smoking. Fay and Ed Carpenter, owners/hosts.

DIRECTIONS: From Maine Tpke. take Auburn Exit 12 and follow Rte. 4 to Rangeley. From NH Rte. 2, take Rte. 16 north to Rangeley. Inn is at southern end of village on Rte. 4 (Main St.).

INN EVENTS: FEBRUARY 14—Valentine's Day Dinner and Ball
MARCH—last sled dog race & Musher's Ball
JUNE—grand opening of "Oscar's Outdoor Cafe"
JULY EARLY—Outdoor Fiddler's Contest
DECEMBER 31—New Year's Eve Celebration & Dance

THE SQUIRE TARBOX INN
Westport Island, Maine

Karen Mitman and I were walking through the woods behind the Squire Tarbox Inn toward Squam Creek. We were two people being escorted by seven lively, handsome Nubian goats in various shades of brown and beige. It being June, we passed through patches of buttercups and lupine, and our group occasionally paused while one of the goats decided to nibble.

"Come on, Garbo," Karen called. "We call her Garbo because she thinks she's kind of dramatic. We arrived at the serene saltwater inlet that has a little dock and a screened-in shed for just sitting and looking through the binoculars provided. A rowboat waits patiently for the energetic guest.

"Most of our guests are from the city, and it's just nice for them to

come here and sit. The combination of the water, the sky, the clouds, the little marshy island, and the trees offers a special quiet privacy."

The Squire Tarbox is in a section of Maine that is sufficiently off the beaten track to be unspoiled and natural. The main house has both the wainscoting of the early 1800s and the rustic wide-board construction of the 1700s. It is quite small—eleven guest rooms have a cozy "up country" feeling with Colonial prints and colors and some working fireplaces. A large hearth with the original bake oven, pumpkin pine floors, and hand-hewn beams set the tone for this rambling Colonial farmhouse.

There are several choices for sitting around in front of fireplaces to enjoy reading or conversation, especially in a captivating three-story barn with large doors that open out on a screened-in sundeck. There is a player piano, an antique music box, Colonial wooden toys, and English wooden puzzles for further amusement.

Karen and her husband, Bill, are very friendly, conversational people, who make innkeeping seem almost deceptively simple. Their background at the Copley Plaza in Boston must have much to do with this.

Karen and I sat in the little shed and continued our conversation while the goats cavorted on the pine needles. "I know you remember when we brought in our first goats," she said. "We were a little hesitant, but they have been a most rewarding experience for our guests. Now we have a new cheesemaking room and have packaged some goat cheese for sale to our guests. The cheese is served every night before dinner as well. Dinner is at seven o'clock in an intimate Colonial dining room and usually begins with a soup that could be made with fresh fruit or vegetables. The second course is a salad, and the main course is usually local fish or chicken or an occasional roast, always served with three vegetables that reflect some creative thinking, such as mint-glazed carrots, cranberries with red cabbage, or spinach with cheese and pasta. One of the most popular desserts is a chocolate concoction known as the Squire's 'Sin Pie.'"

THE SQUIRE TARBOX INN, Westport Island, R.D. 2, Box 620, Wiscasset, ME 04578; 207-882-7693.

An 11-guestroom (private baths) restored Colonial farm midway between Boston and Bar Harbor on Rte. 144 in Westport, 10 mi. from Wiscasset. All size beds available. Modified American plan—includes continental breakfast and full leisurely dinner. Open late May to late Oct. Within a 30-min. drive of L.L. Bean, beaches, harbors, shops, and museums of midcoast Maine. Eleven animal pets outside. CCs: Visa, MC, AE, Dis. Bill and Karen Mitman, owners/hosts.

DIRECTIONS: From Maine Tpke., take Exit 9 and follow Rte. 95 to Exit 22 (Brunswick, ME). Take Rte. 1 to Rte. 144, 7 mi. north of Bath. Follow Rte. 144 for 8-1/2 mi. to inn.

THE WATERFORD INNE
Waterford, Maine

"There is no textbook definition of a country inn," Barbara Vanderzanden exclaimed. "We are in the country—not located in a town; we are historic—built in 1825; and we are small—ten rooms, and a mother-daughter team does it all. I believe our guests really love us because our inn is small and intimate, since it is a converted family home. When they say they feel like an honored guest in our home we know we've succeeded."

Rosalie, Barbara's mother, added, "We frequently have guests comment on how clean everything is." We were sitting on the porch enjoying the view.

What they failed to mention was their constant attention to detail and their guests' comfort.

My eye happened to travel to what was one of the most sumptuous-looking vegetable gardens I have ever seen, and it prompted a question: "What are some of the things that you grow in your own garden for your kitchen?"

"Well, we grow practically all our own herbs," explained Rosalie, who is the cook. "We like fresh herbs in the salad dressing. We also have tomatoes, brussels sprouts, broccoli, peppers, squash, and pumpkins."

"We serve tenderloin of beef with béarnaise, shrimp Pernod, and various veal and pork dishes as entrées. Dinner is fixed-price every evening for both houseguests and visitors. We do all our own baking, and our guests seem to enjoy it very much."

At the Waterford Inne, located in the little-known Oxford Hills area of western Maine, "small and tidy" is beautiful. Merely an hour northwest of of Portland, it's a region of rolling countryside, pristine lakes, active streams and rivers, farms and forests. To city-dwellers looking for an escape from congestion, noise and bustle, it's a paradise. The pace is slower, with no freeways and very few traffic lights. There are no shopping malls here, although the shopping havens of Freeport and North Conway, just across the New Hampshire border, are less then an hour's drive away.

All of the bedrooms have been carefully decorated, usually with some theme in mind. For example, the Chesapeake Room has a fireplace stove and a private porch. The decorations are in the Eastern Shore theme, with duck decoys and waterfowl. Even the sheets and towels have colorful waterfowl on them. The Nantucket room, complete with whaling prints and harpoon; the Strawberry room, bright with red accessories; the Safari room with...well I'll let you wait and see—all of the rooms have either antiques or attractive country furniture.

THE WATERFORD INNE, Box 149, Waterford, ME 04233; 207-583-4037.

A 10-guestroom (7 private baths) farmhouse-inn in the Oxford Hills section of southwest Maine, 8 mi. from Norway and South Paris. All size beds available. Closed March, April, and Thanksgiving week. Breakfast and dinner served to travelers by reservation. European plan. Within a short distance of many recreational, scenic, and cultural attractions in Maine and the White Mountains of New Hampshire. Cross-country skiing and badminton on grounds. Lake swimming, golf, rock hunting, downhill skiing, hiking, canoeing nearby. Alcoholic beverages not served. Well-behaved pets welcome; however, advance notification is required and a fee is charged. Two cats in residence. CCs: AE. Rosalie and Barbara Vanderzanden, owners/hosts.

DIRECTIONS: From Maine Tpke.: use Exit 11, follow Rte. 26 north approx. 28 mi. into Norway, then on Rte. 118 west for 8 mi. to Rte. 37 south (left turn). Go 1/2 mi., turn right at Springer's General Store, up the hill 1/2 mi. From Conway, NH: Rte 16 to Rte. 302 east to Fryeburg, ME. Take Rte. 5 out of Fryeburg to Rte. 35 south, thence to Rte. 118, which is a left fork (with Rte. 35 going right). Continue on Rte. 118 east, past Papoose Pond camping area, then watch for right turn onto Rte. 37. Go 1/2 mi. to Springer's General Store. Take immediate right turn, 1/2 mi. up hill.

THE WHITE BARN
Kennebunkport, Maine

A welcome and an "excellent table" have greeted the guests at The White Barn Inn since 1880 when it operated as a popular Boothby boardinghouse. Settled in a residential area, the luxurious inn and renowned restaurant are just a short stroll from the beach and charming township of Kennebunkport.

Kennebunkport is a post-card Maine village. Rustic fishing boats, with barnacled hulls, lobster pots, gliding seagulls, and Victorian, shingled cottages settle compatibly with art galleries and fashionable boutiques.

In 1988, Laurie Bongiorno and Laurie Cameron purchased the property, completely renovating and restoring the old inn. Both Lauries, husband and wife, embraced the project well prepared from outstanding careers in the hospitality industry.

The original industry was erected in the 1840s. As farming became secondary to housing guests, annexes and wings were added. The gatehouses and cottage were built in the early 1900s.

"We really were adamant about preserving the character sensitive to the inn," the male Laurie told me. "We wanted to meet the expectations of our guests with decor in keeping with the period of the furnishings, unique art work, and little touches that create individual, personable service."

Those little touches, like fresh flowers from the inn's floral cutting gardens, and homemade sweets on the pillow, appear throughout the guest rooms.

The rooms within the main inn are cozy and quaint with coordinated fabrics and wall coverings, accenting the New England period furnishings. All rooms have private baths stocked with fluffy bathrobes and scented toiletries.

Queen Anne furnishings highlight the elegant gatehouse suites. Plump overstuffed chairs, fireplaces, king-sized, four-poster beds, and

roomy, marble bathrooms with whirlpools and separate showers, offer the ultimate in pampering and comfort.

Besides the expansive, open air front porch, where afternoon tea is served in the summer, the inn has four living rooms. Guests can read, sample complimentary brandy and port or, in the chilly months, sidle up to a roaring fire for tea and conversation.

The inn's exceptional New England cooking can be enjoyed in the main dining room contained within two restored barns or in the more traditional dining room of the main house.

Featuring exposed wood walls, a soaring three story ceiling, views to the woods, and a lively piano bar, the barns beckoned to me. Candles played soft shadows on the polished, plank pine floors as I studied the menu, which changes weekly, to provide guests with the freshest seasonal produce and fish.

I started with an appetizer of bacon-wrapped sea scallops in an unusual maple mustard cream. The scallops, melt-in-the-mouth juicy; the mustard, tart yet maple sweet, was just the right accompaniment to my entrée, Lightly Grilled Native Salmon. Perfectly grilled it was, with a dollop of salmon roe, morel sauce and crisp-steamed asparagus tips. A glass of California Chardonnay completed my enjoyment. All dinners include a lovely, composed salad or delicately flavored sorbet. A variety of desserts are available.

Included in the room rate, a hearty continental breakfast is served in the breakfast room. Lots of chintz and lace curtains create a cheerful morning environment.

Miles of wooded trails can be explored pedalling bicycles complimentary from the inn, or hike the extensive nature preserve of the Kennebunks. I spent one whole afternoon wandering the gardens of the sixty-acre monastery directly across the street from the inn.

The White Barn is romantic, relaxing, and a gastronomic pleasure

---

THE WHITE BARN INN, P.O. Box 560C, Beach Street, Kennebunkport, ME, 04046; 207-967-2321. A 24-room New England country inn & restaurant on the rugged Maine coast. Private bath, all size beds. Suites with fireplaces and whirlpool baths. Hearty continental breakfast included. Dinners available, dinner jackets requested for gentlemen guests. Two night minimum weekend and holiday stays. Smoking restricted. Not suitable for children under 12. Walk to beach, galleries, boutiques and antique shops. Bicycle and hiking trails & gardens. No pets allowed. CCs: AE, MC, V. Laurie Bongiorno & Laurie Cameron, owners/hosts.

DIRECTIONS: From northbound I-95, take Exit 2, Ogunquit/Wells. Follow Rte.9 east to Rte.35. Turn right on Beach St. Inn located 1/4 mi. on the right. From south I-95, take Exit 3, to Kennebunk. Follow Rte.35 south 5 mis. to Rte. 9. intersection. Continue straight onto Beach St. Watch for inn on right.

Penobscot Bay and Acadia National Park

EVENTS

JANUARY–MARCH (SUNDAYS)	Blue Hill Winter Chamber Music Concerts (info: 207-374-2161)
MARCH (LAST SUNDAY)	maple sugarhouses statewide open doors to public (info: 207-289-3491)
APRIL	Kenduskeag Stream Canoe Races, Bangor (info: 207-942-9000)
JUNE–AUGUST	Surry Opera (info: 207-667-9551)
JULY 4	lobsterboat races, Jonesport (info: 207-497-2804)
JULY, LATE	Belfast Bay Festival (info: 207-338-2896)
JULY	Full Circle Fair, Blue Hill (info: 207-374-2313)
JULY	Camden Art Festival
JULY–AUGUST (SUNDAYS)	Kneisel Chamber Music Concerts, Blue Hill (info: 207-374-2811)
AUGUST, MIDDLE	Blueberry Festival, Machias (for info, write: Blueberry Festival Committee, Machias ME 04654)
AUGUST	Blue Hill Days (info: 207-374-2281)
AUGUST	Rockland Lobster Festival
AUGUST	Union Antique Show
OCTOBER, EARLY	Fall Festival, Camden (info: 207-236-4404)
NOVEMBER, MIDDLE	Down East Jazz Festival, Rockport (info: 207-594-7374)
DECEMBER, EARLY	Christmas Week with open houses and concerts, Blue Hill (info: 207-374-2844)
DECEMBER	Christmas by the Sea, Camden

SIGHTS

Acadia National Park

Farnsworth Art Museum, Rockland (info: 207-596-6457)

Haystack Mountain School of Crafts

Holbrook Island Sanctuary

Isle Au Haut

Owls Head Transportation Museum (info: 207-594-4418)

Penobscot Marine Museum

Wooden Boat School

BAY LEDGE INN & SPA

Bar Harbor, Maine

The brochure read "A unique fitness retreat", and that it was. Tucked
away on three wooded acres fronting the Atlantic Ocean on Mt.
Desert Island, Bay Ledge is definitely not your typical health resort.
From dense pine forests, ragged cliffs drop down to gravel beaches.

Soaking in the bubbling warm waters of the outdoor jacuzzi and
gazing out over the expansive ocean view, I had no reason to refute the
claim. I was participating in the fitness adventure program, which is
available between November and June each year. I had come to work

off those extra holiday pounds, and was actually having fun doing it! Owner Dee Srinivasan promotes a program of whole health. Boredom was not a problem with an exercise agenda, both on and off the property, offering brisk hikes on the beach, water aerobics in the outdoor pool, rock climbing, kayaking, mountain biking, ice skating, tennis, and cross-country skiing. For indoor types, there is a weight room with plenty of individual instruction.

Upon arrival, each of the six fitness adventure participants—no more are allowed—is evaluated and a personal program designed for his or her level of fitness. No failure here. The three nutritious meals included with the program proved to be appetizing and filling. I always ended my day with a long soak in the jacuzzi, some meditative time in the sauna, or a deep-tissue massage. A variety of seminars on stress reduction, personal power, and inner body cleansing are offered in the evening hours.

During one of our evening walks, Dee told me that Bay Ledge was built in the early 1900s as a farmhouse. In the 1940s it became a motel, so Dee and her husband Lucky were able to utilize their background in real estate construction and covert it to an inn upon their purchase in 1986. The weathered-shingle cottage, trimmed in forest green and dark grey with black shutters, blends well into the three acres of natural landscaping.

There are only ten plush guest rooms available year-round, and three efficiency cottages, which are closed during the winter months. My room, on the second floor, had a peaceful view of the Atlantic from an old rocking chair. The four-poster feather bed had a goose down duvet, and the floral print throw pillows along the headboard matched the cornice above the window. I had been lucky enough to get one of the two rooms that have a jacuzzi tub in the adjacent bath. A personal touch was the fluffy bathrobe hung on the back of the door.

A toasty fire in the second floor sitting room combated the chilly ocean breeze sweeping through the trees. The living room, on the first floor, has a large brick fireplace flanked by natural wicker chairs. Breakfast might include quiche, strata, delicious crepes with fruit or cheese fillings, sweetbreads or muffins. Lunches are available, but are not included with the room.

Guests staying during the spring and summer months have full use of the fitness facilities. A short drive to Bar Harbor offers shopping and sight-seeing. Acadia National Forest provides many hiking trails.

BAY LEDGE INN & SPA, 1385 Sand Point Road, Bar Harbor, ME 04609; 207-288-4204 or 800-848-6885.

10-guestroom (private baths) B&B with spa, unlike any other overlooking the Atlantic above Bar Harbor. Open all year. Breakfast included with room. Three cottages available during warmer months. Limited facilities for children, please call ahead. Fitness Program offered Nov.-May by advance reservation. All meals included as well as instruction. Pool, hot tubs, sauna, massage available. Plenty of Inn activities available, or Acadia National Park and Bar Harbor nearby. No pets. CCs: Visa, MC, AE. Dee and Lucky Srinivasan, owners/hosts.

DIRECTIONS: Rte. 1A to Rte. 3 to Bar Harbor. Turn left at signs for Sand Point. Bear right and follow to water.

THE BLUE HILL INN
Blue Hill, Maine

This home of dignified brick and clapboard was built in 1830, and was converted to a village inn ten years later. I was standing on the front lawn, admiring the lovely Federal-style architecture, and counting the many chimneys, when innkeeper Donald Hartley came around the corner with a load of wood. "Good afternoon!" he said. "I see you're here for our sailing excursion." I was excited about the day sails arranged for guests aboard the 50-foot New England pinky schooner *Summertime*, but didn't realize my new white deck shoes would be such a giveaway.

Donald told me more about the inn's history as we entered the front hallway. "We've celebrated its sesquicentennial in 1990, as a matter of fact. The inn has been in continuous operation now for 150 years." I also learned that the inn's wonderful granite foundation had been quarried locally, and that the inn is listed on the National Register of Historic Places.

Mary and Donald Hartley, prior to their careers as innkeepers, were both active in the management of community-based programs for the developmentally and mentally disabled. "The inn offers us the opportunity to meet and enjoy people, and to broaden our span of skills," Mary explained, as she readied the tray of scrumptious-looking hors d'oeuvres for the nightly innkeepers' reception. The reception is held in the two cozy parlors, or the perienaill garden where cocktails, wine, and soft drinks are available.

The inn's common rooms, dining room, and eleven guest rooms are decorated with 19th-century furnishings. The parlors offer comfortable easy chairs and couches grouped around attractive, working fireplaces. Oriental carpets accent polished wood floors, and colorful print wallpapers contrast with crisp, white trims. Many of the guest rooms have fireplaces, and all have private baths, some with old-fashioned tubs.

New to the Inn is an 1850 pump melodian, a hammock for the garden and packages with a pinky schooner for a day of sailing and overnight aboard.

When Mary and Don took over the inn, they made it a priority to provide the most wonderful food possible and hired a new chef de cuisine who specializes in contemporary foods prepared with classical French techniques.

When I returned, feeling like an old salt with an enormous appetite, the aromas were even more tantalizing. Dinner is served by candlelight and includes six courses, beginning with homemade soup. I was served a subtle chicken and lentil finished with chive broth. My entrée of sea scallops and spinach and mushrooms with tomato-basil coulis was melt-in-the-mouth tender. A sorbet was offered to clear the palate before a crisp, colorful salad of watercress and tomatoes dressed with walnut vinaigrette was served. A slice of rich flourless chocolate torte with a dollop of coffee cream made me wish I had room for seconds, but I knew morning would bring a full breakfast.

The Blue Hill Inn is in the center of the village, so galleries, antique shops, and fine stores are within walking distance. A weekly concert series takes place all summer at Kneisel Hall, and the famous Haystack School of Crafts is only a short drive away. In the winter, Blue Hill Mountain has cross-country skiing and snowshoeing. But I think I'll stick to the water, and keep my deck shoes handy. Maybe I'll even add a captain's hat next year!

THE BLUE HILL INN, P.O. Box 403, Blue Hill, ME 04614; 207-374-2844.
An 11-guestroom (private baths) historic inn located in the center of the village of Blue Hill. All-size beds. Open year-round. Modified American plan, and B&B rates. Wonderful food. Water sports, music festivals, and Acadia National Park nearby. No pets. Smoking not permitted. Mary and Donald Hartley, owners/hosts.

DIRECTIONS: From Augusta, take Exit 95. Take Rte. 3 south of Belfast, through Bucksport; 2 mi. east of Bucksport, take Rte. 15 south to Blue Hill. From Bangor, take Rte. 5 south. From Ellsworth, take Rte. 172 west.

INN EVENTS: FEBRUARY—Wine Dinner Weekend

MAY—Wine Dinner Weekend

MAY—Stress Reduction Weekend

MAY—Artist-Gallery Talks

JUNE—Pinky Schooner Sails

JULY–AUGUST (SUNDAYS)—complimentary tickets for Kneisel Hall Chamber Concerts

NOVEMBER, EARLY—Wine Dinner Weekend

DECEMBER, EARLY—Open House and Concerts

DECEMBER 24–25—horse-drawn sleigh rides, tree trimming

DECEMBER 31—sleigh rides

THE CROCKER HOUSE COUNTRY INN

Hancock Point, Maine

Finding a beguiling, secluded place for an overnight stay on a trip to Canada via U.S. 1 would delight many a weary traveler. And it could be the perfect solution for those who enjoy the activity and excitement of Bar Harbor, Acadia National Park, and Blue Hill, but also want a quiet hideaway nearby. On Hancock Point, three minutes from the ocean, the Crocker House Country Inn is all of the above.

The entrance leads into a living room that is electric, to say the least, with good comfortable old wicker furniture, a big window seat, some rather striking modern primitive paintings, a very handsome rug of Indian design, a backgammon set, and lots of growing plants. At the very moment I walked in I was greeted with a flute concerto by Jean Pierre Rampal wafting from the stereo. It all seemed quite casual and quite natural.

The guest rooms are bright and cheerful. Almost all of them have been redecorated and some have stenciling on the upper walls. They are large enough to accommodate two people very comfortably.

Innkeeper Richard Malaby told me a little bit about the past history of this part of Maine. "Hancock was once a thriving shipbuilding community and also the terminus of the Washington, D.C., to Bar Harbor express train. It was the port from which the famed Sullivan Quarry shipped its cobblestones to pave the streets of Boston, New York, and Philadelphia. I'm afraid that the Crocker House is a lone survivor of those days of the past."

One might expect the dinner menu to consist of good hearty upcountry Maine food; therefore, I was quite surprised to find some international dishes such as poached salmon Florentine, gray sole meuniére, and veal Monterey, which I ordered. It was very thinly sliced veal, sautéed in Madeira with avocado and tomato and topped with Monterey jack cheese. The menu also had filet au poivre, scallops in sorrel and cream, broiled swordfish, broiled halibut Dijon, and other treasures from the sea.

———

THE CROCKER HOUSE COUNTRY INN, Hancock Point, ME 04640; 207-422-6806.

A 10-guestroom (private baths) secluded country inn about 8 mi. north of Ellsworth, ME. Queen, double amd twin beds. Breakfast and dinner served daily. Open from May 1 to Thanksgiving. Bicycles and dock moorings available for guests. Tennis, swimming, and walking nearby. Just 30 min. from Mount Desert Island, Acadia National Park, and Bar Harbor. Blue Hill and the east Penobscot peninsula easily accessible. Richard Malaby, owner/host.

DIRECTIONS: Follow Rte. 1 approx. 8 mi. north from Ellsworth. Turn right at sign for Hancock Point and continue approx. 5 mi.

DARK HARBOR HOUSE
Island of Isleboro, Maine

———

I called one of my more adventurous friends and told him I was travelling his way to review some inns on Maine's Island of Isleboro.

"Oh, wait, wait! Hold on a minute." The receiver clunked in my ear. A few seconds later, he returned to the phone.

"Dark Harbor House," he spurted excitedly between breaths. "You

just have to stay at Dark Harbor House. I've got this great book by Louise Rich, a 1950s classic. She writes about the swimming in a pool right across from the Dark Harbor House!"

I still wasn't sharing his level of excitement. So he went on, "Listen, I'll read it to you: 'That was the only place north of Portland that I ever had comfortable ocean swimming...the water is always at the same level, always calm, and always warmed by the sun.' Sound delightful? Ocean water that's warm and calm!"

Apparently this natural condition is due to a hanged gate that separates the pool from the sea. It opens when the tide comes in, and closes when it ebbs, leaving the trapped water for the sun to heat.

I caught on to his enthusiasm. Even though I'm not much of an ocean swimmer, I appreciate ingenuity and wanted to investigate this idea. I called Dark Harbor House and made my reservation.

As the Isleboro Ferry chugged the twenty minute ride to the island, I leaned against my rental car and enjoyed the spectacular views of the Camden Hills.

Just three miles off the coastline, the island is a refuge for city-weary folks. Harbor seals loll in the sun and wildflowers blossom bright colors along the narrow, seaside lanes.

Presiding over twenty-four acres of lawn and gardens, the regal Dark Harbor House is a wonderful example of Georgian Revival architecture built as summer mansions in the 1890s.

Dark Harbor's dramatic entrance hall, with its sweeping staircase, set the mood for the elegance within.

Fireplaces warmed the public rooms: a spacious library (filled with a blend of books, puzzles, games, and magazines), a drawing room (opening to a splendid veranda), the living room (with a summery sisal rug and windows overlooking the lawn), and the oval dining room with adjoining sun porch.

High four-poster, iron, or sleigh beds, and 19th century antiques decorate the guest rooms. I had a difficult time deciding between a cozy, intimate room with a fireplace or the one with French doors opening onto a sun-drenched upstairs porch. All the rooms are gracious and comfortable with private baths and individual controlled heating. Some baths had classic clawfoot tubs and marble basins.

Immediately after cocktails served in the library, guest adjourn to the eight table dining room for a prix-fixe, four course dinner, which could include entrées like Chinese Steamed Halibut or Breast of Duck Cabernet. A full wine list is available.

Following a breakfast of bacon, fresh fruit and French toast, I claimed one of the inn's bicycles for a little touring. Snapping up the kick-stand, I walked the bike across the road to Dark Harbor Pool. The water was still and inviting, but not quite inviting enough, as I trailed my fingers just beneath the tepid surface.

Climbing back on the bike, picnic lunch tucked into the wire basket, I pedalled along free of worry of passing autos edging me off the road. Louise Rich obviously knew the island and would have understood my pleasure.

Finally, as I boarded the ferry home, I mirrored her sentiments: "It's a great relief," she said of this place. And so it was.

DARK HARBOR HOUSE, Dark Harbor, Island of Isleboro, ME, 04848; 207-784-6669.

A 10-guest room country estate with private baths. Open May through October; 2 night minimum stay on some week-ends and holidays. Breakfast included. Prix-fix, four-course dinner available Wednesday through Monday. Bicycles provided. Schooner sailing, picnics, boating, and golf. Limited smoking areas. Most appropriate for children over 12 years old. No pets. CCs: MC, V. Matthew Skinner, owner/host.

DIRECTIONS: Take the Ferry from Lincolnsville Beach. The Inn is 4 miles north of Camden on U.S. Route 1

EDGECOMBE-COLES HOUSE

Camden, Maine

At some point we have all had the desire to give up our jobs, leave the rat race behind, and move to an acre of land on a beautiful hillside. Terry and Louise Price did just that. Without any plans to move, they visited New England to view the rich fall colors and fell in love with the area near Camden, Maine. Six months later, with San Francisco and jobs as an engineer and advertising executive behind them, they settled in Camden and opened the Edgecombe-Coles House.

Each of the six guest rooms commands a lovely view, whether of the ocean or the forest and garden area. The rooms are furnished with country antiques and original artwork, mostly late-nineteenth-century

oils. Oriental tribal rugs decorate the floors of the predominantly peach- and blue-toned rooms.

Louise's commercial-art background and interest in antiques are obvious in the common rooms of the house, also furnished with Oriental rugs and antiques. "We've collected some exceptional art," she told me. "You may want to spend some time looking at what I call 'the cream' of our collection in the living room." In addition to the artwork, the living room houses a library and has a spectacular ocean view. Moving to the den, a popular place for guests to gather by the fire, I enjoyed the simple craft of the sampler collection on the wall. A television set and stereo are discreetly hidden inside an ancient oak roll-top oil tank.

Breakfast is served at the ten-foot cherry dining room table, which is set with Louise's antique blue and white china. A roaring fire on a chilly morning may accompany coffee and tea, juices, fresh fruit, two different fresh baked goods, and blueberry pancakes with farm eggs and bacon, or a hearty dish of poached eggs over roast beef hash.

EDGECOMBE-COLES HOUSE, 64 High Street, HCR 60 Box 3010 Camden, ME 04843; 207-236-2336.

A handsome 6-room (private baths) inn overlooking the islands of Penobscot Bay. All size beds. Open year-round. No pets. One dog in residence. Limited smoking. CCs: Visa, MC, AE. Terry and Louise Price, owners/hosts.

DIRECTIONS: From the south take Hwy. 95 to Hwy. 1 exit at Brunswick. Take Hwy. 1 approx. 60 mi. north to Camden. Go north of the harbor 7/10ths of a mile; the Inn is on the left.

THE INN AT CANOE POINT

Bar Harbor, Maine

Perched at the edge of Frenchman's Bay, the Inn at Canoe Point offers tranquility on two wooded, secluded acres surrounded by water. The English Tudor-style inn was built as a family summer cottage in the late 1800s and still retains a relaxed air. It was, in fact, a private residence until 1986 and has since been modernized. I found it difficult to remember that Bar Harbor, with its tourists and crowds, was only two miles away, so quiet and restful is the atmosphere.

Even though the mood is relaxed, the inn's interior is an elegant mixture of antiques and traditional furnishings. The main entry hall/living room has a fireplace and a baby grand piano that is always in need of exercise. In the Ocean Room, a magnificent fieldstone fireplace anchors one side, and an equally magnificent 180° view of the ocean and mountains dominates the other. A full breakfast, which can include blueberry French toast, pancakes, or a cheese-and-spinach quiche, is served here, or on the adjacent deck in sunny weather. One morning I made an attempt to finally read Hemingway's *The Old Man and the Sea* while I curled up in front of the fire, but the ever-churning sea itself continually drew my gaze, so I just gave up and enjoyed the thrill of the show.

The five guest rooms mirror the rest of the inn's warm, casual style and overlook either the water or the rocky shoreline and dark pines. All the rooms have spotless modern bathrooms. The Garret Suite, the inn's largest, takes up the third floor and includes a sleeping room with French windows that open to the ocean, and a sitting room with a small balcony. The room can comfortably sleep four.

Innkeeper Donald Johnson had been coming to Bar Harbor for almost twenty years before buying the inn. Therefore, he is quite familiar with the surrounding area and makes an excellent tour guide.

THE INN AT CANOE POINT, Box 216, Bar Harbor, ME 04644; 207-288-9511.

An elegant 5-guestroom (private baths) secluded summer cottage on Maine's coast. King, queen and twin beds. Full breakfast. Open all year. Near Bar Harbor, Acadia National Park, and the Bluenose Ferry Terminal. Not appropriate for young children. No pets. Donald Johnson and Esther Cavagnaro, owners/hosts.

DIRECTIONS: The inn is 15 mi. from Ellsworth, ME off Rte. 3; 2 mi. from Bar Harbor.

JOHN PETERS INN
Blue Hill, Maine

Driving down a country road in Maine, I was more than surprised to come upon an impressive, formal structure positioned on top of a grassy knoll: the John Peters Inn. Built in 1815, this historic Greek Revival mansion, with its columns and brick facade, is surrounded by twenty-five beautiful acres on the tidal waters of Blue Hill Bay.

Hosts Rick and Barbara Seeger recently renovated the inn and added a new carriage house. As Rick took me on a tour of the carriage house, he detailed the six units: small kitchens, queen-sized beds, fireplaces, and decks for lounging.

The Seegers' bouncy Welsh terrier welcomed us as we strolled into the inn's common room. A baby grand piano, beautiful antiques, and two large fireplaces create an elegant, yet comfortable, atmosphere. The guest rooms, with views of Blue Hill Bay and the countryside, reflect tasteful charm. Each is artfully decorated in a different color and has antique country furniture and Oriental rugs. Five rooms have cozy fireplaces.

Breakfast is served on the lovely enclosed porch overlooking the harbor, where you can view yachts and Maine's famous schooners. Amid crystal, silver, and linens, you will idle over Barbara's eggs Benedict, muffins, fresh-squeezed orange juice, pecan waffles, special-blend coffee, seasonal fruits, and a most marvelous treat, lobster omelets with fresh asparagus or artichoke hearts.

JOHN PETERS INN, Peters Point, Box 916, Blue Hill, ME 04614; 207-374-2116.

A 14-guestroom (private baths) Greek Revival mansion and a 6-room (private baths) newly built guest house, beautifully situated on Blue Hill Bay. All size beds. Open all year. Walk to village of Blue Hill; 40-minute drive to Bar Harbor. Canoeing and sailing; biking and hiking on Blue Hill or in nearby Acadia National Park. Breakfast included. No pets. One dog in residence. CCs; Visa, MC. Barbara and Rick Seeger, owners/hosts.

DIRECTIONS: From the south, take coastal Rte. 1 from Camden or Rte. 3 from Augusta to Bucksport. Turn right after crossing Bucksport Bridge. Follow combined Rtes. 1 and 3 for 6 mi. to Rte. 15; take Rte 15 south to Blue Hill. Inn just 1/2 mi. north of village, just off Rte. 176 east.

THE KINGSLEIGH INN
Southwest Harbor, Maine

Reluctant to surrender my Peeping-Tom position behind the telescope, I coerced my wife into getting us some coffee, available on a help-yourself basis, from the large country kitchen downstairs. The telescope, placed in our third-floor turret, was providing afternoon entertainment with panoramic views of the harbor, the activity of arriving and departing boats, and people wandering in the narrow streets below.

Our suite, the largest of the eight rooms, was on the third floor. Cotton and lace valances capped the double-hung wood windows. The rooms were furnished simply, with refinished antiques and rugs over the hardwood floors. Like several of the other rooms, it had a view of the harbor below.

The inn, a grand Colonial Revival built in 1904, is nestled on the edge of Southwest Harbor on the main road. Burgundy and beige window awnings offer shade to the flower boxes overflowing in multi-col-

ored bouquets. On summer afternoons, guests relax on white wicker chairs with bright pillows to enjoy fresh lemonade served in the shade of the veranda.

Refinished antique furnishings and lace restate the colonial theme in the common rooms. There is a comfortable living room with a fireplace and a lush carpeted sitting room with a loveseat, an ideal place for quiet reading or conversation. The dining room tables, accented with flickering candles and fresh flowers, help make breakfast a special occasion. Mouth-watering sausage and egg souffle, cinnamon French toast, or blueberry pancakes highlight the list of daily full-breakfast specialties; a continental breakfast of delicious homemade muffins and coffee cake is offered as well.

The owners of Kingsleigh, Nancy and Tom Cervelli, left high-tech computer careers in New York to fulfill a dream when they purchased the inn in 1989. Their ready smiles and hospitality invite guests to make themselves at home.

THE KINGSLEIGH INN, 100 Main St., P.O. Box 1426, Southwest Harbor, ME 04679; 207-244-5302.

An 8-guestroom (private baths) elegant Colonial Revival inn overlooking the harbor. King & Queen beds. Full breakfast included. No smoking. Open year-round. Shops & restaurants within walking distance. No pets. No CCs. Nancy and Tom Cervelli, owners/hosts.

DIRECTIONS: Rte. 3 from Ellsworth to Mt. Desert Island. Go right onto Rte. 102 to Southwest Harbor. Watch for the inn to your left.

MANOR HOUSE INN

Bar Harbor, Maine

Built as a summer cottage in 1887, you might say Manor House Inn is still being used for just that purpose. The welcome mat is placed out the beginning of May and pulled inside as final guests depart on Nov. 15th, just as the Atlantic chill becomes bearable only to the locals residents.

Owner, Mac Noyes, is used to the winters being a "local" himself. Mac told me he was a Bar Harbor banker for 14 years before purchasing Manor House from a friend in 1989. He appeared to be loving every minute of his new occupation.

"You know," he stated, much like a proud father, "the Inn is on the National Register of Historic Places."

There was no doubt in my mind that the elegant three story Victorian was deserving. The mansion, affectionately called "Boscobel" was the first building that greeted me as I pulled into the circular driveway, however, I later discovered there were additional rooms in a Chauffeur's Cottage and two separate guest cottages. The well-kept buildings sit upon a meticulously landscaped acre, just minutes from the water. "Boscobel's" first floor has two sitting rooms, both with Victorian wallpaper of deep burgundy, fireplaces, hardwood floors and hand-picked antique furnishings. A baby grand piano tempts any musicians. One of the rooms opens out onto the veranda.

"There's a TV in the sitting room on the third floor, if you want to catch up on the morning news," Mac informed me, as I was finishing my breakfast the next morning. It was not tempting enough to make me leave the secluded surroundings of the outdoor breakfast garden just yet. I had stuffed myself with warm banana bread and a hearty omelet. Savoring a final cup of coffee, I visited with some of the other guests before climbing up to my room to retrieve a camera for the jaunt downtown.

My room, typical of the entire inn, was neatly furnished with antiques of the Victorian era, again with the rich color of burgundy predominant. Large windows looked out over the gardens, the two story chauffeur's cottage, and toward the porches of the guest cottages.

Camera secured around my neck, I walked the short distance to downtown to sightsee and shop. Sunset found me at the waterfront attempting to capture the magnificent colors of the evening sky on film.

MANOR HOUSE INN, 106 West St., Bar Harbor, ME 04609; 207-288-3759.
14 guestroom Victorian, including 2 suites and 2 guest cottages with kitchenettes. All sized beds. Breakfast included. Two night minimum stay during busy season, reservations recommended. Open May 1-Nov.15th. No smoking. No pets. No facilities for small children. Short walk to town and waterfront. Acadia National Park just a short drive away. V,MC,AMEX. Malcolm C. Noyes, Owner-host.
DIRECTIONS: From I-95 (Bangor) take Route 1A to Ellsworth, then Route 3 to Bar Harbor. Follow signs to the "waterfront" which is West St.

MIRA MONTE INN
Bar Harbor, Maine

As we turned toward the spacious porch that wraps around the clapboard Victorian, Marian Burns, owner of Mira Monte, told me that the inn was built in the early 1800s as a summer retreat.

She had been involved in teaching Special Education and developing classroom curricula. Mistakenly, she believed a summer inn would allow her time to continue her work in this field. She purchased Mira Monte in 1981, and its subsequent success persuaded her to leave teaching and become a full-time innkeeper. Her acute attention to detail, a carryover from the classroom, is apparent in the renovation of Mira Monte.

"Architects who have stayed here say I missed my calling," she said, seemingly embarrassed by the compliment. The dormers, balconies, bay windows, and porches which now enhance the structure are all of her design.

"Let me give you a tour," she invited, pushing open the front door.

As we approached the living room I heard the plinking of piano keys. Entering, I saw a guest seated before a piano attempting to revive an old tune. A fire beckoned. Brocade cushioned chairs awaited the return of the guests for afternoon refreshments. Nearby, the library provided a quieter atmosphere, with richly colored area rugs offsetting the elegant hardwood floors and antique furniture.

Reflected on the polished sheen of the dining room's large mahogany buffet were the place settings for tomorrow's breakfast guests.

"We have a diet-breaking selection of homemade pastries with our continental breakfast," Marian said. "We can also serve you on any of the balconies or porches."

We climbed the stairs to the guest rooms. I had requested a room with a balcony and was told that all rooms have some combination of balconies, fireplaces, porches, or bay windows. My room, like several others, was located over the expansive lawn and garden area. Wallpaper of soft ivory, mauve, and deep rose accented the dark wood furnishings. Gathered lace curtains, tied back from the windows, allowed afternoon sunlight to stream across the floor. I settled into a white wicker chair on the balcony to listen to the distant sounds of the sea.

MIRA MONTE INN, 69 Mt. Desert St., Bar Harbor, ME 04609; 207-288-4263 (inside ME), 800-553-5109.

An 11-guestroom (private baths) Victorian Colonial Revival inn located in the Historic Corridor of downtown Bar Harbor. King, queen, and double beds. Open May-

Oct. Two-night minimum stay. Restricted smoking. Easy drive to Acadia State Park. Short walk to waterfront, restaurants and shopping. No pets. CCs: Visa, MC, AE. Marian Burns, owner/host.

DIRECTIONS: Rte. 3 from Ellsworth. Turn left on Mt. Desert St.

NORUMBEGA
Camden, Maine

Poised dramatically near the edge of Penobscot Bay was "a castle to call home," as promised in the brochure. Dense stone walls and turrets captured my immediate attention as I approached Norumbega.

"Looks like I should have packed my black suit," I thought as I walked toward the imposing inn. But I soon found I was in error, for the interior of the castle, which was built in 1886, is informal.

I was staying in the Warwick Room, where I could gaze over Penobscot Bay from my bay windows or private deck. A fire was already crackling in the fireplace; the flames were reflected in the polished gleam of refinished hardwood floors.

"This is our most popular room," the manager commented, "next to the penthouse, which is up on the fourth floor and has its own private staircase. It books up months in advance." I assured him that these accommodations were perfect, just for the view alone.

"If you are hungry, we keep a pot of homemade soup on the stove, and the jars in the kitchen are packed with fresh-baked cookies. Please

help yourself. There are always cold drinks in the refrigerator, too." He left me to unpack and to do some exploring.

The common rooms have dark wooded panelling on the walls, typical of old English manors. English Victorian antiques fill the spacious rooms. On my visit, all the fireplaces had glowing fires within to ward off the coastal chill from the bay. A guest was playing the old baby grand piano sitting in the corner of one of the rooms. The lounge has a restored antique billiard table and a television. A sign requests guests to stop play by 9 P.M.

Tea, sherry, and wine were served in the late afternoons. I usually wandered out onto the back veranda, sipping and enjoying the beautiful landscaping which surrounded the inn, before I went into Camden for dinner.

A full complement of fruits, homemade breads and muffins, in addition to main courses of various egg and meat dishes, are presented at breakfast.

NORUMBEGA, 61 High St., Camden, ME 04843; 207-236-4646.

A 12-guestroom 1886 Victorian castle with an exquisite penthouse. All have fireplaces. Some views of the bay. Breakfast included. Afternoon wine and sherry. Open year round. Near Camden Hills State Park; walk to the harbor, shops or restaurants. Downhill or cross-country skiing nearby. No pets. Murray Keatinge, owner; manager on premises.

DIRECTIONS: From Boston, take Rte. 95 north to Coastal Route Exit 22, at Brunswick/Bath. Continue north to Camden on Route 1. Norumbega is 1/2 mi. north of the center of Camden, on the ocean side of Route 1. Trip from Boston about 3-1/2 hours.

THE PENTAGOET INN

Castine, Maine

For many years I regarded Castine as one of the best-kept secrets in the world. I also discovered that when I ran into other people who knew about Castine, we felt as if we belonged to an exclusive club—something akin to people who have climbed Mount Everest.

I'm sure that many people do stumble on Castine, but it's not on the road to anywhere. Its principal claim to fame is the fact that originally it was settled by British Loyalists, who, after the American Revolution, decided they preferred to remain under King George and so moved from Boston up to this lovely out-of-the-way location. There are many markers in the town reminding us that such an exodus did take place.

One of the first things that Lindsey and Virginia Miller and I found

that we have in common was a love of porches. I've spent many a happy hour rocking on porches of country inns all over North America. "That's just the way we feel," said Virginia. "As a matter of fact, that's why we have extended the porch all the way to the back of the main building. You'll notice that we've put window boxes and standing flowerpots in as many places as possible, and our new green awning has been a real blessing."

Well, the talk went on from porches to breakfast. "I must step in here," Lindsey declared. "This morning, besides a cup of fresh tropical fruit, we had a fresh herb omelet. Our French toast is filled with cream cheese and fresh orange, and topped with blueberry sauce. In addition to that there are sausage links or grilled rib eye steak and we continue with our famous Pentagoet muffins."

In the ensuing conversation we talked about many other interesting changes the Millers had made. "When we first arrived in the fall of 1985 we became aware that the inn needed more dining space and more common areas for the guests," Virginia recalled. "We spent the first winter correcting this by creating a very inviting library with an upright Bosendorfer piano and most of our personal collection of books." I agreed that it provides a good place for guests to relax with a book, play the piano, or listen to some classical music.

"The addition of the back dining room was an inspiration," Virginia said, "and I'm happy to say we are well known for our dinners. Part of this is because we have an excellent chef and we offer a variety of main dishes including Maine lobsters, lobster pie, grilled fresh salmon steak with dilled hollandaise, a peppered rib eye steak, and a roast leg of lamb. It's part of a five-course meal which includes soup and dessert."

Some exciting things have happened above the first floor of the Pentagoet, too. For example, by redesigning the second- and third-floor guest rooms, the Pentagoet now has twelve guest rooms with private baths and two with half-baths. In addition, the annex next door, 10 Perkins Street, also has very attractive guest rooms.

THE PENTAGOET INN, Main St., P.O. Box 4, Castine, ME 04221; 207-326-8616.

A 17-guestroom (private baths) inn in a seacoast village on the Penobscot Peninsula, 36 mi. from Bangor. King and queen beds available. Modified American plan includes breakfast and dinner. Dinner available to outside guests by reservation. Open May to Oct. Tennis, swimming, backroading, village strolling, craft shops, chamber music concerts, Maine Maritime Academy, Acadia National Park, and Blue Hill nearby. No pets. One orange tabby cat in residence. Smoking on porches only. Lindsey and Virginia Miller, owners/hosts.

DIRECTIONS: From the south, follow I-95 toward Augusta and use Rte. 3 exit to Belfast. Follow Rte. 1 to a point 3 mi. past Bucksport. Turn right on Rte. 175 to Rte. 166 to Castine. Look for Maine Maritime Academy sign; turn left onto Main St.

THE PILGRIM'S INN
Deer Isle, Maine

Originally a rambling Colonial-style home, today you can enjoy a unique inn here. Travelers really have to be looking for Deer Isle and the Pilgrim's Inn. It's a good hour's drive from U.S. 1, east of Bucksport, to the Blue Hill Penninsula. Deer Isle sits just off the southern flank of the mainland, and no matter how you arrive, it's necessary to cross over the suspension bridge at Eggemoggin Reach.

A four-story, gambrel-roofed red house, this building has overlooked the long harbor on the front and the millpond in the rear since 1793. Jean and Dud Hendrick moved here a few years ago after acquiring the Pilgrim's Inn. Much of the original building has remained almost completely unchanged, with the original Colonial feature of two large rooms and a kitchen on the ground floor still intact. One of these rooms is the Common Room of the present-day inn.

Most of the guest rooms are quite large and feature richly hued pine floorboards, wood stoves, country furniture, and a selection of books and magazines. They are enhanced by coordinated Laura Ashley fabrics, used for curtains, lampshades, quilts, and cushions.

Number 15 is an enchanting house in the village. It sits over the

harbor, affording the occupants unparalleled sunset views from its back deck. It is completely furnished and equipped so that guests may choose to prepare their own meals if they are so foolish as to pass up Jean's fabulous cuisine. It is the quintessential honeymoon cottage or retreat for four friends (it has a hide-a-bed in front of the fireplace in the living room in addition to the upstairs bedroom).

Turning one of the first-floor parlors of the main inn into a warm reading room and library has also worked well allowing guests to quietly read.

The mail boat run to Isle au Haute is a most romantic day trip, and the sailing here is terrific.

THE PILGRIM'S INN, Deer Isle, ME 04627; 207-348-6615.

A 13-guestroom (8 private baths) inn in a remote island village on the Blue Hill Peninsula on the Maine coast. Queen, double, and twin beds available. Modified American plan, May 15 to Nov. 1, includes a hearty breakfast and a creative dinner. In season, outside dinner reservations are accepted. A 4-day minimum reservation is requested in Aug. Bicycles, badminton, table tennis, regulation horseshoes, croquet, and a rowboat for the millpond on the grounds. All types of cultural and recreational advantages, including golf, fishing, sailing, hiking, and browsing nearby. No pets. One English Springer Spaniel in residence. Dud and Jean Hendrick, owners/hosts.

DIRECTIONS: From Boston, take I-95 to Brunswick exit. Take coastal Rte. 1 north past Bucksport. Turn right on Rte. 15, which travels to Deer Isle down the Blue Hill Peninsula. At the village, turn right on Main St. (Sunset Rd.) and proceed one block to the inn on the left side of the street, opposite the harbor.

PULPIT HARBOR INN

North Haven, Maine

At Pulpit Harbor Inn, pint milk bottles holding colorful bunches of fresh flowers are reminders of the dairy it used to be, supplying North Haven Island families with milk. The cows and barn are gone, but innkeepers Christie and Barney Hallowell have maintained the wonderful country feeling of the original 120-year-old farm house.

North Haven Island is one of Maine's least commercial islands, and one of its most lovely. Surrounded by tall spruces and pastoral views of the Hallowells' sheep pasture and the Camden Hills beyond, Pulpit Harbor Inn sits just across from the town's old grange hall. The village of North Haven is small, and virtually traffic-free, a real treat to those who enjoy evening walks and early-morning bike rides.

Christie and Barney were teachers in North Haven for some time before deciding to open their inn. Barney is still active in the community as a full-time teacher and assistant principal at the high school.

The Hallowells' commitment to their community can also be seen in their collection of wonderful local artwork that hangs throughout the inn. Christie is particularly pleased with the new custom-made mantlepiece in the living room. Both the living room and library are casual and comfortable. Two large couches and a wood-burning fireplace invite quiet conversation or evening reading.

In the simply furnished bedrooms, tiny calico prints are a unifying theme in bureau scarves, quilts, pillows, and pillow shams.

Christie is quite a cook and baker. Breakfast and dinner are both served in one of the inn's three dining areas: the dining room, sun porch, or outside on the brick terrace. A continental breakfast that may include two lemon poppy seed or Maine blueberry muffins, juice, coffee, tea, or cocoa is included in your room fee. An omelet or eggs and bacon are available at extra cost. Sandwiches with a creamy garlic herb spread and brown-sugar coconut bars can be made into a picnic lunch to take to the beach. Dinner has four courses and includes two entrées. Ripe garden produce is an integral part of summer dinners, and Christie makes use of the fresh fish in season.

Even though the farm's old barn has been torn down, be sure to visit the inhabitants of the creamery: four sheep, a rooster and hens, two ducks, and the rabbits, Mr. and Mrs. Claus.

———

PULPIT HARBOR INN, Crabtree Point Rd., North Haven, ME 04853; 207-867-2219.

A 6-guestroom (3 private baths) century-old farmhouse on the lovely island of North Haven, in the middle of Penobscot Bay. Open all year. Double and twin beds. Continental breakfast included with tariff; a picnic lunch and dinner available. Quiet and solitude. Hiking on Ames Knob, golf, tennis, beachcombing. Winter xc skiing and ice skating. Pets by advance arrangement, plus a $5 cleaning fee. Christie and Barney Hallowell, owners/hosts.

DIRECTIONS: From Boston, take Rte. 95 north. In Brunswick, take Rte. 1 to Rockland. In Rockland, board the ferry to North Haven Island.

WINDWARD HOUSE BED AND BREAKFAST
Camden, Maine

I'll always remember Jon and Mary Davis. Not only are they a warm couple who own the Windward House B&B, but they actually *almost* got me, a confirmed landlubber, onto a windjammer. Just when I thought I had an excuse—not remembering my wind breaker—Mary thoughtfully offered to get one for me. That thoughtfulness continued throughout my visit.

Jon spent thirty years as a corporate director with AT&T before moving to Camden in 1986. During those years, Mary spent her time as a registered nurse and the owner of a gourmet catering business. They both loved Camden, "where the mountains meet the sea," as Jon says, and decided Windward House would meld their talents into a wonderful way of life.

The home is located in the heart of Camden in the delightful High Street Historic District that overlooks the harbor. Fine restaurants, shops, and performing arts venues are all within walking distance, and just by stepping off the back deck hikers can tread some great trails.

A light blue-gray, the stately clapboard Greek Revival has harmonious cream trim and burgundy windows and doors. Colorful flower beds frame the front porch and deck. The beautifully renovated home was placed on the National Historic Register in 1989.

The first floor is suited to the comfort of Windward's guests. All the rooms are attractive and furnished with antiques and local art. Whether you choose the large living room with its soapstone fireplace crackling on cool days, or the comfortable library filled with books, magazines, stereo and television, you'll find much to do during a stay-at-home evening. Refreshments, including port and sherry, are an appreciated extra.

Quilts, fresh flowers, period furnishings (including wonderful antique beds), and soft colors create a quiet, restful atmosphere in the guest rooms. All rooms have private, modern baths.

I know you'll enjoy Mary's super breakfasts, served by—who else?— Jon. Her peaches and cream French toast is exceptional. Sitting on the back deck with my fourth cup of coffee, I was amused by the youthful antics of Muffins, the inn's senior citizen cat, as she fearlessly stalked wild birds on a tree limb some fifteen feet above the ground. With her example in mind, I thought again about sailing the windjammer...then had another cup of coffee.

———————

WINDWARD HOUSE BED AND BREAKFAST, 6 High St., Camden, ME 04843; 207-236-9656.

A 6-guestroom (private baths) inn overlooking Camden Harbor. Queen, double and twin beds. Full breakfast. Open all year. Children over 10. Smoking restricted. No pets; boarding arrangements available. One dog in residence. CCs: Visa, MC. Mary and Jon Davis, owners/hosts.

DIRECTIONS: Once in Camden, inn is just one blk. north of Camden Harbor.

PROPERTY INDEX

RATES

Space limitations preclude any more than a general range of rates for each inn, and these should not be considered firm quotations. All inns serve full breakfasts unless noted as CB which is a continental breakfast, AP which is American Plan (must purchases your meals separately) and MAP which is modified American plan (Breakfast & Dinner included in rate for two.)

Please check with the inns for their various rates and special packages. It should be noted that many small inns do not have night staffs, and innkeepers will appreciate it if calls are made before 8:00 p.m.

Connecticut

Deep River, RIVERWIND INN	$80–135
Essex, GRISWOLD	$80–125
Greenwich, HOMESTEAD INN, THE	$90–185
New Preston, BOULDERS INN	$130–230
Norfolk, MANOR HOUSE	$80–160
Ridgefield, WEST LANE INN	$135–175
Salisbury, UNDER MOUNTAIN INN	$150–180

Maine

Bar Harbor, BAY LEDGE INN & SPA	$65–190
Bar Harbor, INN AT CANOE POINT, THE	$65–200
Bar Harbor, MANOR HOUSE INN	$50–150
Bar Harbor, MIRA MONTE INN	$80–140
Blue Hill, BLUE HILL INN, THE	$110–165
Blue Hill, JOHN PETERS INN	$80–125
Camden, EDGECOMB-COLES HOUSE	$80–155
Camden, NORUMBEGA	$95–395
Camden, WINDWARD HOUSE BED AND BREAKFAST	$65–125
Castine, PENTAGOET INN, THE	$159–179
Deer Isle, PILGRIM'S INN, THE	$90(B&B)
	$140–180(MAP)
Freeport, 181 MAIN STREET BED AND BREAKFAST	$75–95
Freeport, BAGLEY HOUSE, THE	$80–95
Hancock Point, CROCKER HOUSE COUNTRY INN, THE	$60–70
Isleboro, DARK HARBOR HOUSE	$135–165
Kennebunkport, BUFFLEHEAD COVE	$75–130
Kennebunkport, CAPTAIN LORD MANSION, THE	$125–195
Kennebunkport, INN AT HARBOR HEAD, THE	$85–170
Kennebunkport, MAINE STAY INN & COTTAGES, THE	$85–185
Kennebunkport, WHITE BARN INN	$125–300
Naples, CHARMWOODS	$100–110

Newcastle, NEWCASTLE INN, THE $80–90(B&B)
                                                   $120–170(MAP)
North Haven, PULPIT HARBOR INN $60–95
Portland, INN ON CARLETON $50–80
Prouts Neck, BLACK POINT INN $230–340
Rangeley, COUNTRY CLUB INN, THE $87–97(B&B)
                                                   $132–148(MAP)
Rangeley, RANGELEY INN $65–110
Southwest Harbor, KINGSLEIGH INN, THE $55–155
Waterford, WATERFORD INNE, THE $55–85
Westport Island, SQUIRE TARBOX INN, THE $60–135(B&B)
                                                   $110–170(MAP)
York, DOCKSIDE GUEST QUARTERS $55–129

Massachusetts

Auburn, CAPTAIN SAMUEL EDDY HOUSE COUNTRY INN $65–95
Barnstable, ASHLEY MANOR $100–165
Barnstable, CHARLES HINCKLEY HOUSE $115–145
Boston, LENOX HOTEL, THE $125–210
Chatham, CAPTAIN'S HOUSE INN OF CHATHAM, THE $89–169
Chatham, OLD HARBOR INN $95–150
Concord, HAWTHORNE INN, THE $95–160
Deerfield, DEERFIELD INN $106–122(B&B)
                                                   $131–175(MAP)
Eastham, OVER LOOK INN, THE $65–110
Eastham, WHALEWALK INN $90–150
Edgartown, CHARLOTTE INN $85–350
Falmouth, CAPTAIN TOM LAWRENCE HOUSE $75–94
Falmouth, MOSTLY HALL $80–105
Falmouth, VILLAGE GREEN INN $70–110
Lenox, BLANTYRE $200–500
Lenox, GABLES INN, THE $60–195
Lenox, GARDEN GABLES INN $65–170
Lenox, VILLAGE INN, THE $40–150(B&B)
                                                   $110–215(MAP)
Nantucket, ANCHOR INN $55–125
Nantucket, WAUWINET, THE $200–400
Rockport, LINDEN TREE INN $60–88
Rockport, OLD FARM INN $68–108
Rockport, SEACREST MANOR $74–102
South Lee, MERRELL TAVERN INN $65–140
Stockbridge, INN AT STOCKBRIDGE, THE $75–225
Stockbridge, RED LION INN, THE $56–149
Vineyard Haven, THORNCROFT INN $99–299
Vineyard Haven, TUCKERMAN HOUSE, THE $85–190
Yarmouth Port, WEDGEWOOD INN $90–145

New Hampshire

Bradford, MOUNTAIN INN LAKE	$85–95
Conway, DARBY FIELD INN, THE	$60–140(B&B)
	$104–184(MAP)
Etna, MOOSE MOUNTAIN LODGE	$160
Francestown, INN AT CROTCHED MOUNTAIN, THE	$60–70(B&B)
	$100–120(MAP)
Hart's Location, NOTCHLAND INN, THE	$130–140
Henniker, MEETING HOUSE INN, THE	$65–93
Jackson, CHRISTMAS FARM INN	$136–164
Jackson, INN AT THORN HILL	$110–180 MAP
Lyme, DOWD'S COUNTRY INN, THE	$65–105
New London, NEW LONDON INN	$70–95
North Sutton, FOLLANSBEE INN	$70–90
Snowville, SNOWVILLAGE INN	$80–150(B&B)
	$110–180(MAP)
Sugar Hill, SUGAR HILL INN	$90–105(B&B)
	$140–175(MAP)
Sunapee, DEXTER'S INN AND TENNIS CLUB	$100–140(B&B)
	$125–165(MAP)
Temple, BIRCHWOOD INN, THE	$60–70
West Chesterfield, CHESTERFIELD INN	$99–159

Rhode Island

Newport, MELVILLE HOUSE, THE	$45–95
Newport, WAYSIDE	$95–125
Wakefield, LARCHWOOD INN	$60–80

Vermont

Bridgewater Corners, OCTOBER COUNTRY INN	$70–85(B&B)
	$115–135(MAP)
Chelsea, SHIRE INN	$70–85(B&B)
	$140–180(MAP)
Chester, CHESTER HOUSE	$50–75
Chester, INN AT LONG LAST, THE	$160
Chittenden, TULIP TREE INN	$120–210
Dorset, BARROWS HOUSE, THE	$130–210
Dorset, CORNUCOPIA OF DORSET	$80–165
Fair Haven, VERMONT MARBLE INN	$145–185
Gaysville, COBBLE HOUSE INN	$80–100
Goshen, BLUEBERRY HILL	$168–222
Jamaica, THREE MOUNTAIN INN	$75–125(B&B)
	$100–190(MAP)
Lower Waterford, RABBIT HILL INN	$88–159(B&B)
	$130–190(MAP)
Ludlow, GOVERNOR'S INN, THE	$180–190

Manchester Village, 1811 HOUSE $100–170
Manchester, BIRCH HILL INN $90–112
Middlebury, SWIFT HOUSE INN $85–150
Newfane, FOUR COLUMNS INN, THE $95–170(B&B)
                                                 $195–275(MAP)
Pittsfield, INN AT PITTSFIELD, THE $95–130
Shelburne, SHELBURNE HOUSE $100–230
Simonsville, ROWELL'S INN $70–90(B&B)
                                                 $140–160(MAP)
Stowe, INN AT THE BRASS LANTERN, THE $60–120
Waitsfield, INN AT THE ROUND BARN FARM, THE $85–125
West Dover, INN AT SAWMILL FARM $260–310
West Townshend, WINDHAM HILL INN $170–180
Wilmington, TRAIL'S END $85–150
Woodstock, CHARLESTON HOUSE, THE $75–135

INDEX BY ACTIVITY

SHIRE INN, Chelsea, Vermont
THORNCROFT INN, Vineyard Haven, Massachusetts
WAUWINET, THE, Nantucket, Massachusetts
WHALEWALK INN, Eastham, Massachusetts
WHITE BARN, Kennebunkport, Maine
WINDHAM HILL INN, West Townshend, Vermont

Fishing

BIRCH HILL INN, Manchester, Vermont
BLUEBERRY HILL, Goshen, Vermont
CAPTAIN LORD MANSION, THE, Kennebunkport, Maine
CHARLESTON HOUSE, THE, Woodstock, Vermont
CHARLOTTE INN, Edgartown, Massachusetts
CHRISTMAS FARM INN, Jackson, New Hampshire
COUNTRY CLUB INN, THE, Rangeley, Maine
DOCKSIDE GUEST QUARTERS, York, Maine
FOLLANSBEE INN, North Sutton, New Hampshire
INN AT LONG LAST, THE, Chester, Vermont
INN AT THORN HILL, Jackson, New Hampshire
INN AT SAWMILL FARM, West Dover, Vermont
LARCHWOOD INN, Wakefield, New Hampshire
NEWCASTLE INN, THE, Newcastle, Maine
PILGRIM'S INN, THE, Deer Isle, Maine
RED LION INN, THE, Stockbridge, Massachusetts
ROWELL'S INN, Simonsville, Vermont
SHELBURNE HOUSE, Shelburne, Vermont
SHIRE INN, Chelsea, Vermont
THREE MOUNTAIN INN, Jamaica, Vermont
TULIP TREE INN, Chittenden, Vermont
VERMONT MARBLE INN, Fair Haven, Vermont

Golf

BIRCH HILL INN, Manchester, Vermont
BLACK POINT INN, Prouts Neck, Maine
BUFFLEHEAD COVE, Kennebunkport, Maine
CAPTAIN LORD MANSION, THE, Kennebunkport, Maine
CAPTAIN'S HOUSE INN OF CHATHAM, THE, Chatham, Massachusetts
CHARLESTON HOUSE, THE, Woodstock, Vermont
CHARLOTTE INN, Edgartown, Massachusetts
CHRISTMAS FARM INN, Jackson, New Hampshire
CORNUCOPIA OF DORSET, Dorset, Vermont
COUNTRY CLUB INN, THE, Rangeley, Maine
DARK HARBOR HOUSE, Isleboro, Maine
DEXTER'S INN AND TENNIS CLUB, Sunapee, New Hampshire
DOCKSIDE GUEST QUARTERS, York, Maine
FOLLANSBEE INN, North Sutton, New Hampshire
INN AT CROTCHED MOUNTAIN, THE, Francestown, New Hampshire
INN AT LONG LAST, THE, Chester, Vermont
INN AT SAWMILL FARM, West Dover, Vermont

INN AT THORN HILL, Jackson, New Hampshire
MANOR HOUSE, Norfolk, Connecticut
NEW LONDON INN, New London, New Hampshire
PILGRIM'S INN, THE, Deer Isle, Maine
PULPIT HARBOR INN, North Haven, Maine
RABBIT HILL INN, Lower Waterford, Vermont
RED LION INN, THE, Stockbridge, Massachusetts
ROWELL'S INN, Simonsville, Vermont
THREE MOUNTAIN INN, Jamaica, Vermont
TRAIL'S END, Wilmington, Vermont
VERMONT MARBLE INN, Fair Haven, Vermont
WATERFORD INNE, THE, Waterford, Maine
WEST LANE INN, Ridgefield, Connecticut
WHALEWALK INN, Eastham, Massachusetts

Hiking

1811 HOUSE, Manchester Village, Vermont
BARROWS HOUSE, THE, Dorset, Vermont
BIRCHWOOD INN, THE, Temple, New Hampshire
BLUEBERRY HILL, Goshen, Vermont
BOULDERS INN, New Preston, Connecticut
BUFFLEHEAD COVE, Kennebunkport, Maine
CAPTAIN SAMUEL EDDY HOUSE COUNTRY INN,
    Auburn, Massachusetts
CHARLESTON HOUSE, THE, Woodstock, Vermont
CHESTER HOUSE, Chester, Vermont
CORNUCOPIA OF DORSET, Dorset, Vermont
COUNTRY CLUB INN, THE, Rangeley, Maine
CHRISTMAS FARM, Jackson, New Hampshire
DEXTER'S INN AND TENNIS CLUB, Sunapee, New Hampshire
DOWD'S COUNTRY INN, THE, Lyme, New Hampshire
FOLLANSBEE INN, North Sutton, New Hampshire
FOUR COLUMNS INN, THE, Newfane, Vermont
INN AT THORN HILL, Jackson, New Hampshire
JOHN PETERS INN, Blue Hill, Maine
NOTCHLAND INN, THE, Hart's Location, New Hampshire
PILGRIM'S INN, THE, Deer Isle, Maine
PULPIT HARBOR INN, North Haven, Maine
RABBIT HILL INN, Lower Waterford, Vermont
RED LION INN, THE, Stockbridge, Massachusetts
ROWELL'S INN, Simonsville, Vermont
SHELBURNE HOUSE, Shelburne, Vermont
THREE MOUNTAIN INN, Jamaica, Vermont
TRAIL'S END, Wilmington, Vermont
TULIP TREE INN, Chittenden, Vermont
VERMONT MARBLE INN, Fair Haven, Vermont
WATERFORD INNE, THE, Waterford, Maine
WHITE BARN, Kennebunkport, Maine

Horseback riding

Skiing

SHELBURNE HOUSE, Shelburne, Vermont
SHIRE INN, Chelsea, Vermont
THREE MOUNTAIN INN, Jamaica, Vermont
TRAIL'S END, Wilmington, Vermont
TULIP TREE INN, Chittenden, Vermont
UNDER MOUNTAIN INN, Salisbury, Connecticut
VERMONT MARBLE INN, Fair Haven, Vermont
VILLAGE INN, THE, Lenox, Massachusetts
WATERFORD INNE, THE, Waterford, Maine
WEST LANE INN, Ridgefield, Connecticut
WINDHAM HILL INN, West Townshend, Vermont

Swimming

181 MAIN STREET BED AND BREAKFAST, Freeport, Maine
BARROWS HOUSE, THE, Dorset, Vermont
BAY LEDGE INN & SPA, Bar Harbor, Maine
BIRCH HILL INN, Manchester, Vermont
BLACK POINT INN, Prouts Neck, Maine
BLANTYRE, Lenox, Massachusetts
BLUEBERRY HILL, Goshen, Vermont
CAPTAIN LORD MANSION, THE, Kennebunkport, Maine
CAPTAIN SAMUEL EDDY HOUSE COUNTRY INN,
    Auburn, Massachusetts
CHARLOTTE INN, Edgartown, Massachusetts
CHRISTMAS FARM INN, Jackson, New Hampshire
COUNTRY CLUB INN, THE, Rangeley, Maine
CROCKER HOUSE COUNTRY INN, THE, Hancock Point, Maine
DARBY FIELD INN, THE, Conway, New Hampshire
FOUR COLUMNS INN, THE, Newfane, Vermont
GABLES INN, THE, Lenox, Massachusetts
GARDEN GABLES INN, Lenox, Massachusetts
INN AT CROTCHED MOUNTAIN, THE, Francestown, New Hampshire
INN AT LONG LAST, THE, Chester, Vermont
INN AT THORN HILL, Jackson, New Hampshire
INN AT SAWMILL FARM, West Dover, Vermont
INN AT STOCKBRIDGE, THE, Stockbridge, Massachusetts
INN AT THE ROUND BARN FARM, THE, Waitsfield, Vermont
LARCHWOOD INN, Wakefield, New Hampshire
MANOR HOUSE, Norfolk, Connecticut
NEWCASTLE INN, THE, Newcastle, Maine
PENTAGOET INN, THE, Castine, Maine
RABBIT HILL INN, Lower Waterford, Vermont
RED LION INN, THE, Stockbridge, Massachusetts
SHIRE INN, Chelsea, Vermont
VILLAGE INN, THE, Lenox, Massachusetts
WAYSIDE, Newport, Rhode Island
WEST LANE INN, Ridgefield, Connecticut
WINDHAM HILL INN, West Townshend, Vermont

Tennis

ASHLEY MANOR, Barnstable, Massachusetts
BARROWS HOUSE, THE, Dorset, Vermont
BIRCH HILL INN, Manchester, Vermont
BLACK POINT INN, Prouts Neck, Maine
BLANTYRE, Lenox, Massachusetts
CAPTAIN LORD MANSION, THE, Kennebunkport, Maine
CAPTAIN'S HOUSE INN OF CHATHAM, THE, Chatham, Massachusetts
CHARLESTON HOUSE, THE, Woodstock, Vermont
CHARLOTTE INN, Edgartown, Massachusetts
CHRISTMAS FARM INN, Jackson, New Hampshire
CORNUCOPIA OF DORSET, Dorset, Vermont
COUNTRY CLUB INN, THE, Rangeley, Maine
CROCKER HOUSE COUNTRY INN, THE, Hancock Point, Maine
DARBY FIELD INN, THE, Conway, New Hampshire
DEXTER'S INN AND TENNIS CLUB, Sunapee, New Hampshire
DOCKSIDE GUEST QUARTERS, York, Maine
FOLLANSBEE INN, North Sutton, New Hampshire
GABLES INN, THE, Lenox, Massachusetts
GRISWOLD, Essex, Connecticut
INN AT CROTCHED MOUNTAIN, THE, Francestown, New Hampshire
INN AT LONG LAST, THE, Chester, Vermont
INN AT SAWMILL FARM, West Dover, Vermont
INN AT THORN HILL, Jackson, New Hampshire
MANOR HOUSE, Norfolk, Connecticut
PENTAGOET INN, THE, Castine, Maine
PULPIT HARBOR INN, North Haven, Maine
RED LION INN, THE, Stockbridge, Massachusetts
ROWELL'S INN, Simonsville, Vermont
SHELBURNE HOUSE, Shelburne, Vermont
SNOWVILLAGE INN, Snowville, New Hampshire
THORNCROFT INN, Vineyard Haven, Massachusetts
THREE MOUNTAIN INN, Jamaica, Vermont
TRAIL'S END, Wilmington, Vermont
VERMONT MARBLE INN, Fair Haven, Vermont
WAUWINET, THE, Nantucket, Massachusetts
WEST LANE INN, Ridgefield, Connecticut

Wheelchair access

BIRCHWOOD INN, THE, Temple, New Hampshire
BLUEBERRY HILL, Goshen, Vermont
DOCKSIDE GUEST QUARTERS, York, Maine
HOMESTEAD INN, THE, Greenwich, Connecticut
RANGELEY INN, Rangeley, Maine
RED LION INN, THE, Stockbridge, Massachusetts
WINDHAM HILL, West Townshend, Vermont

Let Me Hear From You ...

Please use this page to let me know about your reactions—positive and negative—to your stay at any of the inns recommended in *Country Inns and Back Roads: New England*, and to tell me about the inns you've enjoyed that I may have overlooked. Just tear out this page and send your comments to me at the address below.

_____

_____

_____

_____

_____

_____

_____

_____

Thanks for your help, and happy traveling!

Jerry Levitin
1565 Partrick Road
Napa, CA 94558